American Psychological Association • Washington, DC

How To Manage Your Career In Psychology

Richard R. Kilburg, Editor

First printing June 1991
Second printing September 1992

Published by
American Psychological Association
750 First Street, NE
Washington, DC 20002

Copies may be ordered from
APA Order Department
P.O. Box 2710
Hyattsville, MD 20784

Cover design: Paine Bluett Paine, Inc.
Typesetting: Easton Publishing Services, Inc., Easton, MD
Printing: Princeton University Press, Lawrenceville, NJ
Technical Editing and Production Coordination: Deborah Segal and Susan Bedford

Library of Congress Cataloging-in-Publication Data

How to manage your career in psychology / edited by Richard R. Kilburg.
p. cm.
Includes bibliographical references and index.
ISBN 1-55798-117-5 (acid-free paper)
1. Psychology—Practice. I. Kilburg, Richard R., 1946-
BF75.H69 1992
150′.23—dc20 91-4219
CIP

Printed in the United States of America.

Contents

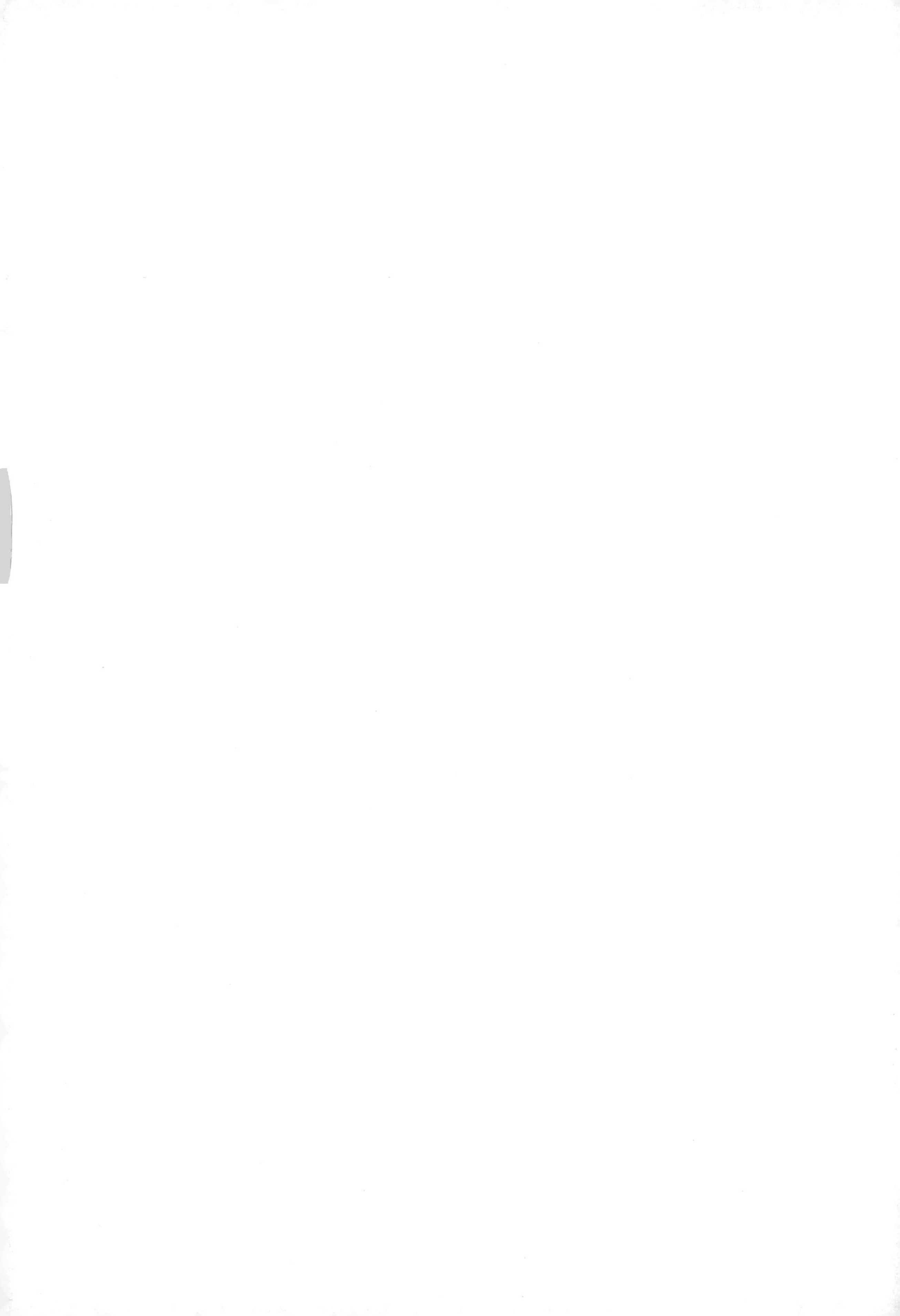

Contributors

Richard R. Kilburg, PhD The Johns Hopkins University and Hospital Faculty and Staff Assistance Program, Baltimore, MD

Dory Hollander, PhD New Options, Inc., St. Louis, MO

Elliot Blass, PhD Department of Psychology, Cornell University, Ithaca, NY

Georgine M. Pion, PhD Institute for Public Policy Studies, Vanderbilt University, Nashville, TN

Michael Owen Miller, PhD, JD Lewis and Roca, Tucson, AZ

Bruce D. Sales, PhD, JD Department of Psychology, University of Arizona, Tucson, AZ

Preface

Approximately 11 years ago, I attended a dinner for the Board of Professional Affairs of the American Psychological Association (APA). I was working as a staff member in the Office of Professional Affairs at the time. The conversation during the meal turned to various activities the members of the Board were pursuing. I was sitting across the table from Bruce Sales who proceeded to describe a handbook he was editing for psychological professionals. I asked him if he had included any material on the topic of management, and he said that he had not. I believed strongly that psychologists and other professionals suffered needlessly in the pursuit of their goals because they simply lacked the appropriate knowledge and skills in management. We spent several minutes discussing these issues, after which Bruce invited me to put together a chapter on the topic for his book.

Several months after I submitted the chapter, Bruce called me. He said that he had decided to use the material for a session in his professional development course. He figured that the material would be good for several hours of discussion. He then told me that he had to force the students onto a new topic after three class sessions were spent reviewing the material in depth. He asked me if I had ever thought about putting together a book on the topic. I said that I had, but felt that I needed editorial assistance for a project that size. Bruce volunteered to help, and a book was born.

During the next several years, we produced about eight chapters in draft form. The central idea for the volume focused on the application of management concepts and skills to the work and careers of psychologists. I believed then as I do now that success in anyone's career is due as much to thoughtful management as it is to training, skills, or knowledge in the field. The book-length version expanded on this central idea.

Both Bruce and I had extremely busy schedules, which slowed the pace of the writing. Eventually, Bruce encouraged me to pursue the project alone. After I left the staff of the APA central office and resumed a career in clinical administration, I had several conversations with Gary VandenBos about the book. Gary was and still is responsible for the publishing activities of APA. He encouraged me to submit a proposal to the Publications and Communications Board of the association. I finally did so in 1987. I was put into the capable hands of Brenda Bryant, then Director of Book Acquisitions and Development. Brenda suggested a number of detailed revisions, and after several drafts, the Board approved the project and the work started in earnest. The past 3 years have seen contributors come and go, and there have been many frustrations and pratfalls along the way. But, after a decade of effort, we have finally produced the book.

The central concept of the original project remains, namely, that psychologists must apply managerial knowledge and skills to their practices in order to become truly successful. The field of management has much to offer the entrepreneurial practitioner, the beleaguered academician, and the climbing administrator. Because our own field has contributed a great deal to the field of management itself, some of the material in the book will be familiar to many readers. However, throughout the volume, I have tried to keep the emphasis on our own field of psychology. The examples and exercises have all been constructed with a desire to assist psychologists with many of the routine problems and decisions that beset us in our work. The whole idea is to improve what we do, how we do it, and, in the process, to increase our levels of satisfaction, skill, and success.

The book is divided into four sections with a total of 10 chapters. In the first section and chapter, I provide an overview of many of the fundamental problems facing psychologists as we go about our work on a daily basis. In chapters 2 and 3 of the second section, I give a succinct summary of many of the general concepts and managerial approaches that psychologists need to practice successfully. In chapter 4, Dory Hollander adds a solid overview of the general approaches to career development and of her unique strategy and method of career management. Elliot Blass describes the managerial challenges and approaches he has used during his successful academic career in chapter 5. I apply the concepts and skills to practitioner careers in chapter 6, and in chapter 7, review the issues and methods you can use to manage career transitions. In the final section, a variety of issues are discussed. Mike Miller and Bruce Sales give an overview of the legal issues psychologists routinely face in chapter 8. I add a chapter on financial management in chapter 9. This is a subject psychologists are seldom exposed to during their training. Georgine Pion ends the volume with a description of the job market in psychology.

Throughout the book, I have tried to emphasize the practical side of working in the field of psychology. All of the authors here provide examples from the many subareas of the field, in recognition of the fact that these management concepts and skills can be applied by any psychologist to improve both what he or she does and how he or she does it. I have taken the stand that every psychologist is a practitioner and that our work and careers can be understood as businesses that must be well managed in order to succeed. Although I fully understand that the content of the field and the subareas of practice vary widely, I try to emphasize that we share a great deal as we pursue our own goals and paths.

Any project that takes as long as this one has to be completed accumulates a number of friends and supporters along the way. I would like to acknowledge the following people, without whom the book could not have been possible. First, my son Ben and wife Gail provided a great deal of encouragement and support all along the way. They also tolerated a large number of hours spent away from them as I hunched over a video terminal. Second, Bruce Sales has been incredibly helpful over the decade it has taken to produce the book. From his first words of encouragement to the lunches at the APA conventions during which we talked about strategy and the publishing business, Bruce has been a good friend and advisor. Third, the APA governance structure, through its Publications and Communications Board, supported bringing this project to life. The considerable assets and talents of the APA central office staff have been available to me for the last 3 years. Gary VandenBos has always been a wise colleague and a quiet supporter. This book would not have been possible without his willingness to take it through the APA process. Brenda Bryant was incredibly helpful, revising the initial plan and endlessly reading and commenting on the draft chapters as they were produced. The design of the book is as much hers as it is mine. Julia Frank-McNeil, Director of Acquisitions and Development, and Ted Baroody, Acquisitions and Development Editor, inherited this project after Brenda left APA to pursue her career in North Carolina. They have been tireless in their effort to produce the book and make it as useful to the field as possible. Barbara Chlan, my secretary for the last 4 years, has helped me with many of the details of preparing the manuscript. Finally, I would like to thank my coauthors, Dory Hollander, Elliot Blass, Georgine Pion, Mike Miller, and Bruce Sales, who did wonderful work and tolerated the usual editorial hectoring with good humor and timely revisions.

I sincerely hope that you, the reader, find this book helpful as you pursue your career as a psychologist. The field and the members of the profession have been good friends to me over the past 2 decades. The following chapters represent a distillation of many of the important things I have learned during that time.

Richard R. Kilburg

Part I

Introduction

1

Richard R. Kilburg

Issues in Psychological Careers

The Problem

Think back over the past few weeks or months. Undoubtedly, you have had a work situation or interpersonal problem in which you found yourself thinking, "they don't teach you about this in school: I wish they had." It could be anything, a client with a tough question at 2:00 AM, an argument with a business partner, or a difficult tax decision. If you are like me, you have faced these kinds of issues many times, like an exhausted and hurt boxer in the 15th round of a championship fight.

Sometimes, your coping efforts succeed and you feel like a winner, a world-champion psychologist. At other times, you fail. You experience the pain of self-doubt and, frequently, the torture of someone's judgment that you are totally inadequate. Most often, you simply muddle through, a mediocre performance that never succeeds or fails.

If you have ever felt as if you were a ship without sails and rudder, adrift in a career that seems as if it's going nowhere, then you are like the rest of us in wanting a better way to develop professionally, to put your life, job, and career in perspective. You want to master one of the most critical problems facing us all, *how to manage your psychological career.*

The Solution

If you are like us, this book was written for you. We cannot keep you out of championship fights. In fact, it is our intention to ensure that you have the opportunity and ability to fight more of them, more successfully, and with fewer injuries and bigger rewards.

As I see it, the answers to the problems in psychological careers come, first, from the ability to know what to expect in a normal professional life span. Knowing what is around the corner lets you anticipate and plan for major and minor events.

Second, it is imperative that we develop specific skills that make us better managers of life events. I am not talking about the skills required to be a good psychologist. These are also vital to victory. Graduate training and professional supervision concentrate on these skills and do a good job. Rather, I am describing a set of general managerial skills applicable to your professional life. Obtaining these skills will make you more effective at whatever you choose to do in the field of psychology. In addition, it is my contention that we all must be effective managers in order to succeed in life. Developing management skills need not be a painful and prolonged experience. I hope that this book will give you a running start in gaining this knowledge.

Finally, there is a set of interrelated issues that you should master. Some of the issues are dealt with in training at an abstract level. Others are never explicitly mentioned except when students or faculty get together in small groups to discuss their fears and commiserate with each other. You must learn to face these issues directly in order to surmount them.

Acquiring this knowledge and these skills is the equivalent of equipping your drifting psychologists' boat, not only with sails and a rudder, but also with a compass and maps of where the shoals and passages are. Appropriately outfitted, a psychological career, even on stormy seas, can become an invigorating and successful journey.

Key Issues

Stop for a moment and think about the following question. What are the major problems that confront or will confront you as a psychologist? Take a pen and jot down whatever comes to mind. When you have finished, compare it to the list below.

1. Developing and maintaining a professional identity.
2. Identifying and understanding your environmental context.
3. Surviving in a power-oriented world.
4. Developing managerial skills.
5. Developing short- and long-range planning skills.
6. Identifying and solving conflicts as they arise.
7. Developing adequate negotiating skills.
8. Managing money.
9. Developing technical competence.
10. Understanding the law as it pertains to your work.
11. Practicing ethically and within the regulatory framework of the profession.
12. Coping with burnout and career renewal.

This list identifies 12 key issues that confront every psychologist regardless of who he or she is and how he or she makes a living in the field of psychology.

How does your list stack up to this one? Where are the similarities and differences? Which problems have your training and education prepared you to handle? If you are lucky, your educational program has addressed four to six of these issues. The others were ignored. Are they any less important to professional growth? I think not. Let's explore them through brief examples.

Your Identity

As an undergraduate, Andrea Moses discovered an abiding interest in the development of children. The oldest of seven siblings, she found herself fascinated with her developmental and personality classes. Her favorite teacher encouraged her to go to graduate school to study developmental psychology. She followed this advice and is now preparing to finish writing her dissertation.

Over the past year or so, she has begun to think about her first job in psychology. Her research and teaching skills have prepared her for a life in academia. She would prefer a teaching post at a small university that would allow her to do some high-quality research and get involved with graduate education. Discussions with recent graduates have highlighted just how difficult it is to find such a position.

Already anxious about the dissertation, she decides to concentrate on the task at hand. She defers action on the job front until she feels she has the writing well underway. Several months later, at the end of a particularly good supervision session with her mentor, she asks her mentor's advice about conducting a job search. The supervisor reassures her and suggests that she consider a post doc with a colleague in a different section of the country. Andrea's stomach flops at the thought of two more years of student life. She asks if there are alternatives. A realistic discussion follows in which Andrea begins to learn the steps she must take beyond the doctorate if she is to succeed. She returns home shaken and tries to sort out what has happened.

Questions to address.

1. Do you know anyone like Andrea?
2. What do you think went wrong?
3. Was your training experience any different?
4. What help would be beneficial to a psychologist about to graduate?
5. When should graduate students begin to plan for their first position in psychology?
6. How does one's job in psychology relate to questions of professional and personal identity?

The Environmental Context

In what kind of environment is your present job? Is it a university, a private corporation, a government bureaucracy, a hospital, a multinational corporation, a nonprofit organization, or your own business? Regardless, each of these environments is organized around a structure, information, resources, decision-making processes, and a network of human relationships that regulates how people behave. Work systems set goals, monitor performances, reward successes, and theoretically punish or extinguish failures. They consume ½ to ⅔ of our waking lives and a significant part of our social experience. Adaptation to work environments is vitally important to professional success. The following example should illustrate this issue.

Bruce Niven is a clinical psychologist who has been working as the director of outpatient services in a medium-sized, nonprofit, community mental health center. He carries a half time case load and supervises the work of a multidisciplinary staff of ten professionals. His boss is a social worker who gives him a lot of room to run his own shop. As a result, the outpatient service has been a productive, supportive, and intimate unit, much like a little club.

Bruce has enjoyed his job for 5 years; however, 6 months ago, he became disillusioned with several administrative decisions his boss was forced to make. He was also a little bored with the clinical work. He began to look for another job.

After several months, his clinical reputation and evaluation skills land him an offer as an assistant director of information services in the central office for mental health programs in the county. He moves to his new position with no real regrets about leaving the outpatient service.

Approximately 6 months into the new job, Bruce becomes aware that his boss is hardly ever around. A political appointee with solid connections, his boss never comes to work on Fridays or Mondays. Bruce now knows and understands the way the operation is organized. His boss has given him the complete responsibility for running the evaluation systems in the county. Although Bruce enjoys the responsibility and influence of the job, he also resents the fact that he is doing the work of two people. He does not know how to handle the situation, because his boss has a reputation for firing anyone who disagrees with him.

Questions to address.

1. What do you think are some of the differences between the work environments of a nonprofit, community mental health center and a large county government?
2. Would Bruce be able to use the same approaches to interpersonal and work-related problems in his new position that he used at the mental health center?
3. What would you advise Bruce to do?
4. If you were in this position, where would you turn for help?

A Power-Oriented World

Jean Stevens is the new chair of a four person department of psychology in a school of education of a state teachers college. Each of her staff carries a teaching load of four courses each semester, which includes practicum supervision for counseling majors in another department. Jean realizes that she and her colleagues will have limited career flexibility unless they can make the time to do research and write.

Jean discusses the situation with her colleagues at a faculty meeting. It is a familiar topic to them. Jean's determination to do something gives them all a lift in their morale.

Jean prepares her arguments and makes an appointment with the dean of the school. She presents the faculty's position well. The dean is sympathetic, listening to her without interruption. He then asks her if she has discussed her proposal for reductions in teaching loads with any of the other chairs in the school. She says no. He asks her where the money will come from to hire another faculty member to take up the slack of the course reductions for her staff. She replies that she had thought the two of them could work on that together. He also asks what areas of research she and her colleagues are planning to explore and what the funding opportunities are in these areas. Jean suggests several possible topics, but has no idea about whether funding support is available.

The dean tells her that he will consider her request. She leaves the appoint-

> ment feeling dissatisfied with her performance and doubtful that any additional funds will be forthcoming. She also thought that the dean was not very supportive, but finds it hard to criticize him because of his questions.

Jean's predicament is played out over and over in the lives of psychologists. We are bright, creative, energetic professionals who frequently work in other peoples' organizations. We want and need to obtain resources to do our jobs and succeed. Frequently, we are forced to "play games" to get what we need. We have a tendency to moan and groan about politics and powerlessness, but rarely do we know what to do to empower ourselves. This is another important area for professional mastery.

Questions to address.

1. What sources of power were evident in Jean's interaction with the dean?
2. Was Jean's position weak or strong? Why?
3. What, if anything, would you have done differently from Jean?
4. What do you think makes these situations so difficult for people in general and for psychologists in particular?

Management Skills

> Thomas Hill is a young child psychologist who has been working in the outpatient service of a suburban community mental health center. He has developed excellent clinical skills. He is particularly adept at helping adolescents in turmoil and those who have begun to experiment with drugs. In the past several months, he has been asked to do some private evaluations and treatment for other professionals who have come to know his work. He is flattered and excited, agreeing to do the jobs with a sense that this is a whole new set of opportunities for him. Initially, he used his office in the center on Saturdays. This did not prove to be a problem because no one else was there. One of the first clients he served was the child of a neighborhood clergyman. The case went smoothly. Over the next 6 months, the minister started to send him more of his parishioners with problem children. Thomas' knowledge and skillful, reassuring way of relating to parents enabled him to be very helpful in the vast majority of situations he encountered.
>
> After about a year, Thomas discovered that he no longer had time to see people on Saturdays. His billing records for the clients that he did have were a mess. He now faced either taking cases during the week or referring them to other colleagues. One of his associates at the center had recently come in to do some paperwork on a Saturday and found Thomas there. He raised a question about whether Thomas had permission to use the center facility and about the legal liability to the organization and to Thomas for conducting a private practice out of his office.
>
> Somewhat bewildered, tired, and confused, Thomas approached the director of the center with these problems. In a friendly way, his boss told him about the policies of the organization. He also suggested that Thomas had built a business without ever having the deliberate intention of doing so. His boss suggested that Thomas would need to make some critical choices and learn to manage the private practice better.

Graduate education does a fairly good job at teaching us to be good psychologists. However, the ability to use your knowledge effectively requires that you are a good manager as well. In this example, we see that creating a psychology business is one of the most exciting and challenging tasks a professional can undertake. Success depends as much on how well you manage as it does on how much you know and can do as a psychologist.

Questions to address.

1. Do you know any psychologists who are full-time managers?
2. How do they spend their time?
3. What are some of the tasks that Thomas will need to address if he is to continue his successful, small psychology business?
4. Have you ever thought of yourself as a manager? Why? Why not?

Planning Skills

> Barbara Martin is a first-year assistant professor of psychology at a major research university. She teaches two courses and serves on several psychology department committees. She knows that she must publish in high-quality research journals if she wants to get tenure and stay at the university. She has many good ideas for research projects in her area of interest, but needs financial support to accomplish them. She talks to her department chair about the problem, and her chair suggests that she prepare and submit a grant application to a federal agency.
>
> Barbara obtains the necessary forms from the university office of sponsored projects. She looks through the forms and begins the task of preparing an application. She finds the work difficult and challenging. She is constantly juggling her schedule trying to teach, supervise students on their own research projects, serve on her committees, and work on the grant application. She discovers many new obstacles while trying to complete the application, including department reviews that suggest revisions and a school-wide Human Subjects Experimentation Committee that also forces several changes in the project. Six months after she started, she finally gets the application in the mail.
>
> To her total delight, she hears several months later that she has scored high enough to be funded. Money will start to flow in the middle of the second semester. After the initial excitement wears off, she now faces the reality that she has just added the equivalent of another half-time job to her schedule. She is expected to continue her teaching, supervising, and committee loads as well as conduct the research project. The research requires her to find space to house the new staff she must hire, to prepare budgets, and to work with the university administration around financial, personnel, and general managerial tasks. Overwhelmed, Barbara turns to the chair once again for advice. He talks to her about project management, and together, they outline a plan for the next 3 months.

This example illustrates a major issue for us as psychologists. Most of us never receive any formal training in planning. We learn it by trial and error through a series of graded tasks given to us in school. Homework assignments, papers, and dissertations force us to learn how to set objectives, anticipate problems, and manage time. In this case, Barbara manages to acquire the grant and move into her research career. However, it is only with a great deal of difficulty that she overcomes a series of problems that she could have anticipated. The more effective we become at planning and implementing, usually, the more successful we will be as professionals.

Questions to address.

1. What could Barbara have done differently to better prepare her for submitting and managing the grant?
2. How do you approach major tasks in your professional life?
3. Have you ever developed a multistaged plan to help implement a project?
4. What kinds of professional tasks in your life could be improved with the application of some effective planning skills?

Conflict Management

> Joan Lane is the chair of a moderately large department of psychology at a major university. Approximately 6 months ago, she and her program directors decided that the undergraduate curriculum needed to be reviewed and revised because of declining enrollments. They solicited the advice of the faculty members, who provided a never ending stream of suggestions, comments, and criticisms.
>
> The effort went smoothly as long as they were just brainstorming and collecting information. However, as soon as they started to try to make decisions about what to keep and what to eliminate of the required and optional courses, their work group became bogged down in a series of arguments. Two camps emerged. The traditionalists wanted to maintain the status quo core courses and add several new alternatives from which students could select. The innovators wanted to eliminate sections of the required courses and replace them with a lattice of options that could be selected by any student.
>
> The meetings degenerated into jousting sessions with everyone working to protect their own program interests. Joan found that appeals to reason, suggestions for compromise, and threats to scrap the initiative were equally ineffective at redirecting or stopping the conflict. Joan finally agreed to table the project in the face of mounting evidence that the department was coming apart over the issues.

This example highlights how difficult it is to change anything. Conflict is always possible and frequently visible in human interaction. Psychologists study conflict and practitioners learn to help others come to grips with the battles in their lives. Applying this knowledge and skill in our own professional lives is somewhat more difficult, but very important.

Questions to address.

1. Have you ever experienced a seemingly unresolvable conflict? Jot down some of the details.
2. Who was involved? What were the issues? What did you do to try to resolve or manage the conflict?

3. Is there anything you would suggest for Joan to try in the previous example before throwing in the towel?
4. What are the most difficult aspects of managing a conflict for you?
5. What would you like to learn about conflict management?

Negotiation Skills

Mary Holtzman was a clinical psychologist just finishing her internship. She was looking at several job possibilities. The one that attracted her most was to affiliate with a growing group of private practitioners. They painted an optimistic picture of full caseloads of paying patients, posh offices, talented colleagues, and the promise of a partnership in the practice if she worked out. She had met with the senior partner over lunch in several nice restaurants. He was charming and persuasive. Everything went well until she received a lengthy contract in the mail full of legal terminology. The senior partner politely pressured her to sign.

She consulted her favorite supervisor who recommended an attorney. Mary and her attorney reviewed the major problems. The contract specified a noncompetition clause that would prohibit her from leaving the practice and setting up her own practice in the city for 5 years. She also had to agree to buy into the group after 3 years at a cost of 15% of her fee collections over a 10 year period. They outlined their concerns, and Mary went to meet with the senior partner. He listened attentively, but made no response other than that he would need to discuss it with his partners. Mary felt uncomfortable haggling over the details. She felt that this nonsense was beneath the dignity of well-trained professionals.

The senior partner made a counter offer several days later. Mary became truly discouraged. They made some minor concessions on outside revenues, guarantees of referrals, and percentage of profits during the buy-in period. The other problems remained.

Simultaneously, she was pressured to accept a salaried position in a community mental health center for which she had applied. After consulting her lawyer, Mary accepted the mental health center job. Months later, she met the senior partner at a professional meeting. Over lunch, she described her frustration with the whole process. He expressed regret about her decision, but stated that he and his partners felt justified in bargaining hard to protect themselves and their business. He said that they had very much wanted her to join them and would have made further concessions had she continued to push. Mary left the lunch feeling chagrined that she had not persisted in the negotiations.

Questions to address.

1. How has your training prepared you to negotiate on your own behalf?
2. Do you feel comfortable asking for what you want?
3. Would you recognize bargaining ploys if they arose in a negotiation?
4. Have you ever been in a position like the one Mary was in? What did you do?
5. Would you have handled Mary's situation differently? How?

Managing Money

> Cal Burrows was a psychologist in a small group practice in a major urban area. This group had developed a high level of technical and professional skill in successfully treating psychosomatic problems. They decided that they could expand their practice by offering to teach others to use their techniques and to supervise training in a clinic they would operate from their practice.
>
> The group spent months planning their program. They put the courses together, designed supervision sessions, assembled an advertising campaign, and attracted successfully a number of practitioners to fill their first class. They did all of this without calculating how much capital they were investing in the project, or without anticipating what a reasonable rate of return on their investment would be, the break-even point, or their financial liabilities for conducting the program. Thus, 2 weeks before the first class, they found themselves not knowing if they would make money or be wiped out by someone's negligence.
>
> They ran around in a frenzy in the final days trying to cover their exposed position. By the end of the first training cycle, they could not tell if they had made or lost money. The final agony came in the next 2 months when the business had to pay its taxes and they could not honestly say how much they had invested in the program. Needless to say, they consulted their accountant and built a basic budgeting and accounting system after the debacle. What a way to learn!

Professionals concentrate on providing state-of-the-art services and meeting client needs. For years, most professionals had no real financial worries in this regard. Their services were in such demand that some solid years of practice were enough to overcome the most heinous of mistakes. This is no longer the case.

In every field, the past two decades have seen a dramatic rise in the number of professionals. It is now difficult to establish a practice in many metropolitan areas. Individuals finish training with enormous debts. It is becoming increasingly important to have strong financial skills in order to succeed professionally.

Questions to address.

1. Before you start a project, do you work out a budget, anticipate profit and loss, and think about when to stop if the financial targets are not being met?
2. Have you ever had any specific training in financial management?
3. Do you have personal financial goals? What are they? How do you know if you are reaching them?
4. Do you avoid discussing financial issues? Why?
5. What would you have done in this example to foresee the problems this group encountered?

Developing Technical Competence

> Robbi Lowman was a new assistant professor in a large, dynamic department of psychology at a major midwestern state university. She had just completed a post doc at another institution, honing her research skills in neurobiology to perfection.

She knew that developing a major research program was crucial to success in this faculty position and felt that she was well prepared for the task.

By the end of her first semester, she had interested several students in working with her. She developed a grant application to the National Institutes of Health (NIH) and submitted it with the support and admiration of her program and department chairs. She knew from experience that it was a good proposal in a highly competitive field.

One month after she submitted the application, a different research team published successive studies that spoke directly to two of the three major foci of her application. Robbi was greatly disappointed upon discovering the articles. She was not surprised when she received a letter of rejection from NIH 2 months later. The rejection encouraged her to further develop the third element of her proposal and to integrate the other research team's findings into her new design. Robbi went back to work on the grant with increased determination, but was somewhat more anxious about the sophistication of her competitors in other institutions.

Maintaining technical competence in an era in which the size of the field of psychology has grown beyond anyone's imagination has become increasingly difficult. The flood of information, competition from colleagues in psychology and related professions, changes in funding patterns, and the sheer complexity of the field make it difficult for even the most dedicated psychologists to stay on top of their areas of specialization. It is a problem that every one of us must come to grips with in our careers.

Questions to address.

1. Could Robbi have done anything to foresee this problem?
2. What sources of information are important to gather in areas of research or practice in which there is intense competition?
3. Have you devised a strategy to maintain your own technical competence in psychology?
4. If you have a strategy, what are the five key elements?
5. If you do not have a strategy, what are the major sources of information in which you will need to monitor developments in the areas you have an interest?

Understanding the Law

Jo Hastings was an independent practitioner in a rural state. She had been in business for a long time and had several associates and assistants work with her. Two years ago, the state medicaid regulations changed. Prior to the new ruling, the state would only reimburse services offered in institutional agency settings. The modifications allowed psychologists in private practice to serve medicaid clients and to bill the state directly for their services. Jo had successfully pushed her business into this new market and was billing tens of thousands of dollars per year for the services they provided.

Recently, a question arose as to whether licensed psychologists could bill for the services provided by assistants or other professionals working under their supervision. An investigation was initiated by the state in the context of a heated reelection campaign. The sitting governor had been accused of being lax in the administration of state-funded programs by his opponent. He was determined to demonstrate that his administration was completely on top of these issues.

The investigation revealed that a number of psychologists had been billing the state for the services of assistants for several years, even before the new regulations had been established for some agencies. However, there had never been a ruling or written clarification that such a practice was permissible. Jo had been one of three psychologists who had sought verbal assurances about the billing procedures as the new rules were put in place. None had taken the precaution of obtaining the clarification in writing. No one had contacted an attorney at the time. The state attorney general's office initiated an investigation of "fraudulent billing practices" that severely threatened the business Jo had built over many years.

Legal literacy is a must for all psychologists in this great era of litigation and regulation. The legislative, administrative, and judicial branches of government are producing laws affecting psychology at an incredible rate. The adversarial nature of our legal system produces increased risks for everyone. This is another key problem for each and every one of us psychologists regardless of where we work in the field.

Questions to address.

1. Do you have an understanding of the areas of law that pertain to your specialization in psychology?
2. Have you developed any local resources to help you monitor laws, regulations, and court rulings that might affect you?
3. Do you have an attorney available to you that understands some of the basic issues that affect research and practice in psychology?
4. What different ways would help you improve your knowledge and resources in this area?

Practicing Ethically

Marv Kuntsler was a private practitioner. He did an intake evaluation on a new client who asked him if the session would be confidential. Marv assured him that, within the limits of the law, everything said would be held in confidence. The client then informed him that he was a high school teacher and that he had been arrested on charges of molesting one of his students. He had been quietly suspended pending the outcome of the legal proceedings. The parents of the adolescent knew about the incident.

Marv faced a dilemma. He knew that, by law, he was supposed to report the situation to the state authorities. The teacher described the situation to him in detail. The student had been in trouble numerous times before, running away and acting out sexually with boyfriends and other older men in periods of tension at home. The teacher had befriended her and her family, becoming quite close to them over the school year. A series of personal reversals, including his wife contracting a life-threatening illness, had left him depressed, anxious, and extremely vulnerable. The girl had offered herself in a moment of weakness for both of them, and he had entered into the affair with great trepidation.

Marv decided to consult his attorney who described his duties under the law, and together they reviewed the specifics of this particular case. The attorney said that he had two options, to report the situation or not to. The fact that the court system had already taken the case left Marv with a legally defensible position if he chose not to report it. Marv felt very torn. He knew that the strict letter of the law required him to call the state protection authorities. If he did that, the client would leave him and not seek treatment. After discussing the situation with his state association ethics chair, who recommended that he report the case, Marv decided not to report it and to continue to provide services.

As the case unfolded, the legal system put the individual on probation, and the school system took him back in an adult education position. The case never came to the attention of the media, and the teacher responded successfully to treatment. Marv made sure to document each and every step he made. He felt very comfortable with the outcome of the case, because the teacher would no longer be involved with adolescent students, and the criminal justice system had taken appropriate action.

Practicing ethically frequently means deciding what to do in very complicated situations where questions of right and wrong, legal and illegal, and effective and ineffective become incomprehensibly intertwined. Making these difficult decisions is the hallmark of a fully functioning professional.

Questions to address.

1. Do you agree with the decision that this psychologist made?
2. How did Marv provide safeguards for himself?
3. Have you ever been confronted with a situation that required this type of complicated decision making?
4. What kind of support system do you have for helping you to make decisions like this?

Burnout and Renewal

Jan Peterson was a full professor in a small psychology department at a liberal arts college. She had been teaching the same courses for years. Although she kept up with developments that were relevant to her areas of responsibility, increasingly, she felt bored.

Over the course of a year or so, she found herself having difficulty getting up in the morning and staying awake at night. She eventually diagnosed the problem as fatigue and took a long vacation over the intersession break. However, when she returned, she found herself becoming irritated at the slightest problem. Students who couldn't write, colleagues who said the same things over and over again in meetings, and the endless stream of exams and papers to grade now caused her to become furious.

Jan began to drink more. She snapped at her colleagues and was demanding and unforgiving with students. One morning, she woke up with a splitting headache, nausea, chills, cramps, and all of the other signs of the flu. After 2 days of

> sitting in front of the TV with no improvement in her symptoms, Jan began to realize that something else was wrong. Slowly, over the course of several months, she began to see that she was burned out and fed up with her job. After thinking about it for some time, she formulated a plan for dealing with the situation. She made major modifications in the amount and types of work that she did. She also began to make time for herself and expanded her life outside of work. She took the opportunity to do many of the things that she had promised herself long ago.

Burnout can and does happen to every psychologist with varying degrees of severity. Some cases end well like Jan's. Others lead to more serious forms of impairment, including mental illness, alcoholism, and severe marital problems. We all need to address these issues of career transition and management. Doing so without the agony of becoming professionally or personally impaired is the major purpose for which this book was created.

Questions to address.

1. Have you ever had the experience of becoming extremely bored or dissatisfied with what you were doing professionally?
2. What did you do about it?
3. Have you thought about the normal phases of a career and the points at which you might become more susceptible to problems like this?
4. Do you have a support network to which you can turn if you get into trouble? Who is in your network?

Exercise 1.1 Tasks and Questions

Go back to the list you made at the beginning of this chapter.

1. Modify it according to what you think you have learned.
2. Make another list of areas you think you might find helpful to explore now that you have started to think about these problems.

Pick the key issue that disturbed or excited you the most.

1. Jot down the reasons why it disturbed or excited you.
2. Think of examples in your own life or a colleague's life that relate to the issue.
3. Seek out your closest professional colleague, schedule lunch together, and discuss what you have been thinking about.

Take a moment and think about your career. No matter where you are in the course of your professional life, try to answer the following questions.

1. What are your goals (contributing to the field, changing society, earning money, publishing, or helping people)?

2. If you are in the middle of your career, what changes do you want to make? Why?
3. Identify three specific steps you can take to begin to accomplish your goals. TAKE THEM!

Plan of the Book

Now that I have introduced you to the central problems and to the key issues that I believe we all face as psychologists, I hope that your appetite for some concrete suggestions and ideas has been sharpened. The rest of this book comprises three sections. Part II provides a conceptual overview, which I believe you can apply to problems already mentioned and many others you may face in your professional life. My next two chapters follow and concentrate on the management skills and concepts that are essential to professional success. Dory Hollander's chapter then gives a good introduction to the major issues and themes involved in developing and maintaining a professional career.

Part III applies the concepts and skills introduced in Part II. Elliot Blass covers the issues facing academicians and researchers in their careers. I cover the same topic for practitioners, and then I explain how career transitions are made successfully. All three of these chapters apply the lessons from the first two sections to problems in the real world—problems which psychologists regularly have.

Part IV addresses three specific problems. In chapter 8, Michael Miller and Bruce Sales give an excellent and practical introduction to the law–psychology interface. In chapter 9, I cover the basics of financial life for psychologists. And finally, Georgine Pion provides an excellent summary of employment trends in the field of psychology and where jobs and careers are likely to be found.

I hope that you find the materials in this book useful in your career as a psychologist. Remember, before we can help anyone else understand their behavior or take steps to improve their lives, it is best if we have some understanding of ourselves and what we want from our careers.

Part II

Conceptual Overview

2

Richard R. Kilburg

The Art of Self-Regulation

Very early in my career, I was consistently bewildered by what was going on around me. Oh, I understood a lot about psychology. I could discuss different conceptual systems and research methodologies, and as my training unfolded, I became comfortable with patients, psychopathology, ways of changing lives, and even myself. However, I remained ignorant about how things were accomplished in the organizations in which I worked.

As I watched some of my colleagues, they seemed to possess a secret that I did not. They knew when events were going to unfold. They were unfazed by political and program developments, and they seemed to get more for themselves and their staff than I could. I knew they had a set of rules they were going by and some power to regulate events, but the rules and this source of power were secret. No one took the time to teach me or even seemed interested in helping others learn how to play the game.

Looking back, I can understand why the rules and this power were guarded so jealously. Those who had the knowledge advanced more rapidly, received higher salaries, got caught in fewer petty squabbles, and participated in the major decisions made in the organization. The rest of us stood around anxiously wondering what would happen next.

Koestler (1978) said, "it seems that life in all its manifestations, from morphogenesis to symbolic thought, is governed by rules of the game which lend it order and stability but also allow for flexibility; and that these rules, whether innate or acquired, are represented in coded form on various levels of the hierarchy, from the genetic code to the structures in the nervous system associated with symbolic thought" (p. 43). He captured the problem in this beautiful sentence. What are the rules of the game in professional life? How can we succeed, grow, achieve our goals, and protect ourselves? How do we play the game? Increasingly, I have come to believe that the key to success in professional life is found in the art of self-regulation.

This chapter focuses on developing a conceptual overview of professional self-regulation. In addition to chapters 1 and 3, it will serve as the foundation for exploring many more specific and concrete issues and skills with which you can successfully manage your psychological career. Let's go on now to discover the major rules of the game that will directly influence the degree of your professional success. Our discoveries will be limited by the current state of knowledge applicable to career management and by the size of this book.

Self-Regulation

Our evolution as a species and our success as individual human beings depends increasingly on our ability to regulate our own behaviors. Each of us must become masters of self-regulation. The rules for life described so beautifully by Koestler and the rules of the game followed by my successful colleagues are the tools of self-regulation. Our job is to understand how these tools enable us to manage successfully our psychological careers. Let's start by exploring an example.

Example 2.1 A New Psychologist

Mary Evans was a young clinical psychologist starting her first full-time job as a therapist in a community mental health center. She was very bright and capable. She got along well with her colleagues. She busily immersed herself in helping the large number of patients that were referred to her in the outpatient department.

As time wore on, Mary found herself becoming increasingly interested in working with the large number of women who came for help because they were in difficult marriages, had several children to care for, and wanted to make major changes in their lives, but were baffled and buffaloed by all of the psychological, economic, and social barriers in their way. Mary knew that these women needed more than the occasional psychotherapy session that she could offer.

Mary began to plan the content of a comprehensive program of services to provide the help her clients needed. She spent some of her personal time in the library and on the telephone doing research on what was available and what worked. She wrote a solid description of what she proposed to do and took it to the director of the agency. He promised to look at it.

After a month of waiting, Mary finally tracked him down in his office and asked him if he had read the proposal. He said that he had not had time, but that he would. After another month, she again went to see him. Again, he had not read it, but they made a firm appointment to discuss his views the following week.

Mary was nervous when she went to his office. She didn't know what to expect. After some cordial chit chat, the director proceeded to compliment her on all of the fine work that she had done. He was apologetic for not reading the proposal sooner. He told her that although her ideas for a program were sound, there was no way that sufficient funding could be obtained. He asked her to go back to seeing her clients and to leave the program planning to the administrative staff.

Mary left the meeting feeling baffled and betrayed. She did not believe she had been given a decent hearing. She felt excluded from meaningful participation in the decisions made by the organization. She was angry at the way the whole thing was handled. For the first time since she was hired, she started to think about leaving the organization.

Mary's experience is not unique. It is typical for bright, well-meaning psychologists to want to experiment, grow, and improve. They will try to apply their skills and knowledge to all of the problems they encounter. Unfortunately, Mary's program development skills did not extend to administration, finance, or politics. She failed to develop support for her ideas and suffered a severe blow to her sense of self-worth. She lost enough face and faith in the organization to consider quitting.

How can we as psychologists become sufficiently savvy so that what happened to Mary won't happen to us? How can we move our careers forward to higher levels of achievement and satisfaction without suffering humiliating defeats? Just what are the rules of the self-regulating game, and how can we learn to apply them on our own behalf?

Systems and Self-Efficacy

The first concept you must grasp is that as a provider of psychological services, you are a business system. Whether you educate graduate students, consult to corporations, work in school systems, or provide psychotherapy to patients, you have a set of skills, a collection of resources, and a number of products. To offer your services effectively, you must develop a system of delivery and a structure, accompanied by a set of definitions and guidelines, that will allow you to control the content and quality of your work.

In other words, you need to develop a means of self-regulation that ensures your professionalism. To do this, you need to start by thinking of yourself as a *system* for delivering psychological knowledge and services. You also must provide yourself with the means to grow and change as an individual and as a professional.

My foundation for understanding career management is based on *ecological systems theory*, one of several theories of systems management that are useful in analyzing organizational structures and processes. Von Bertalanffy (1968), Kuhn (1974), and Piaget (1971) described the concepts of systems theory most effectively.

In this context, I see psychologists as extremely complex biological, psychological, and social systems. They are self-regulating individuals who adapt to environments within an understandable and predictable conceptual framework. As systems, we have a structure in the form of roles, relationships, tasks to be performed, and personal, organizational, and communal boundaries within which we operate. We incorporate processes such as communication within ourselves and with others, physical transactions of various sorts, and the actual provision of psychological services. The content of our *psychologist system* consists of relating to our world in and through the various jobs that we agree to undertake. The key to success as a psychologist involves learning to *manage* this process of adaptation and self-regulation to achieve the goals you select for yourself.

Psychologists interact with a wide variety of environments. Most frequently, they work in formal (e.g., a university or corporation) or informal (e.g., a collegial-practice network) organizations. These organizations have usually developed more or less well-organized subsystems. The most comprehensible way of understanding the substructure of these organizations is to define the various *niches* that compose them. Defining organizations in terms of their niches is one of the best ways to understand how these systems operate. In effect, when you discuss the niches and system operations within organizations, you are talking about the ways in which people, technology, and money interact.

A niche consists of physical space, resources, structure, processes, and functional role or job in an environment, whether that environment is an organization or community. Formal and informal organizations have large numbers of niches in which you, as a psychologist, can perform successfully. Developing and adapting to niches is the central task of self-regulation for psychologists.

To begin the process of self-regulation, you need to develop and refine your awareness of how elements in your personal and professional life interact to create a system. Exercise 2.1 is designed to help you define yourself as a system.

Exercise 2.1 The Psychologist as a System

Take a piece of paper and a pen and jot down your observations about the following.

1. Nature of Your Interactions
   a. Identify the key people you depend upon. List their names, the role that they play in relationship to you, and the level of importance that they are to you on a scale of 1 to 5, with 5 being the most important.
   b. The list should include people you depend upon for the following items:
      i. money
      ii. information
      iii. intimacy and feelings of self-worth
      iv. exercise
      v. recreation
      vi. food and the other necessities of life
      vii. professional achievement
   c. How frequently do you interact with each person?
   d. What form does each interaction take? Are you in a subordinate, superior, or equal relationship to each person? Does the relationship change and if yes, when, and why?
2. Nature of Your Goals
   a. If you can, identify the major goals you have in life. See the list in 1b for some ideas about various areas in which you might set goals for yourself.

Now that you have completed this exercise, you have begun to develop the tools for self-regulation. You have defined some of the major elements in your interpersonal system, some of the processes you use to relate to these elements, and the goals that form your professional and personal foundation. These tools are actually several of the rules you use to make choices and determine how you implement decisions in your life.

Bandura (1977, 1982) described the concept of *self-efficacy* as a way of summarizing and organizing many of the essential components of self-regulation. He stated that "the basic phenomenon being addressed centers on people's sense of personal efficacy to produce and to regulate events in their lives" (p. 122). Efficacy is the "generative capacity in which component cognitive, social, and behavioral skills must be organized into integrated courses of action to serve innumerable purposes" (p. 122). Bandura clearly identified the art of self-regulation as being at the center of effectiveness in life when he says "perceived self-efficacy is concerned with judgments of how well one can execute courses of action required to deal with prospective situations" (p. 122). The greater you perceive your level of self-efficacy, the more effort and persistence you will display in pursuing achievement in your professional life.

The work of Markus and Nurius (1986) and other self-concept theorists overlaps and extends Bandura's essential idea by exploring the world of *possible selves*. "This type of self-knowledge pertains to how individuals think about their potential and about their future. Possible selves are the ideal selves that we would very much like to become. They are also the selves we could become and the selves we are afraid of becoming" (p. 954). In other words, if we master the art of self-regulation, if we become self-efficacious in our professional lives, we not only learn the rules of the game, we are also able to create ourselves and our careers any way our knowledge, skills, abilities, and social circumstances permit. This is a message of optimism, hope, and the promise of fulfilled dreams and ideals. But how do we translate our dreams into the reality of an effective and exciting psychological career?

Behavioral Transformation/Adaptation

In professional life, a niche is usually what we think of as a job—clinician, administrator, researcher, consultant, teacher—that has been identified by an organization that desires your services. Each niche in an environment is defined by a particular set of requirements—skills, knowledge, experience, attitudes, values, energy, etc. A niche is also an opportunity for you to define one of your possible selves. You can become the person who does that job effectively, and in so doing, you can both explore and create your ideals and dreams.

Once you move into a niche, you go through a sequence of stages to adapt to the job requirements and to develop and create yourself professionally. The degree of success in this adaptation process will determine whether you will survive in that niche and environment. Let us examine the stages in the adaptation process more closely so that we can be more specific about how we regulate and change ourselves.

Adaptive process. Let us assume that you possess the basic skills, knowledge, and ability to be a successful psychologist. Once you choose to work in a given environment, you face the challenge of adapting to a particular niche. In order to adapt successfully, you must begin to change. When you have completed this behavioral transformation successfully, you will find that an excellent *fit* between you and the niche exists. Figure 2.1, following the discussion of Braham (1978) and Kilburg (1983), presents a five-stage flowchart of this transformation process.

Stage 1: Toti-potential. When you enter into a new environment, you are, for all intents and purposes, *toti-potential*. This suggests that your intelligence, skill,

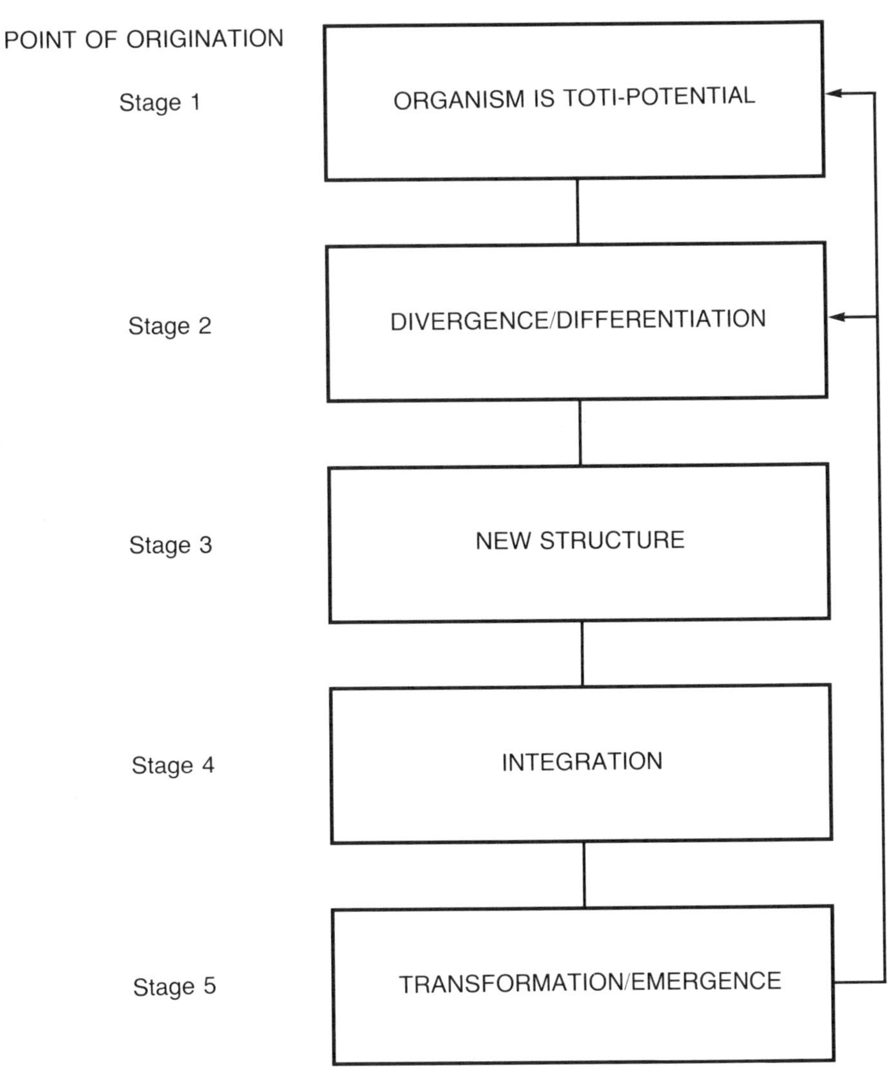

Figure 2.1. The transformational process.

knowledge, motivation, and adaptive capacity are vigorously flexible and can be pushed, pulled, or otherwise molded in a wide variety of directions. To be sure, there are huge differences in the degree to which any individual is toti-potential. Graduate training and early career choices certainly alter your capacity. Yet, when speaking of psychologists, it is reasonable to assume that most have a great degree of behavioral flexibility when entering an environment and niche. Our training helps us develop this flexibility.

Stage 2: Divergence/differentiation. Almost immediately upon entrance into a new environment, you face a new set of demands. For example, a clinical practitioner moving to a new community will face a new circle of colleagues, a new group of challenging clients, a new set of procedures to learn, and a new environment to explore. A new assistant professor will have courses to prepare, students to meet and teach, research projects to initiate, and an administration to comprehend. These requirements force the initiation of stage 2, *divergence/differentiation*. During this stage, new behaviors are added to what you brought to the niche. The practitioner learns new therapeutic techniques, the academician mounts a new course.

Stage 3: New structure. As you perform these new activities, you automatically enter into stage 3, *new structure*. Although still guided by your knowledge and experience, you will develop new schedules, new friends (and perhaps new enemies), new requirements for energy expenditure, re-allocations of time, expanded knowledge about people, new procedures and forms, new organizations, new schedules of events, and so forth. The new structure, which comprises all of the bits and pieces of new information and new behavior that you acquire when adapting to a new niche, is superimposed on what you brought to the niche. The first 3 months in a new niche are like being thrown into a cement mixer in which a psychological and behavioral soup is produced. The differentiation process gradually mixes the new components together. Your sense of what is needed to survive, what your goals and dreams are, and what feels right filter out the valuable and useful components of the mixture and build it into a new structure that, when constructed properly, forms a lasting tool that enables you to *fit* into that niche. Stage 3 ends as the new structure solidifies and begins to aid you in your daily activities.

Stage 4: Integration. As you become accustomed to working in a new environment, the new structure becomes integrated into your way of behaving; it literally becomes a seamless piece of yourself. In a way, a new person or self is created. The structure that preceded the adaptation process accommodates to the new learning. The sense of being all over the place that characterizes the stages of differentiation and new structure is replaced by a feeling of security. You can now trust yourself to do the right thing in the niche almost automatically. The chronic anxiety of not quite being sure about what is right is replaced by a holistic and pervasive understanding of how you have been modified by the recent developments, hopefully, for the better.

Stage 5: Transformation/emergence. Eventually, past experience merges with present environmental mastery and your transformed self stretches outward to encompass different alternatives and beckoning goals. If the process has been successful, you have been changed by the niche and the niche by you. You have a clearer notion of goals and priorities, know what it takes to accomplish the new tasks, and have an increased sense of confidence about your ability to master what faces you. The different parts of your personal and professional life merge and subordinate to this new sense of wholeness. This new identity includes (yet simultaneously transcends) the new niche, because the transformation process adds new skills and confidence that can carry you beyond this position. You have become one of Markus and Nurius' possible selves, and you have exercised Bandura's self-efficacy through this transformational process.

Multiple cycles. Figure 2.1 also demonstrates that new cycles of transformation can be initiated when one is complete, and more than one transformation can occur at the same time. The average psychologist is frequently engaged in several stages of transformation simultaneously as different tasks and activities are undertaken. These multiple cycles of transformation lead you down an evolutionary path. You can stop short of final evolution in a niche and still be very successful and comfortable. You can also go to the end and find that you have outgrown the niche or that you need to move on for other reasons. However, in each niche and at each step along the way, there are decisions to be faced. At times, they are explicit, "Do I take that job?" At other times, they are implicit, "What do I want or need to read?" The molding and shaping forces of the transformation process operate constantly as the individual and the environment interact.

Evaluation. You make an important step toward professionalism when you realize that the adaptation process is inevitable and endless and that implicit in the move from stage to stage is the notion that you are engaged in a continual evaluation process. Evaluation can come in many forms. It may be experienced as a vague sense of doubt or wonder about how things are going. At certain critical junctures, these questions will erupt into full-blown, deliberate attempts to determine where you should move next or just where a situation began to go badly.

At times, it is hard to be objective. Often, you will reach out to others for support, guidance, or simple affirmation. Careful attention to whom you seek out and the advice that seems most relevant can prefigure changes that are coming. These informal efforts can lead to more structured evaluation. To be most effective, periods for formal evaluation and decision making can be built into the process deliberately. Choosing a time to assess your professional progress once a year is a highly effective strategy. This will provide a sense of coherence in what can be, at times, an emotionally draining experience.

How does this process of behavioral transformation work for psychologists? Example 2.2 provides a brief description of the transformational process at work.

Example 2.2 The Adaptation Process

Pat Biondi was a social psychologist just starting out as an assistant professor at a major university. Pat's first weeks on campus were a complete blur of activity and stress—moving into the office, meeting new colleagues, learning the forms that had to be used, trying to get some research started between classes, attending faculty meetings, and responding to student requests. Even finding the way to the classes was a chore.

Pat learned all of these new things rather quickly and settled into the position. Life began to change significantly with the new schedule, responsibilities, and growing sense of identity. The pace of change increased as graduate students began to make requests for research supervision. Immersion in new projects forced Pat to read in many different areas. Some of this exploration led Pat to conclude that there were significant new research opportunities that one of the federal research institutes might be willing to fund. However, Pat did not know much about obtaining such grants.

Pat talked to a wide variety of people about the grant-submission process. There were a great many steps that needed to be completed simply to develop a proposal. Pat outlined an activity plan that could lead to a grant submission in about 3 months. Pat requested a meeting with the department chairman and received strong support. Pat began to implement the plan.

The easy part of the process was designing the research. Drafting the proposal in concise language that would convince a review committee to fund the project, working out the seemingly endless details of the budget, and walking through all of the administrative steps required a great deal of learning and patience.

Finally, Pat submitted the application near the end of the academic year. Pat received a letter in the fall of the second year saying that the project would be funded. Feelings of elation mixed directly with the knowledge that there was now even more work to do. Pat felt sure that the project could be done well and that the last year of work had somehow provided a foundation for the challenge that lay ahead.

My view of behavioral transformation and of self-regulating systems has been enriched by the model provided by Aldrich and Pfeffer (1976). They presented a natural-selection approach to the problem of how organizations grow and develop. This model of environment–organization interaction is applicable here because both organizations and psychologists are controlled acting systems that work to adapt to their environments.

For Aldrich and Pfeffer, the organization and the environment tend to produce a number of random and planned *variations* in behavior. "The general principle is that the greater the heterogeneity and number of variations, the richer the opportunities for a close fit to the environmental selection criteria" (p. 85).

Following this principle, we can see that at each stage of the transformational process, the psychologist and the environment/niche produce behavioral variations. The wider the variation, the larger the possible number of choices will be in a particular job, role, or project. In our example, the reading and the supervising of students that Pat did produced an array of new ideas that led to a grant-funded research project.

As variations are produced, the process of *selection* begins simultaneously. This process of influencing, experimenting, evaluating, and decision making involves extremely complex learning adaptations. The individual tries new behaviors to solve old problems, old behaviors to solve new problems, and varieties of permutations and combinations. The effect of the selected behaviors on the problems confronted influences how that behavior is evaluated. Behaviors that are judged to have solved problems, produced effective adaptations, and increased the probabilities of survival in the niche are evaluated as successful. Successful behavior patterns often become very stable structures. They are *retained* by the psychologist, and, as the environment/niche constantly provides pressures to perform the behaviors, the repeated success in adaptation reinforces the retention of that behavior.

We can readily see the *variation-selection-retention* model at work in Pat's transformation as the successive stages of differentiation, new structure, and integration reflect this trial-and-error process. New behaviors are tried in mastering classes, schedules, relationships, and course materials. Students force variation in reading and thinking and in selecting and adding new skills and knowledge to the repertoire. As gains are made, Pat consciously and unconsciously decides what is working and retains the most successful of the new adaptive skills and knowledge. Pat eventually emerges as a more skillful and experienced psychologist with a new array of abilities as an academician and person to apply to whatever life brings.

We too can invent ourselves anew by deliberately varying, selecting, and retaining aspects of our personal and professional lives. We can also voluntarily enter into cycles of transformation as a strategy for pursuing self-efficacy. As we do this, we demonstrate the art of self-regulation, and we become masters of the game of professional life.

Discipline

The description of psychologists as self-regulating, adapting systems is nearly complete. However, mere knowledge of how the transformation process works to help us create ourselves is insufficient to ensure success. A final and essential feature of our description involves the concept and skills of *discipline* that are vital to mastery of the self and the environmental niche. Peck (1978) described a system of discipline that comprises four techniques: (a) delaying gratification, (b) assumption of responsibility, (c) dedication to truth or reality, and (d) balancing.

Delaying gratification is the first element of discipline. For Peck, "delaying gratification is a process of scheduling the pain and pleasure of life in such a way as to enhance the pleasure by meeting the pain first and getting it over with" (p. 19). Peck's approach is both brutal and refreshingly frank. Professional life is tough, and one of our most important abilities is the capacity to identify our problems and to work on those before attending to pleasure.

Psychologists must be able to delay gratification for themselves and for those with whom they work. Because much of our professional lives centers on solving problems on behalf of, in collaboration with, or as a result of the demands of clients, students, and colleagues, success is often measured by our ability to identify critical problems and to design solutions as rapidly as possible. The straightforward acceptance of the pain involved in this process and the skillful management so that the pain is kept to a minimum while the job is done are hallmarks of a successful, self-regulating psychologist.

The second basic technique of discipline involves the willingness and ability to *accept responsibility*. We must "accept responsibility for a problem before we can solve it" (p. 32). Accepting responsibility for problems is difficult. It is important to avoid traps that arise, to avoid either accepting the weight of the world or blithely refusing to accept any responsibility for events or problems. The central focus of accepting responsibility is to be aware of the choices and decisions that you make. In a true sense, we are the sum of all the decisions we make during our lives. Acknowledgment of the act of making a decision and acceptance of the consequences of the choice selected enhance our adaptation to life and niche.

For Peck, the third technique of discipline is the *dedication to truth or reality*. He urges his readers to construct a map of reality that is free of self-delusion, defensiveness, and lies. The more accurately our view of reality conforms to the actual truth that we confront, the easier it is to discern clear alternatives and to make wise decisions. If our vision of the world is clouded by fabrications, misrepresentations, and half-truths, we cannot truly decide which way is best for us.

The process of building a map of our view of reality is long, arduous, and painful. The choices and events that anchor the major landmarks of our course through life often represent the most difficult phases that we encounter. Coping with these occurrences through behavioral transformation and the learning associated with that process etches features into our character just as surely as major storms modify the land on which we live. Life seems to challenge us constantly with new information, concepts, skills, and experiences that become part of our reality. Peck's requirement for honesty with ourselves and with others and the demand that we constantly challenge our views of reality, our ethics and values, and our willingness to endure suffering while solving problems is critical to our development as psychologists and as people.

Peck's fourth and final technique of discipline is *balancing*. He acknowledges that the process of self-discipline can get out of hand and become an instrument of torture and self-doubt. He encourages discipline of the process of discipline itself so that we remain free to enjoy life spontaneously. Even as we plan for the future and make choices based an careful assessments of the alternatives at hand, we must be able to act on a whim, follow our creative impulses, and react to the world as children do when they find something that fascinates them for the first time. The way to regulate discipline is through balancing.

Balancing provides flexibility for the individual, and the foundation of this process is "letting go." As we move through life, we attach ourselves to people, places, things, events, ideas, and feelings. In order to continue to grow through life, discipline requires that we change these patterns of attachments. We know that change produces anxiety, depression, anger, and so on—in a word, pain. So, we tend to avoid it. Peck believed that the pain must be embraced if we are to continue to grow. We are therefore required to give up much in our lives so that we can enrich ourselves in other ways.

Letting go can be difficult. At its worst, it approximates the process of dying. New growth is often impossible unless the old is swept away. As trees prepare for the stirring rebirth of spring by dropping their leaves in the fall, so we too must be willing and able to let go of what we have created so that we can remake ourselves as needed. The art of maintaining and developing what is essential to life must include the technique of balancing.

We only need to look at the brief example of Pat (Example 2.2) to observe discipline in action. Pat used the four techniques of discipline without really being aware of the process. Psychologists like Pat accept the need for change and the pain of giving up while simultaneously embracing the joy of adaptation and the requirement to maintain equilibrium. We must fight for what we truly believe in while remaining open to the possibility that our beliefs might need modification. When psychologists demonstrate this degree of flexibility and judgment, they approach the attainment of that rarest of all human traits, wisdom. The demands of the environment and the desires of self-fulfillment push us to develop this trait.

Think about these four techniques of discipline. Undoubtedly, you have used each of them in your career and life. Exercise 2.2 will help you to become more aware of how to use these methods.

Exercise 2.2 Learning Self-Discipline

Try one or more of the following suggestions as a way of heightening your awareness of how you are using these techniques and whether you have problems with one or more of them.

1. *Making Choices.* Pick a day and time that is safe for you and decide to go without your biggest meal. Try to be aware of how you feel as you anticipate the activity. Note your physical sensations. Check how you feel at the time of your next meal. Does it taste better? Are you more hungry than usual? What was it like to make a deliberate choice?
2. *Accepting Responsibility.* Volunteer to do a small chore at home that you ordinarily avoid at all costs. Carry through with it fully and try to be good natured about it. Again, be aware of how you feel as you anticipate the chore. Note fantasies, thoughts, and behaviors that push you to delay or to not do the task. Afterward, ask yourself what it was like to accept the responsibility for the chore.
3. *Reality Testing.* Pick a person that you do not get along with or like. Make a list of the characteristics or traits that lead you to your feelings for the person. Now, make a list of positive characteristics. Force yourself to *see* the individual as a whole person. Finally, make a third list of the aspects of your own character that interact with this other person to cause the dislike. Is your new picture of the person and the situation now closer to *reality*?
4. *Balancing.* The next time you have a major project or task to do, find a time that is safe for you, and allow yourself to take a break to do something pleasurable in the middle of working hard on the project. It may be a 30-minute nap, a walk around the block, a lunch with a very good friend, or a dish of rich ice cream. Note the effects on your motivation to do the project. What are your feelings—guilt, anxiety, joy? What happens when you try to go back to work? Do you have any sense of an increase in your ability to decide deliberately what and how to do things for yourself?

Systems, self-regulation, self-efficacy, transformation, and discipline—you have now constructed a description of yourself as a self-regulating person. You possess complex structures and processes that enable you to adapt to a variety of demanding environmental niches. You possess knowledge, skills, and abilities that enable you to transcend difficulties and problems. Finally, you are disciplined. Psychologists are capable of being of service to others because of this unique blend of traits. The extent to which you bring these traits to bear and provide these services in a particular niche will determine how successful you are and how long you survive. You may not be perfect, but you will succeed.

Self-Regulation and the Prevention of Professional Impairment

Every one of us encounters difficulties as we move through our lives. Often, we do not truly notice the strains of a slightly increased workload, the problems of keeping a relationship functioning smoothly, or the issues that our children encounter on their own road to maturity. We skim the surface of our lives like so many skaters, barely aware that the lake just beneath the ice is full of wonders, surprises, and even dangers. Occasionally, however, a crack or hole opens up in the ice, and we might stumble, fall, or take a surprisingly cold bath if we are not careful.

Kilburg, Nathan, and Thoreson (1986) described many of these problems in their work on distressed professionals. They implied that professional performance operates on a continuum:

⟵——————————————————————⟶

Peak   Normal   Distressed   Impaired   Disabled

On the left side, we see peak performance, the place where we would all like to function most of the time. Moving to the right, we find normal functioning. This is just what the term implies, the level of performance most of us reach most of the time. In the middle of the figure, we find distressed performance. This occurs when the problems of daily living overwhelm our capacity to cope on a temporary basis, and our ability to perform is reduced, but not dangerously below what is normal for us. Here, there are no performance failures. However, to the right of distress, we find impaired performance. Physical, emotional, or behavioral problems can affect professional skill and judgment. When a professional is impaired, there may or may not be documented performance failure. Keep in mind that psychologists normally function with a great deal of personal freedom and often with a true absence of accountability. Organizations and colleagues can be slow to recognize that any problem exists, so that impaired performance can continue for long periods of time without consequences for the psychologist. Finally, we have disabled performance, where the physical, emotional, or behavioral problem produces significant and documented declines in skill or judgment.

Types of Impairment

There are many different types of impairment that can affect a psychologist—too many to review in depth here. Lang, Jara, and Kessenick (1989) described most of those that they have experienced with practicing physicians. Psychologists are equally prone to these difficulties. What follows is a brief description of some of the major forms of impairment/disability that you or your colleagues are likely to experience.

Burnout and rust out. In chapter 6, I cover this problem in more detail. Suffice it to say that psychologists are as vulnerable to the burnout syndrome as anyone else. Maslach (1986) and Freudenberger and Richelson (1980) described the symptoms as including emotional exhaustion, depersonalization, and reduced sense of personal accomplishment. The burned-out psychologist finds it increasingly difficult to work effectively. The rusted-out psychologist is beyond burnout. He or she has stayed far too long in a job/niche and has ceased to function with any true effectiveness. Rusted-out people are often trying to hold on until retirement or meet some other internalized goal, and they do not respond well to environmental demands.

Chemical dependence and codependence. Psychologists are not immune to the diseases of alcoholism and drug dependence. Thoreson and Skorina (1986) indicated that approximately 6% of psychologists suffer from alcoholism. Because this disease often takes a long time to manifest itself on the job, psychologists can be drinking or abusing drugs long before it comes to the attention of supervisors and colleagues. Fortunately, chemical dependency is treatable, even though it is difficult to get people with the disease to accept help.

Mental illness. In a study with a small sample of psychologists and psychotherapists, Racusin, Abramowitz, and Winter (1981) found that 100% of them came from families in which there was someone who was chemically dependent, mentally or physically ill, had suffered from child abuse or sexual molestation, or had experienced divorce or other traumatic loss. Many psychologists have struggled with the problems of anxiety, depression, and other forms of mental and emotional problems. We often expect ourselves to be above such problems, especially because we teach people about them, do research in this area, and even treat people who suffer from them. However, we are just as vulnerable as anyone else and, if a problem does occur, it can significantly affect our personal and professional lives.

Sexual impropriety with clients. Psychologists and other mental health professionals are in a unique position in society. Those of us who practice clinically are expected to talk to people about their most intimate thoughts and feelings while simultaneously keeping our own under the strictest of control. At times, our ability to regulate our own behavior disappears under a host of internal or external pressures. At these times, psychologists are vulnerable and may be likely to take advantage of their even more vulnerable clients by engaging in sexual activity with them. Brodsky (1986) reviewed this problem thoroughly. She provided a thoughtful picture of the patients most likely to be victims of this type of affair, the circumstances that make it possible, and a series of recommendations about how to prevent it from occurring.

Legal problems and malpractice stress. Knapp (1980) provided a succinct overview of some of the major problems that lead psychologists to be sued for malpractice. These include physical assaults occurring in encounter groups, sexual improprieties, negligent treatments of suicidal patients, the duty to protect third parties from the violent acts of patients in treatment, and fraud. Although the problem of negligence suits is nowhere near as significant as it is in the medical profession, psychologists who are taken to court are likely to experience "malpractice stress." Pfifferling and Lang (1990) discussed this problem, suggesting that, for some individuals, a malpractice suit can seriously damage their mental and emotional health.

Family and relationship problems. Psychologists learn a great deal about human behavior during their training years. They teach and research the subject of human relationships, and they help others build more effective connections in their jobs and in their personal lives. Psychologists are also humans, themselves. They have their own relationships and are just as prone to the problems of relationship strain, separation, and divorce as is any other group in our society. When these problems arise, psychologists are likely to feel even more responsibility and emotional turmoil than the average person because of their special knowledge and skills. In an extreme case, an individual going through such events can experience impaired or even disabled professional performance because of the mental and emotional problems that are frequently associated with relationship disturbances.

Physical illness and disabilities. Psychologists are subject to the same array of physical problems that affect the rest of the world. When illness or disability occur, they can severely restrict or inhibit someone's ability to practice in the field. Perhaps the problems are not as dramatic as when a surgeon loses fine motor control due to aging, but a stroke, a heart condition, an accident requiring a lengthy recuperation, or chronic illness such as diabetes, multiple sclerosis, or crones disease can present tremendous burdens for a psychologist (Mandell & Spiro, 1987). It is crucial that we understand our vulnerability to such problems, and that we do not underestimate the potential impact that an illness could have on any of us.

Impairment and Self-Regulation

Distressed, impaired, or disabled performance most often indicates failures in physical, emotional, social, behavioral, or professional self-regulation. As we reflect on the model of ecological systems and self-regulation described earlier, several major forms of failure stand out immediately.

First, there is the *failure to anticipate* that problems will and can occur. The knowledge of the adaptation process and the complexity of life should enable us to see that certain events in our lives are unavoidable and require an extra measure of attention. However, we often ignore what we know, secure in the knowledge and in the expectation that we will be able to cope with whatever occurs. This can be a fatal error in some circumstances. For example, if you try to start your own business and do not provide sufficient capital to weather the economic storms that always occur, you could lose your business.

Second, there is the *failure to implement corrections* when problems do arise. Psychologists defend themselves just like anyone else. We deny that problems exist, that they are as serious as they seem, or that anything should be done. We do not take responsibility for our actions. We do not initiate new forms of behavior, build new structures, or integrate the problems into what we know. We often sit and wait until it is too late to do anything constructive except clean up the mess. If our business does fail, we are left to contemplate the failure and look for another job.

Third, there are *failures in discipline.* We don't delay gratification, take responsibility, choose to see reality for what it is, or balance the process of discipline itself. If we watch ourselves struggle with discipline, we can learn a great deal. Often, psychologists do not balance discipline, and they become workaholics. Their families can suffer greatly as they pursue normal lives, while these psychologists think only about grants, papers, clients, or classes.

Fourth, there are *failures in strategy*. Psychologists do not gather enough information about the environments in which they work. They overvalue their own knowledge or skill and often select the wrong approaches to problems or phases in their lives. In short, they get off on the wrong track. When this happens, it can sometimes take years to correct. If you start out pursuing a career as an experimental psychologist in academia and discover that you would rather practice full-time as a child clinician, it will take you a great deal of time and energy to change the situation around.

Finally, psychologists often *cope poorly* just like anyone else. We lack awareness of what is important or what is happening around us, we do not properly understand the issues that confront us, we make poor choices, or we fail to evaluate our performances. As a result, any one of the types of impairment described earlier can occur. For example, some psychologists may experience the difficulties of a separation or divorce and then go on to complicate matters by becoming sexually involved with a client. This can only make matters worse, and yet, despite all of the training and safeguards built into our work, some of us go on to create just this type of craziness and chaos for ourselves.

Let's take the time to explore just what can happen to an individual who experiences one of these failures in self-regulation.

Example 2.3 A Psychologist Under Pressure

Paula Ford was a 30-year-old school psychologist who had just finished collecting the data for her dissertation. She received an excellent job offer as an assistant director of psychological services in a large metropolitan area in a neighboring state. She discussed the offer with her husband, Jim, an attorney who worked for a large law firm that happened to have an office in the same city as Paula's new job. Together, they decided to move to that city. Paula would go first, because she already had the job offer. Jim would follow in approximately 6 to 12 months with their two children, Monica, who was seven, and Jason, who was four. Jim could arrange a transfer within his law firm, but it took a little time, and they had to sell their house.

Paula moved into an apartment in the new city with a roommate who proceeded to drive her crazy with constant visitors and very late hours. Paula found her job exciting and challenging and settled into the routine of it very quickly. The school system was revamping the curriculum and creating several new programs for children with special needs. Paula's boss asked her to lead the psychology department's efforts on these initiatives. As she became immersed in the work, she came home feeling drained and unable to work on the data analysis for her dissertation. She would call home, talk to Jim and the two children, and find herself in bed early.

After 3 months, Paula had enough of her roommate and found a townhouse that she liked. After talking it over with her husband, she took a lease and moved again. Shortly thereafter, Monica, Jason, and Jim came for a long weekend. The children were very glad to see her, but became argumentative, demanding, and whiny as the weekend wore on. Jim told her that he was having trouble selling the house and that the transfer might take longer than expected because of a few of his cases that had troubling complications. They decided that the children could move in with Paula at the end of the school year, which would occur in another 3 months.

> Over the next several weeks, Paula and Jim had several long, argumentative telephone calls. Both of them were irritable and worried about money and the children who were not doing very well. Paula had developed a nice friendship with a male colleague at work who occasionally took her out to dinner. They had long talks about work and anything else that came to mind. Paula wasn't quite sure how it happened, but after a particularly hard stretch at work and another series of arguments with Jim about money, she ended up having a short affair with this colleague, which she believed she could handle fairly well. It was the first time she had been unfaithful to Jim in their 12-year relationship.
>
> A month later, the children moved in with her, and she ended the affair with her friend. Paula became a single parent in a relatively new town during the summer months. She made day-care arrangements, altered her schedule at work, and tried to settle in to finish her dissertation. Jim was still having trouble selling the house because of a very slow market. They decided to lower their asking price significantly, so that the house would sell.
>
> At work, Paula's colleague began to pressure her to resume their love affair. She resisted all of his efforts, but found it increasingly difficult to go to work because of his constant presence. She called Jim and suggested that they put the house up at a fire sale price because both she and the children were missing him. They finally sold the house and Jim moved several weeks later. After 15 months, the family was finally back together.
>
> Within 2 months, Monica began having nightmares. She hated her new school. Paula made accommodations in her schedule to support Monica, because Jim was commuting to two different offices to both finish up his old cases and start at his new location. Paula and Jim were still somewhat short tempered with each other, but managed to buy a house and move in before Christmas. Paula's colleague continued to pressure her, and she began to have anxiety attacks in the middle of the night. She would get up and pace the floor, worrying about Monica, her marriage, and what would happen if her friend called her husband. After several weeks of sleepless nights and a growing feeling that she was becoming depressed, Paula sought assistance from a senior psychologist in private practice who had an excellent reputation. Paula began to put the pieces of her life back together as she stabilized her daughter in school, set firm limits with her colleague at work, and tried to figure out why she had entered into the affair. She continued to do well in her job, and while Jim took care of the children on weekends, she finally began to do some work on her dissertation.

I hope that this example illustrates the complexities involved in successful self-regulation. Paula planned and implemented a major change in her life and the life of her family. She moved into the process of behavioral transformation and created new patterns of work and relationships as she tried to integrate her family life and old role as a graduate student. She managed to create a new structure within which she could work comfortably, but her family continued to have problems adjusting to the situation. Paula tried a variety of adaptations to assist herself and her children. They were partially successful, but they created additional problems, especially when she entered into the affair with a colleague and destabilized her work environment. Paula developed some acute psychological symptoms for which she sought treatment, despite having achieved a great deal in her new job and enabling her family to make the transition to a new town and way of life.

Adaptation failures are seldom complete. We often do some things well even as we create problems for ourselves in other areas. The process of self-regulation and the discipline required for success demand an enormous amount from us. I believe that it is only when we extend our knowledge and skills in the adaptation process that we can truly create ourselves as we want to be and prevent the variety of problems that can lead to impairment or disability. The following questions should help you to develop in these areas.

Exercise 2.3 Some Interesting Questions to Ask

1. Think about the most recent time you were distressed at work or in your personal life. Were you bored, emotionally troubled, physically sick, or having a major struggle with a colleague?
2. What happened during this episode of distress? How did you adapt to the problems that were created?
3. Did any of the failures in self-regulation described in this chapter occur? If yes, which ones?
4. How did you resolve the distress? How was the process of self-regulation involved?
5. Did the events or the process change you or your circumstances in any way? How?
6. Would a better knowledge of self-regulation and the adaptation process have prevented the problem or helped to shorten or simplify it? How?

References

Aldrich, H. E., & Pfeffer, J. (1976). Environments of organizations. *Annual Review of Sociology, 2,* 79–105.

Bandura, A. (1977). Self-efficacy: Toward a unifying theory of behavioral change. *Psychological Review, 84,* 191–215.

Bandura, A. (1982). Self-efficacy mechanism in human agency. *American Psychologist, 37,* 122–147.

Braham, M. (1973). A general theory of organization. *General Systems, 13,* 13–24.

Brodsky, A. M. (1986). The distressed psychologist: Sexual intimacies and exploitation. In R. R. Kilburg, P. E. Nathan, & R. W. Thoreson (Eds.), *Professionals in distress: Issues, syndromes and solutions in psychology.* Washington, DC: American Psychological Association.

Freudenberger, H. J., & Richelson, G. (1980). *Burnout: The high cost of high achievement.* Garden City, NJ: Doubleday.

Kilburg, R. R. (1983). The psychologist as manager. In B. D. Sales (Ed.), *The professional psychologist's handbook* (pp. 495–537). New York: Plenum Press.

Kilburg, R. R., Nathan, P. E., & Thoreson, R. W. (Eds.). (1986). *Professionals in distress: Issues, syndromes and solutions in psychology.* Washington, DC: American Psychological Association.

Knapp, S. (1980). A primer on malpractice for psychologists. *Professional Psychology, 11,* 606–612.

Koestler, A. (1978). *Janus: A summing up.* New York: Random House.

Kuhn, A. (1974). *The logic of social systems.* San Francisco: Jossey-Bass.

Lang, D. A., Jara, G. B., & Kessenick, L. W. (1989). *The disabled physician: Problem-solving strategies for the medical staff.* Chicago: American Hospital Publishing Inc.

Mandell, H., & Spiro, H. (Eds.). (1987). *When doctors get sick.* New York: Plenum Medical Book Co.

Markus, H., & Nurius, P. (1986). Possible selves. *American Psychologist, 41,* 954–969.

Maslach, C. (1986). Stress, burnout, and alcoholism. In R. R. Kilburg, P. E. Nathan, & R. W. Thoreson (Eds.), *Professionals in distress: Issues, syndromes and solutions in psychology*. Washington, DC: American Psychological Association.

Peck, F. S. (1978). *The road less traveled*. New York: Simon and Schuster.

Pfifferling, J. H., & Lang, D. (1990). *The malpractice stress syndrome*. Unpublished manuscript.

Piaget, J. (1971). *Biology and knowledge: An essay on the relations between organic regulations and cognitive processes*. Chicago: University of Chicago Press.

Racusin, G. R., Abramowitz, S. I., & Winter, W. D. (1981). Becoming a therapist: Family dynamics and career choice. *Professional Psychology*, *12*, 271–279.

Thoreson, R. W., & Skorina, J. K. (1986). Alcohol abuse among psychologists. In R. R. Kilburg, P. E. Nathan, & R. W. Thoreson (Eds.), *Professionals in distress: Issues, syndromes and solutions in psychology*. Washington, DC: American Psychological Association.

Von Bertalanffy, L. (1968). *General systems theory*. New York: Braziller.

3

Richard R. Kilburg

The Tools of Management

In order to be effective in the art of self-regulation and address the key problems facing us as psychologists, we must look beyond the concepts presented in chapter 2. We must develop specific skills that enable us to succeed in our careers. I believe that many of those skills can be learned by mastering the tools of management.

Management is usually defined as both a process and a function. In organizations, the function of management is to be responsible for the success or failure of the enterprise. The processes of management or the ways that managers perform their function include planning, organizing, leading or directing, decision making, and controlling (Sisk, 1977; Rakich, Longest, & Darr, 1985; Koontz & Weihrich, 1990). By applying this definition to psychologists, it is clear that our success or failure rides extensively, but not exclusively, on our managerial abilities. The tools of management are our primary means of regulating our professional development, establishing rules for functioning as psychologists, and finding methods for addressing the key issues that face us in our professional lives. In the remainder of this chapter, I will review some of the principal tools of management.

Management Roles

Mintzberg (1973) formulated a taxonomy of the working roles of professional managers (see Figure 3.1) that includes three major categories: interpersonal, informational, and decisional roles. Let's review the characteristics of these roles and focus on their relevance for psychologists.

Interpersonal Roles

In the interpersonal category of roles, a psychologist acts as a figurehead, leader, and liaison. These roles overlap somewhat, but each has characteristics that are worth examining separately.

Figurehead. The central idea is that there is one person who, by virtue of his or her position as figurehead, conveys and commands the image, control, authority, and resources of the organization. That individual functions as the symbol of what that organization represents. In this role, a psychologist presides at ceremonial

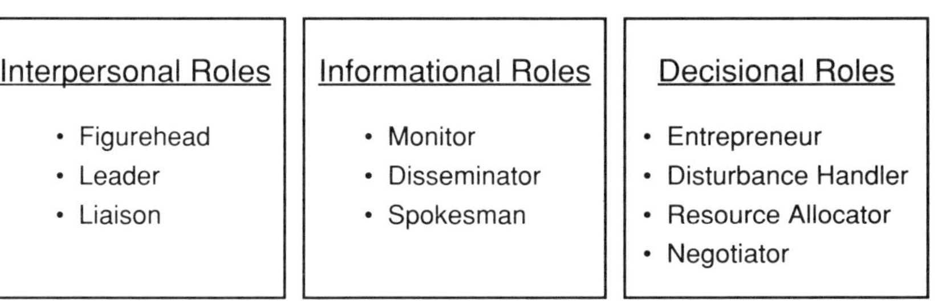

Figure 3.1. The manager's working roles.

occasions; lends prestige, status, and power to subordinates at appropriate times; enters into negotiations; makes commitments; and officially signs documents.

Psychologists who hold positions such as department chairs, directors of health and human service organizations, and executive officers of their own businesses are readily seen as engaging in this role. However, every psychologist also acts as a figurehead when presenting himself or herself to the external world. Whether you are appearing on a panel at a professional or scientific meeting, negotiating an employment contract for yourself, or simply talking to a member of the public as a psychologist, you are a symbol for what you represent professionally. Performing this role calls for sensitivity, tact, and a commitment to effective behavior. If others see you as ill prepared or bungling, or under the worst conditions, dangerous or nefarious, you and everyone else you represent will suffer. Exercise 3.1 will help you look at yourself as a figurehead.

Exercise 3.1 Are You a Figurehead?

Take a few minutes and jot down your thoughts in response to each of the following questions.

1. How would you like to be perceived by others inside or outside the field of psychology?
2. What are the five adjectives you would most like people to associate with you as a psychologist?
3. What are the five adjectives you would least like people to associate with you as a psychologist?
4. Are you ever sought out by colleagues or others for advice? Do others follow your advice? Why?
5. What kind of public presentation do you make (appearance, speaking style, manner of relating to people and new situations)?
6. Have you ever thought of yourself as a figurehead? If yes, what do you expect from it? If no, why not?
7. What attitudes, beliefs, and feelings would you need to change to make yourself effective as a figurehead?

8. How do others respond to you in general?
9. What types of responses from others do you monitor? Do you ever ask about how you are coming across? If you do, what responses have you received?
10. Have you ever modified your own professional behavior based on what you thought someone's response to you was? If yes, how and why?

Leader. When a psychologist acts as a leader he or she is performing one of the most important roles in an organization. Leaders create the climate in which others live and work. Leaders also provide the inspiration and incentives for effective functioning. Mintzberg (1973) stated that some of the most important behavioral components of leadership include staffing–hiring, training, judging, remunerating, promoting and dismissing subordinates, motivating, advising, directing, recognizing, encouraging and chastising employees, and meddling (p. 61). In leading an organization, a psychologist works to pull the efforts of the organization into a coherent and collaborating whole. Most important, the leader tries to ensure that the goals of the individual mesh with those of the organization.

When you act as a leader, your primary responsibility is to establish and maintain the environment in which the business or subunit of the organization operates. In addition to this, you set the goals for that organization. One of your tools is to develop the major niches of your organization. Usually, you do this through job descriptions. A niche is defined by the work expected and the capacities, skills, and experience levels of the person who will occupy it. You start, then, with an abstract idea of the work that needs to be done and the duties that need to be performed. Then, you need to recruit people to perform in the niches.

Finding the right people to fill niches is actually the most complex and important subset of a leader's tasks, because the leader's own success is ultimately dependent on the capacities of his or her colleagues to do the work assigned to them. No other single decision carries quite the amount of weight, because all future activities result from the release of the creative energies of staff members as they work to make the leader and the organization succeed.

Once you select your staff, the process of behavioral transformation begins. In your role as leader, you facilitate and sometimes force the adaptation process in your subordinates. You train, judge, reward, punish, promote, and dismiss people. In addition to these motivational strategies, you use communication skills such as advising, directing, encouraging, chastising, and gently interfering in the work life of your subordinates. When successful, you attain the goals of the organization and develop reasonable fits between subordinates and their niches.

Your facilitation of the adaptation process is based on your beliefs and values. McGregor (1960) outlined the two major belief systems that he thought leaders used in supporting and directing their subordinates. Theory X assumes that people dislike work, must be forced to put forward sufficient effort for the organization to succeed, and prefer to avoid taking responsibility, seeking security more than anything else.

On the other hand, Theory Y assumes that work is just as natural to people as play. Punitive controls are not needed because individuals will direct themselves, seek responsibility, and apply their creative capacities to the work of the organization. The manager's job is to harness the energy and capacity of the employee to the tasks necessary for success. This is obviously a very different picture of what a leader will expect from subordinates. It usually contributes to more participative and supportive leadership styles.

Aside from attitudinal systems, leaders pay attention to hygienic conditions and motivators. Sisk (1977) defined motivators as those factors that foster achievement, positive attitudes, and the willingness to accept responsibility. Hygienic conditions are not directly related to the job and include salaries, work environments, safety conditions, and supervisory effectiveness.

Leaders can use a large variety of techniques to influence morale and to create the conditions for good adaptation. Environments can be designed to provide safety and comfort. Benefit plans can be altered to offer increased rewards for hard work. Jobs can be enriched to increase staff members' self-respect and sense of accomplishment. Supervisors and staff can be trained for a wide variety of purposes. Human relations strategies can be used to build better communication, trust, and teamwork. And, when all else fails, staff members can be disciplined and eventually fired if performance continues to be below expectations.

Establishing good organizational climates and developing effective processes for delegation are the most critical tasks for leaders. In setting the climate, you arrange the general environment in which people work. In delegating, you extend your influence and field of action through the work performed by colleagues.

The *delegation-supervision process* is a subtle, complex, and difficult art. It is hard to teach and even harder to learn. Sisk (1977) described successful supervision as dependent upon the following factors: the maintenance of a good organizational climate, the use of effective delegation practices, an equal focus on tasks to be done and the quality of relationships with the subordinate, and the ability to harness participation in the service of change.

Sisk (1977) identified the following three steps in the delegation process: assignment of responsibility, delegation of authority, and creation of accountability. A leader gives someone a job to do, assigns sufficient power and resources to get the job done, and requires that the individual report regularly on events that affect the job. It seems simple and straightforward. However, a wide variety of issues, events, and problems can interfere with delegation.

It is easy enough to assign responsibility, but leaders are often unclear as to the nature of the task to be done. Sufficient authority to make decisions can be withheld. At times, leaders do not pay attention once a task has been assigned. Subordinates do not communicate when they should. Personality and emotional factors such as an inability to confront problems, a distrust of people, and a fear of failure can also interfere. Delegation is deceptively simple and simply difficult to do well.

For the second major task, Ouchi (1981) provided an excellent description of how organizational climates are developed (i.e., the structure through which delegation is implemented and accountability is established) in what he called Type Z organizations or clans. Ouchi also distinguished between hierarchies and markets, two other types of organizations structured for economic activity, by emphasizing that clans are intimate associations of people engaged in economic work and tied together through a variety of bonds. I believe that Ouchi focused on the familial characteristics that can be seen in any organization. His clans are simply work families that are very good at competing in economic environments.

Ouchi (1981) stressed the subtle and important relationship between the individual and the work team. He believed that organizations must make a long-term investment in their people. It is only after sober reflection on job performance over a substantial period that a person's true value to a company can be determined. Simultaneously, an individual can come to trust the investment the organization has in him or her and make the necessary commitment to achieve at the highest levels possible. The intricate and effective teamwork that evolves out of such trust and commitment puts the individual's efforts in a group context that makes evaluation of individual performance difficult and at times, meaningless. In the organizational climate of an effective clan, when the work group succeeds, the individual succeeds.

Ouchi (1981) emphasized that clans take McGregor's (1960) emphasis on meshing individual and organizational goals very seriously. In effective organizations, individuals come to understand and accept the goals of the enterprise so well that they constantly seek to do what will help the organization succeed. In a sense, clans tell individuals "this is where we are going, do anything that you can to help us get there." The person accomplishes his or her own objectives, but in the selfless pursuit of helping the organization achieve. People feel free to be themselves because the organization asks them to do just that for the widely accepted goals.

There are a variety of ways to create or change an organizational climate. Ouchi (1981) enumerated a series of 13 steps that can be followed to create a Type Z organization. These steps highlight one systematic approach to changing an organization and creating a particular type of organizational climate.

Ouchi's 13 steps are as follows:

1. Understand the Type Z organization and your role.
2. Audit your company's organizational philosophy.
3. Define the desired management philosophy and involve the company leader.
4. Implement the philosophy by creating both structures and incentives.
5. Develop interpersonal skills.
6. Test yourself and the system.
7. Involve the union (or unions).
8. Stabilize employment.
9. Decide on a system for slow evaluation and promotion.
10. Broaden career-path development for employees.
11. Prepare for implementation at the first level.
12. Seek out areas to implement participation.
13. Permit the development of holistic relationships.

Following these steps helps you to define the art of leadership as it creates an organizational climate. It is a most difficult role to play. Example 3.1 demonstrates leadership in action.

Example 3.1 Becoming a Leader

Kyle Panetta, a clinical psychologist with 10 years experience in community mental health centers, recently accepted a position as the director of a center in another state. He arrived to find that the organization and its staff had been through several bruising battles with local governments and neighborhoods over building community facilities for the mentally handicapped. The staff was demoralized. The board of directors was polarized. The organization was lifeless. It was clear that the first task was to listen.

So, in the first 6 months, Kyle met with a number of people and discovered the problems of staff, board members, government leaders, and community groups. In a series of discussions with major funding sources and the executive committee of the board, Kyle eventually introduced a number of goals, action plans, and budget proposals. Kyle was able to obtain support for most of the proposals.

Kyle then met with staff members to suggest that they begin to move the organization forward. The pain of recent events led to a great deal of resistance to change among the staff. The key leaders of the resistance were two of the previous director's principal deputies. Kyle had meetings with the management team and discussed the new agenda. They agreed collectively that the new directions were needed, but the team members did not believe that resources or support could be found to implement them. They promised to work hard if Kyle could find the necessary support.

Kyle had already negotiated most of what they needed. At a follow-up meeting, the news was given to the management team. No one was happy. During the next year, it became clear that several members of the team would not support any change. Kyle made a series of tough decisions and removed these individuals. With new and more enthusiastic team members, the organization soon righted itself and began to forge better relationships with the communities it served.

This example highlights the complexity of the leader function. Kyle modified the goals and climate of the organization and then had problems with staff fitting into the new niches that resulted. Delegation and supervision worked in some cases to help individuals adapt to the changes, but not in others. Eventually, performance was judged to be so bad that some new staff members had to be recruited, and the better fit that resulted moved the organization forward. When psychologists lead themselves and others, these two factors must be handled well.

Liaison. According to Mintzberg (1973), this last role in the interpersonal triad involved building a network of reciprocating relationships that becomes a central resource in the working life of professionals. Information, job offers, political contacts, opportunities to grow or decay, problems, battles, friendships, trust, love, and hate are all part of what the liaison role will bring to you.

Working as a psychologist turns you into an information-processing system, and the liaison role enables you to manage effectively exchanges of information with other people. Information is critical to your growth and survival because without accurate information, adaptive strategies can be mishandled, sometimes creating a disaster. Your major task as a liaison is to obtain sufficient information to help avoid catastrophes that could threaten your life, job, career, and profession.

In crafting a network, you must consider all of the sources of power, such as money, authority, information, personnel, products, services, professional contacts, and other scarce resources that must be obtained and maintained in order to survive in a niche. As a liaison, you systematically review and contact the people associated with these sources of power in your environment. Over time, you build relationships with these individuals.

When possible disasters or opportunities arise in your environment, successful performance of the liaison role provides an early warning system that, if heeded, leads to better strategies and improved problem solving capabilities. Because you have established such a network, friends and colleagues who acquire relevant information pass it on to you, often without knowing that it is intelligence. The suggestion of a new business opening in town, a change in political forces in an organization, or an idea for a new product or project all provide useful leads for an alert psychologist. Exercise 3.2 will help you to identify the ways in which you fill the liaison role in your personal network.

Exercise 3.2 Identifying Your Networking Potential

1. Think for a moment about the four major resources (e.g., money, information, emotional support, job security) on which you depend in your personal and professional life. Write them down.
2. Now try to identify the individuals with whom you most closely associate these resources. Write them down.
3. When was the last time you met with any of these people either socially or professionally? How long has it been?
4. Make plans to meet with everyone on the list in the next 3 months.
5. Finally, try to identify individuals who might have information, ideas, or access to resources that would be helpful to you. Plan to meet with them.

Informational Roles

Mintzberg (1973) also described managers as information-processing systems. In this regard, the essential features of managerial and psychological work are the same—the success, indeed the survival of both, depends on accurate and timely information.

Psychologists are the nerve centers of their own information-processing systems. Information processing is divided into *input* (the process of obtaining information), *throughput* (the process of determining the relevance of information), and *output* (the process of using information to further your objectives). Again, the effectiveness with which you perform this role often dictates the extent to which you will succeed professionally. As an information processor, you act as a monitor, a disseminator, and a spokesperson.

Monitor. When acting as a monitor, you seek to understand the internal and external environments in which you find yourself. Over time, you build the capacity to obtain a broad array of information that you determine is vital to your functioning as a psychologist. The monitor role overlaps with the liaison role described earlier.

As a psychologist, you are constantly on the alert for new sources of information relevant to your areas of interest. You stay abreast of scientific and practice literature to remain current on technical and conceptual developments. You may also monitor other sources of information on political, economic, and legal trends that might affect you. Finally, you track changes in psychology and other professions. Monitoring change is an efficient way to remain aware of issues and trends that could threaten your survival as a psychologist.

Mintzberg (1973) elaborated on this theme by stating that managers usually receive or seek information in five areas: internal operations, external events, analysis, ideas and trends, and pressures. Psychologists managing themselves must collect this sort of information on both their internal and external environments.

Internal operating information comes from the experiences of subordinates and colleagues working in the same environment, as well as from observations of work in progress, standard internal reports, and so forth. Much of this information is routine and tells whether or not events are moving according to plan. In rapidly changing environments, this information is essential in obtaining a good picture of the present and near-future realities likely to affect your niche.

Information on external events centers on market opportunities, capacities of competitors, sources of capital and other supplies, feedback from clients, and other information sources outside of the home environment. The sources include magazines, books, reports, trade journals and other formal channels, rumors, gossip, and the informal speculations of colleagues, friends, and enemies. You must always compromise on the depth of coverage of these sources of information, focusing particularly on issues that are potentially promising or threatening to you.

Analysis usually involves examining more detailed reports of special interest to you and interpreting their value. These reports come from a variety of sources. If you are going to make the time to read them, be sure they are important to you.

Ideas and trends include examinations of technological, demographic, political, and social developments likely to affect you as a psychologist. You attend conferences, talk to colleagues, suppliers, referral sources, and funding agencies, read journals and books, and so forth in an effort to collect this information.

Pressures involve the impact of demands, power tactics, and various social, political, legal, interpersonal, and other strategies used in and on organizations. This information is usually found between the lines of formal reports, letters, and articles. They are often feelings, fantasies, or impressions created as a result of some interpersonal exchange.

As a psychologist, you must work hard at assembling a coherent picture of your environment/niche from the various pieces of information available. From these data, you can build working models of your environment that will enable you to set realistic goals and activity plans for the future. In Exercise 3.2, you evaluated your networking potential. In Exercise 3.3, you will evaluate other sources from which you derive information.

Exercise 3.3 Evaluating Formal Information Sources

1. Make a list of the following sources of information you use to guide your professional development:
   a. Journals, magazines, newspapers, and letters you read.
   b. The last five books you have read.
   c. Professional organizations to which you belong.
   d. Conferences and meetings that you attend either regularly or sporadically.
   e. Internal reports and similar data sources that you have access to in your organization.
2. How good is your coverage of the information, people, and organizations most likely to affect your work in psychology?
3. Are there other sources of information that you believe would help you? Write them down. Develop a plan for gaining access to them.

Disseminator. Once you obtain critical information through the liaison and monitor roles, it is important to communicate the information to those most likely to be helpful to you. In sharing the information you act as a disseminator. According to Mintzberg (1973), you will typically transmit *factual* and *value* information.

Factual information consists of reports of what was said or done in different situations by different people. It can include written documentation of these events in the form of letters, memos, and reports and oral communication. Such data can be verified easily. However, you must develop the means to check on the validity and reliability of all of the information you collect. The more accurate your factual information is, the easier it is to develop strategies, plan for the future, and solve current operating problems.

Value information includes needs, wishes, fantasies, and beliefs of what should be. Opinions, gossip, rumors, and speculations are some of the major sources of value information. Value information adds meaning to factual information. Most important, value information often allows you to sense or anticipate the pressures being brought to bear within an environment. Psychologists must become aware of these pressures and interpret them correctly in order to meet challenges successfully. Value information helps you to round out your model of an organization or environment and makes prediction somewhat easier. Be alert to the unseen ways that value information can influence your decisions (e.g., someone's expressed opinion that another person is a threat). Often, you will be asked to "line up" on someone's side in a disagreement or to do something on behalf of a colleague. Caution is advisable in such circumstances.

Having formed your model of the factual and value information at work in a situation, you will then operate in the disseminator role to distribute various pictures or pieces of the model to key people with whom you work. Although dissemination should advance in all directions in organizations, you must ensure that information is placed in the hands of individuals who can help you professionally and personally and withheld from people you believe will hurt you.

As you let various people know what is happening, you are in a position to collect additional data that enables you to validate your model. This additional information is often both factual and value rich. You must be able to incorporate the new material into your own plans and methods of operation to help you succeed. Exercise 3.4 will help you to evaluate how you function as a disseminator.

Exercise 3.4 Evaluating Your Effect as a Disseminator

1. Make a list of the last five people you talked to about problems, issues, plans, or possibilities you were considering. Who are they? Were the discussions helpful? Did anything come of the talks that was of concrete value?
2. Think for a moment about five other individuals who possibly should know about one or more aspects of your work, interests, or personal life. Why do you think they should be included? How do you think they can help you?
3. Make a plan for talking to at least two of these people. Identify why you want to talk to them and what you want to say. Do you have any requests to make? If they are subordinates, what do you want them to do for you? If they are superiors, think about how you can present yourself in the best light possible.

Spokesperson. As you can see, psychologists can gather a vast array of information from the performance of their many managerial and professional roles. When you are called upon to speak on behalf of yourself or your organization, you become a spokesperson. The information at your command and your status as a professional can make you a forceful advocate for yourself and your organization.

Mintzberg (1973) stated that "the spokesman role requires of the manager that he keep two groups informed. The first is the organization's set of key influences—the Board of Directors in the case of a chief executive and the boss in the case of the middle manager . . . the second group to be informed is the organization's public. In the case of chief executives, this includes suppliers, trade organizations, peers, government agencies, customers and the press" (p. 75–76).

As a psychologist, you must learn to perform this role effectively. No one else can portray you or the status of your organization with as much accuracy or forcefulness as you can. Although the notion of image is an overused concept, you must accept that the image you project into the environment can directly affect how key individuals or other resources relate to and support you. Jobs, sources of information, and finances can all be influenced in positive directions. You cannot just hope that an effective and sympathetic image will be conveyed. You must develop a specific plan to convey the crucial information to the people of influence who surround you and the general public.

Most spokesperson exchanges take place verbally and publicly. You must carefully craft the messages you want to send in order to achieve the intended effects. Accurate information, which can be confirmed, is sent to those with influence and the public. Frequently, you will vary the content and tone of your communication to match your audience. Thus, what you decide to share with your board of directors in a service agency concerning your problems with staff may vary significantly from what you share with a funding source. It is most important to recognize that these exchanges are necessary and that you must carry them out with care and deliberation. Although the circumstances and the motivations of the people involved can unite to decrease the effectiveness of a particular information exchange, you can reduce the number and lessen the impact of such ineffective episodes through the exercise of due caution. Let us explore this role in action through a brief example.

Example 3.2 Influencing the Influencers

Robin Browning was the director of the school psychological services in a large urban school system. At a staff meeting, Robin was informed about a small group of parents of handicapped children who had begun to organize themselves to pressure the system for better services. Robin validated this staff report by talking to teachers and administrators in the affected schools. Robin had wanted to improve the psychological services in a number of schools for some time, and the parent group's activism provided an opportunity to encourage change. Before taking any further action, Robin planned to discuss the issue with the assistant superintendent for operations in their next regular meeting.

Because the meeting presented a somewhat risky opportunity to push tactfully for additional resources for the next year, Robin carefully planned the meeting. The assistant superintendent was both cautious and meticulous and demanded that arguments be supported with solid information. The assistant superintendent was also very close to the superintendent and was the chief problem solver for the school system.

At the meeting, Robin covered a number of routine subjects, but was careful to leave enough time to raise the new issue of expanding services. At the appropriate time, Robin suggested that a new issue had come up and quickly filled in the details. The assistant superintendent probed carefully about the nature of the complaints and the sources of the data Robin had presented and asked if Robin had responded to the parents. Robin said no and went on to suggest a modest plan that might address some of the parents' concerns through improvements in the existing psychological services in the affected schools. The assistant superintendent said the plan would be considered after careful discussion with the superintendent.

Eventually, the superintendent's office arranged for a series of meetings with the parents and school officials to which Robin was invited. At several points in these meetings, Robin was asked for impressions and ideas. At these times, Robin carefully presented several suggestions for increases in psychological services based on recent reported research and discussions held with the school psychology staff. Robin was careful to leave the superintendent's options open and to couch the proposals by indicating that they were only possible solutions to problems.

After months of planning and many more meetings, Robin was pleased to report to the psychology department that the next budget year would provide for a significant increase in the number of staff members to address some of the issues raised by the parents.

In this example, we see the monitor, disseminator, and spokesperson roles in operation. Robin was able to use information obtained from a variety of sources to inform superiors of a potential problem. Simultaneously, the situation presented an opportunity to act as the spokesperson for psychological services, which helped the administration to understand how psychology could solve this newly identified problem. Although the happy ending presented here does not always occur, careful preparation and implementation of the informational roles can greatly increase your possibilities.

Making Decisions

As psychologists, each of us is on a professional journey for which we, like the captains of a ship, chart the course in response to changes in climate and mission. Some of us only have responsibility for ourselves, the communities, clients, and students we serve, and the profession to which we belong. Still others have the responsibility for thousands of employees and a large complex of social, political, economic, and legal obligations. In this context, just as a captain's decisions can affect the success or failure of a voyage, your decisions determine transformation or decay, survival or death in various aspects of your career.

From the first decision to enter the field of psychology, through the selection of courses and mentors, the development of collegial relationships, and most important, the decisions concerning which jobs we take, we are all determining the course and speed for our careers just as surely as the captain of any ship is determining the course of a voyage. As we have seen, these decisions are made in a process of dynamic interaction with complex external environments. As we interact with our environments, nothing is more critical to success than the formulation and implementation of strategies to adapt to the conditions we confront. The foundation for these strategies consists of our decisions.

It is easiest if we think of a continuum of strategic decision making organized around the degree of control exercised in the decision-making process. At one end of the continuum, you have little control over your decisions. For example, you might face a crisis in which there is little time to gather information or engage in the analysis and design phases of decision making. In these situations, you make the best choices you can and prepare for the worst outcomes.

As the continuum extends, circumstances arise in which you have a moderate degree of control. Typically, such situations are day-to-day problems that range from mild to severe. Nevertheless, you usually have some time to gather information and think through some alternatives.

Finally, at the other end of the continuum, there are decisions over which you exercise a high degree of control. These are your entrepreneurial choices that determine the basic goals and objectives you will pursue as a psychologist. Fortunately, you have the maximum amount of time to gather information and consider alternatives before you make the large-scale commitments involved in these decisions.

According to Mintzberg (1973), the strategy-making process involves four dif-

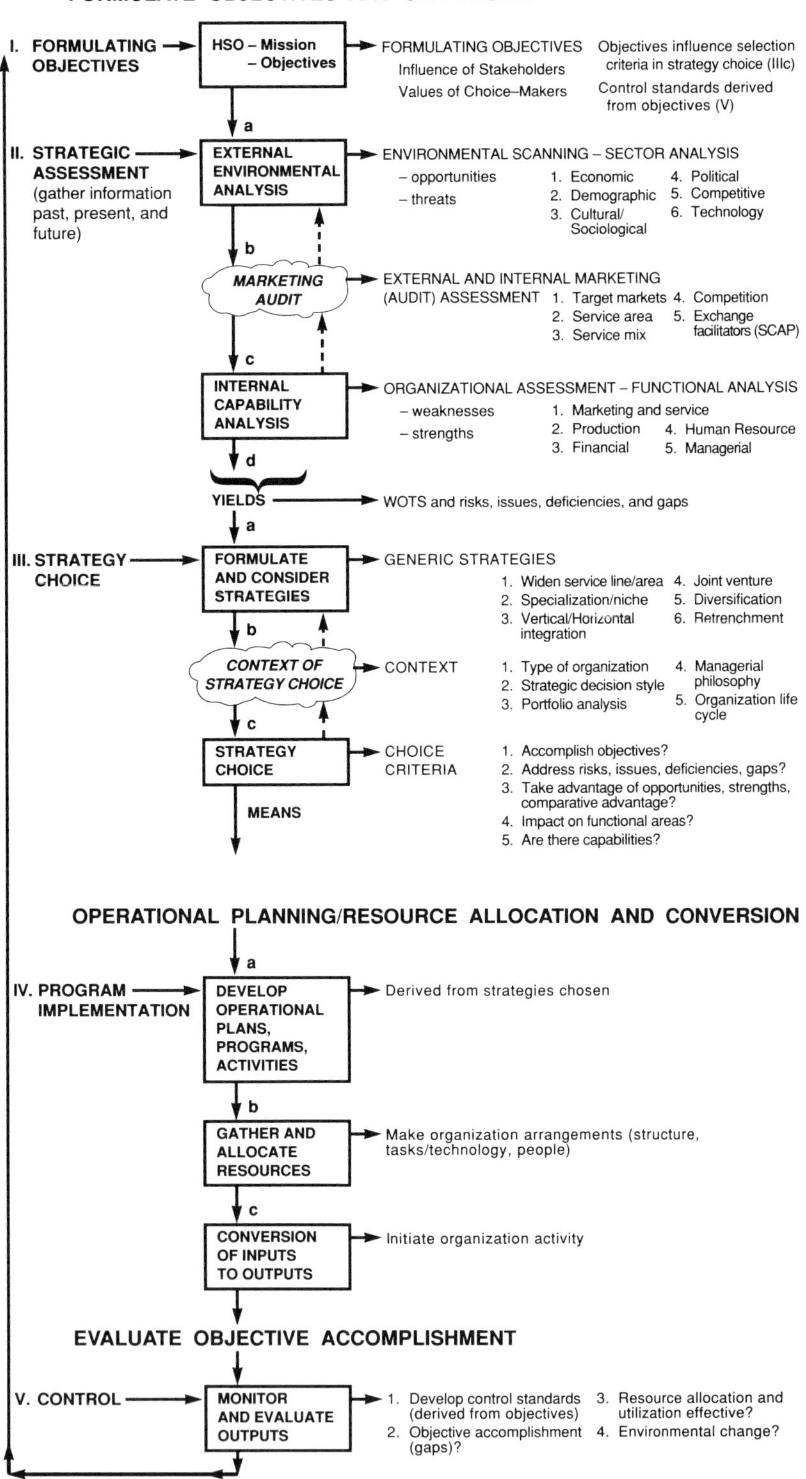

Figure 3.2. The strategic planning process. From Rakich, Longest, and Darr (1985). Reprinted with permission.

ferent roles: entrepreneur, disturbance handler, resource allocator, and negotiator. Let's briefly examine each of these roles.

Entrepreneur. If your career is to prosper, you must become a forward-thinking businessperson. This role, which Mintzberg (1973) called the entrepreneur, requires that thoughtful, informed, and sometimes adventurous decisions be made. The key to making effective decisions is planning, usually referred to in the business world as strategic planning. There are a number of conceptual approaches to strategic planning. Figure 3.2 presents a flowchart of a strategic planning process synthesized by Rakich, Longest, and Darr (1985, p. 229).

This strategic planning model has five major components: (a) formulation of objectives, (b) formulation of strategic assessment, (c) strategy choice, (d) program implementation, and (e) control.

When you, as a major stakeholder, decide what your mission as a psychologist will be, you are *formulating objectives.* For psychologists, this most often involves the choice of specialization.

Next, you put together your *strategic assessment.* You examine the external environment for opportunities and threats, analyze various market possibilities, and evaluate your own strengths and weaknesses. The summation of this assessment provides you with a great understanding of who you are professionally, what the opportunities are in your own environment, and what possibilities are open to you.

With this information, you enter the third stage of the process, *strategy choice.* First, you consider the variety of choices open to you—for a psychologist, this means identifying services to render, courses to teach, research to pursue, and so forth. Then, you consider the environment/niche you wish to inhabit. What will work best for you? Finally, you choose an alternative—that is, you establish an objective—based on the best and most thorough evaluation of the assumptions and criteria that you believe underlie the possibilities.

In the fourth stage of the model, you move forward with *program implementation.* You develop plans to achieve your stated objectives. You decide who will do what, when, where, on what time schedule, and with what resources. Then you act to the best of your ability, step by step.

In the last phase of the model, you *evaluate* the results and ask how well you are doing. Was your strategic assessment correct? Did you choose the correct strategy? How did implementation go? The results of your evaluation can be used to modify and improve your objectives and each of the other components of the planning process.

We all must engage in strategic planning in order to better implement our entrepreneurial decisions. A great deal of information must be considered, and this process takes time. In the entrepreneurial role, we make decisions that affect us tremendously over the long term. In effect, we are determining our identities as psychologists, our missions, choices, specific plans, and the activities that we will partake in our daily lives. Recognizing the need for strategic planning and the necessary steps in the process helps us to understand the complexity and detail that should go into making such important direction-setting decisions.

Let's get some practice with entrepreneurial decisions by doing the central part of the planning/implementation model described earlier. This involves a WOTS (weaknesses, opportunities, threats, and strengths) Up analysis (Steiner, 1979, p. 142), provided in Exercise 3.5.

Exercise 3.5 Wots Up?

Begin with the assumption that you have made a commitment to a specialty area in psychology and that you have a sense of your mission in research, provision of services, consultation, administration, and so forth.

1. Take a sheet of paper and draw two lines, one from the top down the middle and one from side to side in the middle so that the page has four equal sections. Label each of the four sections as follows: (1) weaknesses, (2) opportunities, (3) threats, and (4) strengths.
2. In each quadrant, start making a list of the things that you think will affect the quality of your work and professional life given your mission. Be as thorough as you can.
   a. Weaknesses include such things as areas of knowledge or skills that you lack, poor products or services, lack of controls in accounting, and insufficient time to spend in liaison or monitoring activities.
   b. Opportunities include the ability to improve knowledge or skills, new colleagues, new grant or funding opportunities, underserved populations, new job possibilities, poor performance by competitors, and favorable economic climates.
   c. Threats include strong competition from others, new laws or regulations that alter your environment negatively, inflation, recession, poor health, and anything that can inhibit your ability to operate as a psychologist.
   d. Strengths include excellent products or services, major skills or areas of knowledge, good staff members, financial stability, and the capacity to do research and development to produce innovative products or services.
3. Go through each of your lists and reorder them according to the impact they have on your professional life. At the end of this step, you should have some idea of what the major problems and opportunities you face are and what some of the resources you have to confront them with are.
4. Pick out the two or three items that head your lists of weaknesses, opportunities, and threats. Spend a few minutes thinking about what you could do, using your current strengths, to take advantage of an opportunity or to address a threat or weakness. Could you enroll in some continuing education, develop several new relationships, or submit a grant application? Do not limit your imagination. Write down your options.
5. Get specific now. These options can be restated as your objectives. Make a new list of steps you need to take in order to register for a course, develop a relationship, or submit a grant. Be as detailed as you can, and list the steps in the order in which you think they should be done. Now, opposite each of these steps, create a separate list of dates by which you think you

could complete each step. In other words, develop a schedule. On a clean sheet of paper, jot down any resources you have or need that you believe will help you accomplish each step (information, relationships, computers, money, transportation, telephones, skills, and so forth).

6. You have created a simple strategic plan that you know how to implement. This is the heart of entrepreneurship. Try to implement your plan step by step. Jot down any problems encountered as you go along. Remember your aim is to reach your goals. Spend a short time considering what the process was like to create the goals, the action plan, and to implement what you wanted to do. Evaluate why and how you succeeded or failed to reach your objectives.

Disturbance handler. Entrepreneurial decisions apply to situations in which you exercise a great deal of control. Disturbances usually involve problems and issues that can arise spontaneously. Frequently, you cannot predict when or where they will occur. However, these conflicts and crises usually demand that you address them quickly.

Figure 3.3 presents a flowchart of the stages of a conflict modeled after Walton's (1969) discussion. Conflicts are seen as arising out of a particular environmental context (the interaction between environment, niche, and person). These elements interact, inducing conflict-producing issues.

Figure 3.3 presents the characteristics of conflicting issues by focus and type. This matrix illustrates that conflicts arise from within an individual or between two or more people. The focus can be within an organization and its subunits or between organizations in an environment. Conflicts can also involve larger social systems such as communities or nation-states. Locating the focus of a conflict provides important diagnostic information and may suggest some ways of managing the problem.

Figure 3.4 also illustrates that conflicts arise over substantive or emotional issues. Substantive issues involve problems such as the direction a policy will take in your life or organization, the allocation of resources to a particular project, and the questions of who will make a decision or how a program will be implemented. Emotional issues often involve responses to the process through which some action occurs—how you or someone else is treated as a project is implemented, how people

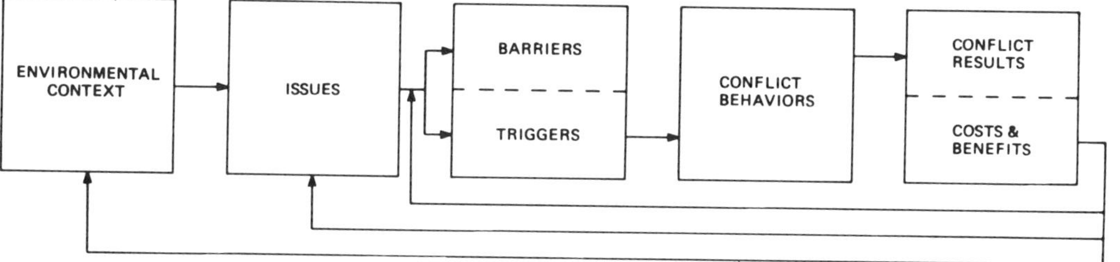

Figure 3.3. The stages of a conflict. Adapted from Walton (1969) with permission.

	TYPE			
	SUBSTANTIVE		EMOTIONAL	
FOCUS OF CONFLICTING ISSUES	MANIFEST	LATENT	MANIFEST	LATENT
INTRAPERSONAL				
INTERPERSONAL				
ORGANIZATIONAL/GROUP				
INTERORGANIZATIONAL/INTERGROUP				
LARGER SOCIAL SYSTEM				
ENVIRONMENT				

Figure 3.4. Characteristics of conflict issues. Adapted from Walton (1969) with permission.

respond to losses or victories, and how people react to criticism. The difficulty with emotional issues is that they are often unseen and unvoiced in professional life. Frequently, individuals do not know they are having a response or what their response really is. Nevertheless, such emotions can have major effects in an organization.

Substantive and emotional issues can be further subdivided into manifest and latent categories. Manifest issues are identified easily, expressed overtly, and on the whole, resolved more easily. Latent issues are neither overt nor stated. At times, they are even hidden from the individuals who are responding to them. Both types can be very destructive if not handled carefully. Identification of the issues involved in a conflict or crisis is the first step in managing the situation.

These issues are connected to what Walton (1969) called barriers or triggers. *Barriers* consist of things that prevent or inhibit conflicts from arising. *Triggers* serve to initiate or inflame an issue or situation so that it becomes a conflict or disturbance. For Walton (1969), barriers and triggers included items such as the following:

1. Task requirements—too little time.
2. Behavioral norms—encourage or dampen conflicts.
3. Personal-role concepts—fighters vs. pacifists.
4. Public images—how people want to be seen by others.
5. Perceptions of others' vulnerabilities.
6. Perceptions of own vulnerability.
7. Fears that your behavior will not be reciprocated.
8. Physical barriers—distance, no communication.

Understanding barriers and triggers give us our most useful tools for managing conflicts. If the barriers are not high enough or the triggers are too efficient, conflict behaviors are initiated. Bernstein (1965) outlined the following range of conflict behaviors usually found in groups:

1. Physical violence—fairly rare in professional life.
2. Verbal violence—the most frequent conflict behavior.
3. Seeking allies—usually occurs in fights over policies, directions, allocation of resources.
4. Seeking an authoritative decision—going to the boss.
5. Creation of disruptions, diversions, and delays—losing papers, asking for committees to explore issues, leaking information to the media.

These behaviors can occur simultaneously or sequentially. The conflict behaviors produce the most difficulty for people. Because we are anxious about whether they will injure us, we often move to reduce these threats without our conscious awareness.

The final phase of a conflict cycle, appearing in Figure 3.3, involves experiencing the costs and benefits of the conflict. Costs include lost time, delayed projects, development of enemies, negative emotional states, loss of status and power, and in the worst cases, loss of position. Benefits include achievement of objectives, defeat of enemies, increased status and power, decreased negative emotional states, and time saved. Most disturbances and conflicts produce both costs and benefits. Being honest with yourself about disturbance outcomes is a helpful tool for self-management.

Figure 3.4 also illustrates that conflicts can be cyclical in nature. Barriers and triggers can affect whether or not an overt battle takes place. The results of a skirmish can change the issues. Characteristics of organizations, such as budget and planning cycles, ensure that struggles will take place regularly. Your knowledge of the issues and the processes provides many tools for managing conflict. At each step, you can use this information to increase or decrease the elements involved in the conflict. Management demands that you evaluate the situation in light of your objectives and act accordingly.

Disturbances and conflicts can create crises for individuals or organizations. Ewing (1978) offered a succinct summary of the stages of a crisis. Initially, you manage any disturbance or conflict by using your basic skills and abilities. Occasionally, the situation overwhelms your capacity for adaptation, and a full-blown crisis emerges. Ewing stated that there are four stages in most crises:

Stage 1—You respond to increased pressure by using your normal problem-solving skills, attempting to produce equilibrium.

Stage 2—Normal problem solving fails. Increased pressure leads to trial-and-error measures.

Stage 3—If trial-and-error measures fail, creative emergency measures can be developed, the problem may be ignored or redefined, or you may give up your efforts to reach an objective.

Stage 4—If the situation continues, a breaking point is reached and your personality and adaptation efforts deteriorate precipitously.

The parallels between this description of a crisis and the process of behavioral transformation are obvious. In most crisis situations, the problems are resolved long before Stages 3 or 4 are reached. However, you must realize that everyone, including brilliantly trained psychologists, has a breaking point. In such circumstances, external assistance in the form of consultation, counseling, education, or psychotherapy can be of enormous assistance.

Skills for managing disturbances are crucial to effective self-regulation. Understanding the evolution of conflicts or crises provides us with a wide range of opportunities to intervene creatively to solve a problem before it gets out of hand. One of the most difficult tasks involves knowing when you must start a conflict in order to solve a problem. There is no easy set of guidelines or chart that will tell you when and how to do this. Experience is the best teacher. Let's explore this issue in Example 3.3.

Example 3.3 Constructive Conflict

Shelley Hawthorne was an industrial organizational psychologist employed by a large corporation to manage employment selection and development. The company had been the target of several lawsuits in which discrimination in recruitment and selection procedures had been alleged. These suits had been settled out of court. In addition, during the past 12 months, the business had suffered from serious financial problems that led the senior management to undertake a series of drastic cost-cutting steps.

When the discrimination suits arose, the organization had responded well to Shelley's proposals to validate all of their procedures with the best current technology. Shelley had been given a substantial research and development budget. She was literally in the middle of collecting data on the tests and procedures when she received a terse memo from the vice president for corporate finance stating that all funding for the project would be halted immediately and that she should prepare for major staff cuts.

Knowing the financial position of the organization, Shelley had anticipated that some cutbacks might be necessary. However, the implications of the memo were much worse than her expectations. For a few days, Shelley worried about what to do and pondered the best ways to make cuts. Finally, Shelley decided that the project and the efforts of the selection and training staff were so important that the decision had to be fought.

Shelley marshalled data and arguments and consulted with colleagues, consultants, and corporate legal staff. She made an appointment to see the vice president for human resources to whom her office reported. After introducing the problem, Shelley quickly sketched out proposed solutions and key issues and sought the vice president's support to turn the decision around. Shelley was surprised to discover that the vice president knew nothing of the decision or memo. Apparently, the finance staff had made a whole series of decisions about how to reduce expenses without communicating with managers of the affected company divisions.

Shelley's boss asked her to prepare and present a response to the memo and arranged a meeting with the finance people. The meeting was long and stressful. After a drawn out debate, the finance people agreed that they had acted hastily and without due consideration of the effects that the cuts might have. Financial targets for the human resources division were identified, and Shelley's boss agreed to present a plan that would meet the targets to senior management. Shelley was then asked to prepare a budget and program plan, as were all of the other directors in the division.

This example provides an illustration of crisis and conflict management. The issues were both substantive and emotional. The financial problems and the memo provided triggers. The organizational structure and process produced barriers that furthered the conflict. Outcomes involved both costs and benefits for everyone. Shelley never faced a Stage 4 crisis simply because she used creative management to avoid the worst consequences.

We will now turn to a consideration of the resource-allocator role outlined by Mintzberg.

Resource allocator. According to Mintzberg (1973), this role is at the heart of your strategy-making operations. When you function in this role, you control a network of resources from which to draw. For example, independent practitioners or academicians in small departments usually have their own time and energy, money, or other forms of capital and expertise. Other resources include equipment, material, reputation, and, in larger organizations, the resources of subordinates. Achievement of the goals and implementation of the action plans, which were established in the entrepreneurial role, depend largely on the effectiveness of resource management.

Mintzberg stated that resource allocation comprises three major elements—scheduling time, programming work (strategic planning, discussed in the entrepreneurial section), and authorizing decisions made by others (the delegation process, discussed in the leadership section). Delegation and strategic planning depend on your ability to schedule your time effectively. Let's discuss this issue in some detail.

The central problem of professional life is learning how to use your time efficiently. When everything else is said and done, productivity and achievement depend upon the wise use of your time. Other resources, such as energy level, intelligence, character, skill, knowledge, and support, come into play as well and can be very effective in helping you use your time.

There is a wide variety of resources now available to help you think about and master the productive uses of time. MacKenzie (1972) wrote a small classic on the subject in which he pointed out that the idea that professionals are overworked is a myth. He concentrated on teaching people to work more intelligently, not harder, and recommended a number of practical steps for evaluating how you use your time.

A major problem that most psychologists share is that they do not know how much time they spend on various tasks. So, the first step in allocating resources and managing yourself consists of constructing a time log with which you can analyze how you use your time. Figure 3.5 presents a sample that you can copy and use. Simply identify the major activities in which you spend your time on a typical day. Do not guess. Keep a daily record. In the cell opposite the category, put the number of 10-minute segments you spent on the activity during the day. Time logs are best kept at the end of the day when major events are still fresh in your mind. Include all of your activities—phone calls, meals, breaks, discussions with colleagues, meetings with clients and students, classes, reading time, and time spent on other professional activities. Keeping daily logs for several weeks allows you to

DAILY PROFESSIONAL TIME LOG FROM TO

	M	T	W	T	F	S	S	TOTALS
ACTIVITY CENTER 1. SERVICE DELIVERY								
(a) Evaluation								
(b) Therapeutic Services								
(c) Consultation								
2. ENVIRONMENTAL RELATIONS								
3. PROFESSIONAL DEVELOPMENT								
4. BUSINESS MANAGEMENT								
TOTALS								

Figure 3.5. A sample time log. From Kilburg (1983). Reprinted with permission.

establish baselines from which you can analyze your current allocation patterns and identify changes that you need to make. Once you construct the pattern of activity that works best for you, you do not need to do the log every day. New goals, changes in jobs, and different implementation plans will call for systematic alterations in time allocations.

Once you know where your time is presently being spent, you can effectively change your allocations or those of your subordinates. The central question is "where do I want the time to go?" Remember, the implementation plans arrived at through the planning process provide a specific list of steps you must take to reach a goal or objective. You can list these activities on your time log or those of your subordinates, and thereby obtain a measure of the time you are spending in each of the activities you identified as necessary in the plan. Because your plan included some notion of the priorities for the activities, you should spend the most time on the most important components of your job.

MacKenzie also recommended several other practical steps for allocating your time resources.

1. Work on one problem/priority at a time.
2. Tackle the toughest problems first.
3. Understand your work style and its strengths and weaknesses.
4. Analyze periodically how you are spending your time.
5. Plan your work effectively (see entrepreneurial section earlier).
6. Say no to spending time on less important matters.

7. Develop a comfortable and functional work space for yourself.
8. Develop a useful filing system.
9. Decide what is essential to read, then read it.
10. Use the waste basket on the rest.
11. Manage interruptions carefully (telephone calls, visits, tours, and social chats should all be coordinated so that work on your top priorities is not disturbed).
12. Manage your meetings (set and stick to an agenda, start and end on time, set time limits for items, summarize results, assign follow-ups, etc.).
13. Use the planning model to make decisions when you can.
14. Delegate whatever you can to subordinates.
15. Hire a good secretary and let him or her help you manage your time.

MacKenzie (1972) treated each of these suggestions in much greater depth than we have room for here. Remember the tasks of resource allocation and that effective time management is at the heart of this role. Now let's practice time management by doing Exercise 3.6.

Exercise 3.6 The Psychologist as Time Manager

1. Go back to Exercise 3.5. Take the material you developed in the last steps that we called your activity plan. Make a copy of the form from Figure 3.5, and place the activities from your plan in the rows. Use as many rows as you need.
2. At the end of each day for the next week, sit down and try to remember the number of 10-minute blocks that you spent on each activity in your plan. Add up the time. At the end of the week, add up the daily records. How much time did you spend on your top priorities? How productive did you feel this week was? Do you feel like you should make some changes? Refer to the list of suggestions earlier, and determine what you could try next week.
3. Keep your log until you have accomplished your objectives or are better able to work effectively.
4. Monitor yourself periodically.

Negotiator. The final managerial role identified by Mintzberg (1973) involves acting as a negotiator. Negotiation skills are a key element in your ability to compete in an environment. When you negotiate, you are arranging the exchange of resources with someone else. An effective negotiator uses the previously described skills and roles to achieve success.

Your information and dissemination roles provide data about yourself, your niche, and your external and internal environments. You are empowered to act in negotiations as the leader of your organization. You develop strategies through your planning and decision-making skills. You manage the negotiation process partially with your ability to handle disturbances. The following brief discussion of negotiation details the conceptual and pragmatic descriptions offered by Kuhn (1974) and Nierenberg (1973). There are also many other good texts available on the subject.

Kuhn described negotiation in terms of the concepts of the transactional basis of power. Power literally involves the capacity to get what you want from an environment. In the simplest version, power transactions/negotiations bring two people together who want something from each other. These transactions can involve information, money, goods, services, time, energy—in fact, anything of value. Let us use an example to illustrate some of the key concepts.

Suppose you want a job in a particular organization. You have a desire for the position and its responsibilities, visibility, salary, fringe benefits, work environment, and colleagues. In this case, the organization also has a desire for you and your knowledge, abilities, skills, experience, and personality. You want to give the organization what you have, but only if it in turn gives you what you want. Similarly, the organization wants you, but only if its conditions are met. In Nierenberg's language, you both have a need that helps to drive the negotiations forward. Kuhn (1974) suggested that the basis of this need is the mutual desire for what the other party has.

Kuhn also stated that your desire for the position in this example combines with your willingness to "give up" yourself to the organization under the appropriate conditions to create your *effective preference*. In simple terms, your effective preference is what you are willing to give for what you want. Similarly, the organization has its own effective preference, what it is willing to give up to get you.

The following are the two main themes in negotiation: (a) Finding a comfortable overlap of your effective preference (or preferences) and that of the other negotiating party so that each experiences the exchange as a fair deal and (b) getting as much of what you want without giving up so much that you are injured in some way.

The characteristics of a negotiation are (a) understanding your needs and developing a preference, (b) preparing for the negotiations, (c) managing the negotiations, and (d) closing the deal.

Assume that the position you want is as an assistant professor in a department of psychology in a major university. You have a need to work in an academic environment, to research, teach, supervise students, and provide services. You believe you need a certain salary to live reasonably well. You also know that there are insurance plans, retirement benefits, vacations, and other benefits provided by the job that you want.

The organization has a position open in an area that appears to be a good fit with your knowledge, skills, abilities, and experience. It can offer a certain salary range, a benefits package, and certain other conditions and resources that you may or may not know about such as lab space, equipment, students, secretarial help, and travel support.

You have been through the recruitment process; interviewed with faculty, students, and administration officials; provided references; given a symposium; and performed other actions to demonstrate your desirability. The department chair calls and says she would like you to come back to negotiate an agreement. Implicitly and explicitly, this is a statement that the organization believes you meet its need for someone to fit the niche in the organization. You liked what you saw and believe that you would also fit in well there. You agree to go for the visit. You are deciding that you want this job. How do you prepare for and conduct the negotiations?

First, recognizing that you already know a great deal about the position and school, use the other managerial roles and skills to collect as much information as you can and to formulate your goals for the negotiations. If you have not yet done so, you need to talk to colleagues and mentors who know academia and can suggest what to watch out for and what benefits to seek. Try to get direct information about the organization from people you trust so that you can anticipate the pitfalls. Try to get as much data as you can about salary and benefits at the institution to guide your decision making. Understand that you represent yourself and prepare to speak on your own behalf. Identify the issues and decide what stance you will take on each of them. Do your homework.

Second, agree on the date, time, and site for the meeting. Find out who will be there. Ask who will make the agreement on behalf of the organization. Find out if you will deal with an intermediary such as a program director or with someone who can negotiate like the department chair or dean.

Third, take steps to ensure it's a good meeting. Prepare mentally and emotionally to handle the strain. Work to set an agenda when you arrive at the meeting. Open the meeting with positive statements and a good attitude, but do not reveal all that you know immediately. In this scenario, the other person will probably reveal his or her position first. Listen respectfully. Watch for tactics and strategies (see following list). Reveal your own position carefully. Remember your objectives and preferences at all times. Most important, determine the other person's maximum and minimum positions. This will tell you about his or her effective preference. Check the degree of overlap with your own goals, objectives, and preferences.

Fourth, read the other person's behavior and tactics. Watch for the following negotiating techniques:

1. Lowball—minimum offers on salary and benefits.
2. Surprises—sudden shifts in method, position, argument.
3. Reversals—forward and backward, "now you have it and now you don't" tactics.
4. Diversions—attempts to make side issues of central importance.
5. Friendship—attempts to make you believe that your goals are theirs and vice versa.
6. Devaluation—statements that reduce your value and your bargaining room and increase theirs.
7. Agents—people who can only speak for the boss and cannot make commitments.
8. Sectioning—taking one thing at a time, when it gets you to agree with everything they want.
9. Confusion—introducing new information, issues, or people that serve to confuse the issues being negotiated.
10. Brackets—attempts to establish ranges and then moving within the ranges to reduce your preferences.

You can use many of these tactics in pursuit of your own preferences or you can use your knowledge to counter someone else's tactics.

Fifth, remember that the purpose of the negotiations is to meet each other's needs in ways that you believe are fair to both of you. Disagreement for its own sake can work against you. Agree whenever you see that your needs are being met.

You will recognize when it is time to close the deal when you have covered all of the issues on your list and you are comfortable with the results. If you are not comfortable, ask for time to consider the agreement before signing it. Do not hesitate to use your liaison network to check the fine points before making a commitment. Remember, you are an active participant in the negotiations and can exert considerable influence if you only try. Sign the agreement with the expectation that it will work for both parties. If you don't believe it is fair for you, do not sign it.

Keep the concepts of negotiating in mind, and enter the discussions with the department chair prepared with information about salary structure, fringe benefits, perks offered to other faculty members, salaries of colleagues in similar organizations, and requirements for your own efforts to succeed. The chair makes an offer. You listen and counter offer as appropriate. Sometimes, you or the chair may use tactics to win negotiating points. Sometimes, the situation is very straightforward. If you get stuck on a point, move on to other issues and come back to it later. When you have what you want, close the deal and hope that you didn't overlook something major.

You will rely on your negotiation skills repeatedly during your psychological career. Work at honing them, for they will serve you well.

Other Tools

By now, you will have recognized the degree of overlap between management roles as described by Mintzberg (1973), the management processes and functions of Sisk (1977) and others, and my own tools and rules. If you can mobilize these tools and roles for your own use, you will go a long way toward setting the rules that will allow you to succeed as a psychologist. There are two other tools that I want to mention briefly before we move on to the next chapter. As you struggle to adapt to your niche and transform yourself into a successful, self-regulating psychologist, you will improve your chances of survival if you know how to assess an organizational environment and how to accumulate and use power. Both of these tools are central to managing a psychological career.

Organizational Assessment

Lawler, Nadler, and Cammann (1979) provided a comprehensive survey of the concepts and technologies available to perform an organizational assessment. Industrial organizational psychologists are trained to use these methods. However, we all work in organizations, even if they are very small, and it is critical to be able to put together a fairly comprehensive view of any organization in a minimal amount of time. When you enter an organization as an employee, a service provider, or even as a guest, asking some or all of the following questions will provide both interesting and useful information. Remember our earlier discussions of systems, rules, and self-regulation. Your basic task is to determine the rules that help an organization survive.

Suggested questions.

1. How large is the organization?
2. How is it organized? To whom do/will you report?
3. What are the goals or missions of the organization?
4. What are the characteristics of the leadership processes used? Are they directive, consultative, or participative?
5. How are goals established for work to be done?
6. How are problems solved?
7. How are employees motivated? Are fears and threats used? Are personal goals linked to the organization's missions? How are money issues handled?
8. How is communication handled? Does it flow smoothly from the top down and back up? Are there blockages or other problems?
9. How do people interact? Does the organization feel friendly? Do people talk at all levels? How do they influence each other (with orders, arguments, or information)?
10. How are decisions made? Will you participate in decisions that directly affect you?
11. What organizational controls are in place? What are the policies, procedures, norms, reporting structures, information systems, and so forth?
12. How is the work organized? How are jobs defined? Who defines your job?
13. How is performance assessed and by whom?
14. What are the chances for advancement? Who decides?

These questions are basic tools for understanding how an organization works. You should know the answers to them before you accept a job in a particular organization, unless your job is to consult with a firm to help them understand how it works. Your other management tools can be helpful to you in collecting and integrating the information. Knowing an environment and its niches before making a commitment to live in it enhances your efforts to succeed there. If you are interested in other issues to explore in an organization, see Likert (1967) and Levinson (1972).

Understanding and Using Power

The concept of power in human affairs has been explored extensively by many scholars and authors. It is recognized as a pivotal issue in most, if not all, human interactions. In my experience, psychologists, despite their extensive training and knowledge about power, worry about, misapprehend, and perform poorly in this area at least as much as any other professional group. It seems uncharacteristic in a field that is so centrally concerned with human behavior. Why is this?

To begin with, power is incredibly simple to understand, but very complicated in how it works. It consists of the ability to get what you want from people or environments. Success in your career absolutely requires you to obtain power and to use it well.

Kotter (1978) suggested that the technique of power/dependence analysis (PDA) be used to identify job dependencies and the power strategies necessary to manage them. He identified a list of questions that can be used to assess the power/dependence features of any position. You should be familiar with them. Ask yourself the following questions:

1. Who are the people on whom you depend?
2. How important is each dependency?
3. What is the basis of each dependency?
4. Are any of your dependencies inappropriate or dysfunctional?
5. If they are dysfunctional, what created this pattern?
6. How much effective power-oriented behavior do you engage in?
7. Is your power behavior sufficient to manage your dependencies?
8. If your behavior is not sufficient, what changes need to be made?
9. Can you change your behavior?
10. Does your creation and use of power have negative consequences for you?
11. If there are consequences, what are they?

At this point, you might be wondering what a dependency is and where you get power behavior. A dependency exists when you rely on the resources of others to accomplish your own goals. Strategies, skills, resources, behaviors, and capacities that decrease your dependency on others and create dependencies on you will increase your power.

Kotter (1979) concretely described some basic forms of power behavior. He suggested the following steps for gaining power and reducing dependencies:

1. Gain control of tangible and scarce resources—budgets, employees, buildings, equipment, decision-making responsibilities, referral resources, and so forth. These are realistic power bases for psychologists.
2. Obtain and control information. This will be your most widely used strategy as a psychologist. Technical information and the ability to apply it will automatically grant you power. Other sources of information in an environment can also increase your power.
3. Establish favorable relationships, build friendships, establish interpersonal obligations, and achieve sufficient expertise to be recognized in your field. All of these will increase power and decrease dependency.
4. Foster identification and dependence. Use the power you have to gain control of resources that others need and then shape their perceptions so that they know that you have the power.
5. Use persuasion and indirect influence. When all else fails, try to structure information that is important to the goals of others who have power so as to change their attitudes, values, and behavior. You can also restructure the environments of people or the evolution of events to bring about significant change.

Having and using power requires you to exercise caution with other people. A strong set of values and ethics is necessary, because you are responsible for the consequences of your actions when you work as a psychologist. Although courage, risk taking, and assertiveness should be valued and used as you develop power, these attributes must be accompanied by equal amounts of wisdom, temperance, and respect for the rights of others.

Summary

When I think about psychologists and their careers, I am constantly amazed by how useful we can be to others and how infrequently we apply what we know to ourselves. In chapters 2 and 3, I have tried to outline the basic conceptual approach that we will take in the rest of the book. Our goal is simple: We aim at regulating ourselves and our niche and environment to ensure a good fit for ourselves. I believe the best methods to use in this effort are the tools of management that enable us to define or negotiate rules for our own lives.

References

Bernstein, S. (Ed.). (1965). *Explorations in group work.* Boston: Boston University School of Social Work.

Ewing, C. P. (1978). *Crisis intervention as psychotherapy.* New York: Oxford University Press.

Kilburg, R. R. (1983). The psychologist as manager. In B. D. Sales (Ed.), *The Professional Psychologist's Handbook* (pp. 495–537). New York: Plenum Press.

Koontz, H., & Weihrich, H. (1990). *Essentials of management* (5th ed.). New York: McGraw-Hill.

Kotter, J. P. (1978, Winter). Power, success, and organizational effectiveness. *Organizational Dynamics,* 27–40.

Kotter, J. P. (1979, July). Power in management. *AMA Management Digest,* 13–17.

Kuhn, A. (1974). *The logic of social systems.* San Francisco: Jossey-Bass.

Lawler, E. E., Nadler, D. A., & Cammann, C. (Eds.). (1980). *Organizational assessment: Perspectives on the measurement of organizational behavior and the quality of work life.* New York: John Wiley & Sons.

Levinson, H. (1972). *Organizational diagnosis.* Cambridge: Harvard University Press.

Likert, R. (1967). *The human organization: Its management and value.* New York: McGraw-Hill.

MacKenzie, R. A. (1972). *The time trap: Managing your way out.* New York: AMACOM.

McGregor, D. (1960). *The human side of enterprise.* New York: McGraw-Hill.

Mintzberg, H. (1973). *The nature of managerial work.* New York: Harper & Row.

Nierenberg, G. I. (1973). *Fundamentals of negotiating.* New York: Hawthorn/Dutton.

Ouchi, W. (1981). *Theory Z: How American business can meet the Japanese challenge.* Reading, MA: Addison-Wesley.

Rakich, J. S., Longest, B. B., & Darr, K. (1985). *Managing health services organizations* (2nd ed.). Philadelphia: W. B. Saunders Company.

Sisk, H. L. (1977). *Management and organization* (3rd ed.). Cincinnati: South-Western Publishing Co.

Steiner, G. A. (1979). *Strategic planning: What every manager must know.* New York: The Free Press.

Walton, R. E. (1969). *Interpersonal peacemaking:confrontations and third party peacemaking.* Reading, MA: Addison-Wesley.

4

Dory Hollander

Understanding Career-Management Issues

Planning Your Career

Your career as a psychologist belongs to you. Your successes, your failures, your personal job satisfaction, and your ability to find your niche in the profession belong to no one else. No devoted advisor is waiting in the wings to orchestrate your postgraduate career development or to help you evaluate which career moves constitute success. Like it or not, in managing your career as a psychologist, you alone shoulder the responsibility for your strategies, tactics, and outcomes. Although this sense of personal responsibility for what happens throughout your career is less pressing early in your professional life when the consequences of poor choices are highly reversible, it eventually becomes clear that your career choices are far too important to entrust to anyone else.

After all, who else besides yourself is qualified to plan your career trajectory over time, to develop appealing alternative career paths, and to know when to stay and when to leave? The dilemma is knowing how to gain enough career savoir-faire to design a reasonable action plan without making too many deadly mistakes along the way.

This chapter deals with the critical issue of how to take care of yourself in your career given changing personal, professional, and cultural contexts. A commitment to taking care of yourself is the heart and soul of successful career management.

Yet this is hard. Few of us have received professional coaching in managing our careers as psychologists. In the absence of know-how, we turn our career decisions over to serendipity. To paraphrase a common bumper sticker, "careers happen." When careers "just happen," people typically substitute some default combination of chance and cultural wisdom about work life for more intentional career management. Often, people put more planning into the purchase of a house or a boat than into their long-term career paths.

Perhaps these observations don't apply to you; but there is little reason to believe that psychologists differ from other professionals. Having made a major "single point in time" career decision (e.g., choosing to be a clinical psychologist), especially one that required substantial commitments of time, schooling, and money, it is easy to turn on the automatic pilot and forget about lifelong career planning—to become haphazard about tracking who you are and what you want. But somewhere down the road, this kind of thinking can lead to major disappointment. Unexpectedly, you may find yourself excruciatingly unhappy or derailed in your job. Belatedly, you may realize that becoming a psychologist is an altogether different process from effectively managing your career once you are one. In choosing to become a psychologist, you structured an action plan. You applied to graduate schools, completed a course of study, got a doctorate, did an internship, became licensed, and took a series of jobs in your chosen specialization. Now your career requires a new intentional action plan based on a new understanding of career issues, work contexts, long-range planning, tenacity, and follow-through.

The academic years typically provide new learning and professional socialization into the field, while ignoring postgraduate, career-survival tactics. Your first few postdegree jobs give you a chance to learn more about which aspects of the profession best fit your academic training and to experience the daily glories of being a psychologist. But these jobs scarcely represent your final career resting place. Rather, they provide a hands-on opportunity to gain valuable information about yourself and

- to field-test your academic knowledge base,
- to collect data about what you still need to learn,
- to understand various organizational contests and politics,
- to explore your likes and dislikes in a hands-on situation,
- to challenge your competencies, and
- to move toward gaining a better career fit in your subsequent positions.

The most well-guarded secret about career management is that you must have these first job experiences securely under your belt before you can successfully tackle more extensive career planning. These first jobs allow you to begin to gather three sets of critical data. The first relates to external factors like job characteristics and knowledge of actual career alternatives. The second relates to internal factors like personal skills, interests, values, and limitations in the workplace. The third relates to contextual factors like institutional culture and politics. Each information base will help you to develop operational strategies and tactics for implementing your career vision.

In fact, it is helpful to see yourself as an undercover participant–observer in each postdegree job. Besides doing your job, your task is to collect data unobtrusively about the workplace, your coworkers, and yourself. Log your reactions to what happens on the job and track data related to your success, including career opportunities, organizational politics, work conditions, and developments in the field. You are accumulating a career data base that you can use to evaluate changing jobs, redefining your career mission, respecializing, or making eventual career changes. This approach fits the Aldrich and Pfeffer principle outlined in chapter 2, which stated that greater heterogeneity and variations in your work environment provide greater opportunities for natural selection, leading to a closer fit.

The principle inherent in successfully managing your career is a willingness to adapt and accommodate to ongoing internal and external changes. No matter how absorbing a particular job may be, you will still need to track macro issues, such as developments in the larger world and in psychology as a profession, as well as micro issues related to particular work environments, personal identity, values, and needs. You will need to weigh how even small shifts in priorities among work, family, and personal life may influence your career decisions at key turning points in your life.

This chapter takes the prescriptive stance that successful careers are managed careers and that thriving in your career as a psychologist requires the primary metaskill of intentional, self-directed career management. This involves systematically collecting and assessing data about yourself and the profession from a framework based on adaption and skill development. Success depends on your personal willingness to stay alert and embrace career development as a lifelong process. Careers are not static.

Consider the following example.

> Manya Walters has been working as a clinical psychologist in private practice for the past 2 decades. Although she still loves the discipline, she has begun to feel restless and trapped in her work with patients. She daydreams about using her expertise to make a bigger impact and applying her knowledge of human behavior to the business world.
>
> When Manya is asked to do stress-management seminars for a local Fortune 500 company, she grabs the opportunity. Then management asks her to consult on a variety of employee situations. They offer her a chance to evaluate executives being considered for promotion. Reacting to the opportunity, she limits her individual practice and redefines and markets herself as an organizational psychologist. Although she never even considered working for corporate clients when she was in graduate school, she feels this is a near-perfect career change that fits her current needs.
>
> Unfortunately, Manya encounters unexpected difficulty. Several colleagues have criticized her for practicing outside her area of professional competence, and she is unsure about whether or not they are right. She has read the American Psychological Association (APA) Code of Ethics and sees their viewpoint. But in applying her original training to new areas, she feels she is learning more professionally than she has since her internship. She has considered "sticking to her knitting" and toughing it out for 20 more years of private practice, but to her this seems like being buried alive.

Manya's discontent with her career after 20 years in the field is not unusual; nor is her solution. If we knew more about psychologists' subjective sense of their own careers, we would probably find that the need for growth into new professional areas is typical. Manya's dilemma highlights problems in managing your professional career as a psychologist in a world where the norm of "one life, one career" has changed, but the expectation for circumscribed areas of clearly delineated, often territorial professional expertise, has not. Adding to the confusion, in highly regulated professional careers, the rules for managing lifelong career growth are often confusing, costly, or both.

If you expect your postdegree career to unfold with stability and predictability, unforeseen twists and turns may throw you off course. To expect to remain happy and satisfied throughout middle and late adulthood in a career that you chose 15 or 30 years earlier is setting yourself up for future disappointment.

The demographics are clear. The average person can plan to change careers three or four times over the course of his or her work life and to change jobs every 3 years. But we have little systematic, longitudinal data about what happens to psychologists or others in their careers over time.

Nor does the career development literature of the past 40 or more years yield much data on these points. It too reflects a historical bias toward viewing occupational fit as being fixed over time, although this is slowly changing. Traditionally, models of career development have centered on how people (mostly men) choose careers in early adulthood—not on how they later adapt, manage, and change their careers. Reading this literature, it is easy to conclude that initial career choice is most critical and that once you have weathered that initial decision, the remainder of your career will be smooth sailing. When this flies in the face of your subjective experience, it is easy to blame yourself, concluding that "if I am unhappy in my job or career, something must be wrong with me."

This emphasis on stasis is reinforced by the fact that many current, midcareer psychologists studied personality and cognitive development in the days when childhood and adolescence were perceived as critically formative, whereas normal adulthood was depicted as a static backdrop for the resolution of remaining childhood conflicts. Similarly, until recently, models of cognitive development and educational psychology primarily addressed learning and thinking in the context of childhood. Consequently, many midlife psychologists missed studying recent development models of personality and cognition that emphasize ongoing postadolescent development and growth.

Yet people's personal experiences no longer confirm one-time career choice any more than they confirm one-time marital choice. Expectations for unexamined career stability over a 50-year period are spurious and potentially damaging. Even factoring out economic upheaval, changes in the profession of psychology, and career reselection issues, personal growth alone may yank us, kicking and screaming, from bland career complacency into confused reexamination of past career commitments.

Pragmatic self-defense dictates that we expect the unexpected and place personal growth needs into our career equation. Priorities shift. You might expect that if at age 30, your career is the cornerstone of your self-worth, then at age 40, your family, a relationship, or your leisure time will suddenly demand precedence. Whatever the specifics, some shift is likely.

Staying open to change is critical. Change may be major, like pursuing a new profession such as law or a new role in psychology such as entrepreneur. Change may be moderate, like Manya Walter's shift from a clinician in private practice to a clinician consulting to private industry. Or change may be minor, like switching jobs using tried-and-true skills and knowledge. Even in this latter instance, change will require that you move, adjust, make new friends, and learn new politics.

In any case, don't allow your identity as a psychologist to trap you in a job or career path that is no longer right for you. If you have not planned for change, you may encounter constraints against crossing over into a new professional specialty or even a new geographic location. State-licensing laws, as well as ethical codes, prohibit psychologists from casually practicing outside their area of professional competency without formal retraining. And due to nonuniform, nonreciprocal state-licensing requirements, often, it is even hard to take a job in a new state. These reasons alone are compelling for prioritizing long-term career planning.

Although a professional identity as a psychologist dictates certain scientific perspectives, a clear-cut academic discipline, and demonstrated professional competence, you have to preserve room to tinker with your career. A discipline is different from an occupation, and an occupation is different from a job. Even without formal respecialization, each psychological speciality has many alternative roles, jobs, and career paths. Psychology provides the underlying theme—jobs provide the variations. Your task is to make choices, then to calibrate these variations with your own development.

Questions to address.

1. What expectations and negative or positive messages did you derive from observing the course of your parents' careers?
2. In which life area—career, personal, or relationships—is more of your personal identity centered right now? How is this different from 5 years ago?
3. Think of a time when you felt trapped in a job or aspect of your professional identity. List the assumptions that contributed to your feeling trapped. If this situation hasn't changed, brainstorm alternative solutions with a trusted colleague.

What Models of Career Development Predict about Change

The field of career development is young. Its structural roots—from the 1906 work of Parsons to the concentrated focus in the 1950s through the 1970s—are in adolescent vocational choice and in theories of occupational selection, rather than in what happens to people after they enter their occupations. Underlying this preoccupation with career selection was the assumption that an appropriate career choice would last a lifetime and that occupational choices, typically, would be made by the early twenties. Until recently, scant theoretical and empirical emphasis was given to adult career management or ongoing career decisions. Over the past decade, this has begun to change. In response to growing evidence of endemic, midcareer change and an increasingly interdisciplinary approach to understanding adult life-cycle issues, a number of recognized career theorists (Ginzburg, 1984; Roe & Lunneborg, 1984; Super, Thompson, & Lindeman, 1988) have revised their earlier approaches somewhat to account for ongoing adult career development. But, as yet, there is no critical mass in the literature for career-development issues pertaining to successful career management, career satisfaction, women and minority career development, and the impact of dual careers. We don't know how individuals are actually socialized into their professions, much less how they actually manage their careers once they are established. Noticeably absent from the literature is any systematic information about effective later career development or management.

In the next section, I have scanned several well-known models for ideas that you can expand on and apply to managing your career.

Learning from John Holland's Personality–Environment-Fit Model

The premise of John Holland's (1973, 1985a, 1985b, 1985c) personality–environment-fit model has intuitive appeal. Who you are and what you do for a living should match. To feel satisfied and comfortable in your work life, you will need a good fit between your personality and your work environment. If the fit is poor, you will chafe and long to change careers.

Because who you are is grounded in your personality, your past experiences, and the complex socioeconomic culture in which you grew up, we can ask certain standard questions to gather data about you. We can then use these data to describe key aspects of your personality type relative to the world of work. We can also gather data about the world of work to find a range of ideal jobs that will suit each personality type we describe. Holland's hypothesis is that careful matching of personalities with occupations leads to career satisfaction. Put considerably less reverently, "there is a profession for every pathology." If you know yourself well enough, you can find it.

According to Holland, a sustaining career choice expresses personality and identity, as well as skills and abilities. Should you find yourself in a profession dominated by people with personality patterns markedly different from your own, your stress levels will rise. This "birds of a feather" approach predicts that when you are with like-minded people, you will be more comfortable. Although Holland's personality–environment-fit model is an occupational choice rather than a career-development model, it offers career managers an opportunity for gathering systematic information about how careers and personalities mesh and for gaining insights and new directions.

The career-management challenge is to get and then maintain the best person–environment fit that you can. To do this, no matter where you are in your own career trajectory or life cycle, you must first identify your personality type. Although Holland doesn't deal with changes in adult personality, it is clear that if personality–environment fit is a key to job satisfaction, you must be vigilant about monitoring any changes in your own personality and interests as well as any changes in your chosen field. To keep your options flexible, it is also a good idea to observe the types of people who occupy a range of potential occupational environments.

Even though Holland's model and accompanying instrumentation in *The Self-Directed Search* (1985a) treat people more or less alike, regardless of age, cohort, developmental stage, sex, and ethnicity, his personality–environment-fit approach remains one of the most widely used and researched theories of career selection. There are reasons for this.

Its self-help instrumentation is easy to use. But what gives Holland's theory its utility and intuitive appeal is its well-supported assumption that what a person does for a living is a critical, nonrandom expression of that individual's personality. People of all ages use what they know of occupations, even general, cultural occupational stereotypes, to find work environments that fit who they think they are. This makes sense. Who hasn't experienced a private "aha" upon learning that someone is a teacher, an accountant, or a psychoanalyst? Right or wrong, most people believe that an occupational title imparts important information. Although Holland didn't address why people develop their personality and occupational preferences, he asserted that people in given occupations share common past experiences, expectations, and personal histories that permit successful prediction of which person–environment fit will produce the best results. Decades of research lend general support to his hypotheses.

Because Holland sees occupations as a central means of defining adult identity and life satisfaction, he developed a set of practical approaches to help people identify their personality types and find an appropriate group of matching occupations.

His schema categorizes people into six personality types. Occupations are categorized into the same six types. The key, obviously, is to discover the optimal fit between a person's personality and work environment. Holland made this easy by describing empirically work environments via the modal personality preferences of people who populate them. Holland's six personality types, which are represented by the acronym, RIASEC, are typically diagramed on a hexagon that schematically places compatible personality types (e.g., AS or EC) adjacent to each other and less compatible types (e.g., AC or RS) opposite to each other. A very brief description of each type follows:

- *Realistic types* (R) are practical and prefer handling tools, machinery, and animals and performing physical skills (e.g., machinists, agriculturists, and construction workers).
- *Investigative types* (I) are task-oriented problem solvers who want to understand the scientific world (e.g., research psychologists and technical writers).
- *Artistic types* (A) prefer self-expression in original, unstructured environments that often involve working alone (e.g., authors, actors, and photographers).
- *Social types* (S) prefer to help others in positions that involve discussion, leadership, and group skills (e.g., counselors, teachers, and social workers).
- *Enterprising types* (E) prefer to lead, influence, and dominate in order to achieve organizational and personal goals (e.g., consultants, executives, and managers).
- *Conventional types* (C) prefer highly structured, systematic activities where their work is directed by a clear authority (e.g., accountants, secretaries, and traffic managers).

When you scan these six categories to find your own traits, one category is likely to be dominant. Then you can rank the remaining categories based on degree of resemblance. The three categories that best define your personality pattern yield a three letter code (e.g., IAS) that can be arranged in six possible combinations (e.g., IAS, ISA, ASI, AIS, SAI, and SIA). Using Holland's *The Occupation Finder* (1985b), you can compare your codes with the 500 common occupations that Holland classified according to the RIASEC schema. The assumption is that social types dominate and belong in social work environments, artistic types dominate and belong in artistic environments, and so on.

Although these codes compare different occupations with different personality types, they can also be used to match personalities with specialty areas within a profession. This involves more fine tuning and knowledge of a given field. For example, should you so choose, you can find many appropriate and alternative person–environment fits within the field of psychology, thus avoiding a radical shift to a different occupation. You can combine a knowledge of your personality type and interests with an understanding of the concept of fit to find your particular niche within psychology.

Let's suppose you are dissatisfied with your current work as a psychologist, but aren't sure that you wish to leave the field. Although psychology is coded as an investigative (I) profession in the Holland typology, clinical and counseling psychologists are classified as SIA, industrial/organizational psychologists as SEI, educational psychologists as IER, and experimental psychologists as IRS. With only a little extrapolation using *The Occupation Finder* or with just plain common sense, it can be seen that a psychologist with an ESA profile—associated with management and directorship jobs—might be happiest as a department chair or a director of a program, agency, or consulting firm, depending on the particulars. As an SAE psychologist, you would probably fit better in an independent-practice setting than in a research setting. If a well-defined shift in setting weren't feasible, you might tinker with the emphasis of your current job, focusing more on one-on-one counseling of students or applying for a hands-on grant permitting more innovation, visibility, or community interaction. Suppose your Holland code indicated that you were an ICR psychologist. Even though you might feel more at home in a laboratory research or industrial setting than in an agency or teaching college environment, you might cope with an agency or teaching job by intentionally pursuing more investigative work.

In short, you can use the meaning of your Holland code to fine tune your selection within the field of psychology, modifying your roles, tasks, or projects on a given job. Too often, Holland's codes are narrowly interpreted to indicate that an individual whose profile doesn't match his or her occupation must make a large-scale career change. Knowing how your personality type relates to occupational typology allows you to revise and mold any work setting to better fit your traits.

In this sense, Holland's codes have not yet been sufficiently explored and adapted to the nuances in a given job that remain under individual control and that can be altered for a better fit. If you are thinking of changing your career path, a good rule of thumb is

- First think small; consider innovative ways to tinker with your particular position, so that you shift priorities or change the actual content or focus of what you are doing.
- If that doesn't help, think about a more radical career change.

A simple but interesting inventory for exploring the evolution of your own work preferences is Holland's *The Self-Directed Search* (1985a). This self-scoring instrument encourages people to determine systematically which RIASEC types they most resemble by asking questions related to past experiences, preferences, and occupational daydreams.

The personality–environment-fit model has liabilities. It is "a one size fits all" nondevelopmental model. People cope with different objective and subjective career issues at different stages of career and life development. When people make career choices in early adulthood, they often have limited knowledge of occupations and jobs—other than occupational stereotypes. Experience is limited and governed by gender, culture, and socioeconomic status. It is easy to make a serious life choice based only on a restricted range of familiar ideal jobs (e.g., teacher, counselor, lawyer). Or faulty career decisions can be based on widespread, but inexact or even inaccurate, occupational stereotypes (e.g., psychologists help people). Because awareness of alternatives dictates choices, a person who insufficiently investigates and explores lesser known career possibilities may choose from too small a pool of career options—even if the options match in terms of personality parameters. The complacent may believe that they can plunge into matched careers, forgetting change for the millennium. A one-time read out of traits and interests scarcely justifies settling into a matched job or career-specialty area for a lifetime.

The glue that holds the personality–environment-fit approach together is the view that personalities and careers are stable entities that we can measure, match, and then shelve. If each match is stable, then its shelf life should be stable too. Unfortunately, we don't actually known how stable any initial match will be over the barrage of events, experiences, and personal perceptions that constitute a lifetime. When people seeking career change apply this approach, we can reasonably assume that they are experiencing incongruence between their personalities and their work environments. Perhaps, they didn't get the right fit in the beginning. Or is career dissatisfaction and change just part of a grander, predictable developmental shift? If you are curious and always learning, will you experience personal transformations that will eventually redefine your occupational priorities? Finally, we all know people who have experienced life crises that have propelled them to seek career changes or to radically rebalance their work and play to satisfy their needs for congruence in both areas.

Successfully matching your personality to an occupational niche demands more than a cursory "know thyself" snapshot. You must simultaneously track your own evolving personality and the evolving world of careers over years and even decades. The most effective use of the personality–environment-fit model demands rematching—not matching. The repeated use of a rematching approach over time will help prevent you from wearing career blinders.

The Developmental Career Models

Developmental career models place career-management issues into a life-cycle framework where the past, present, and future interact. These models look at how childhood antecedents of career choice (Roe, 1956; Roe & Lunneborg, 1984), stages of development in childhood and adulthood (Ginzberg, 1984; Ginzberg et al., 1951), and how an individual's identity and self-concept affect later career behavior (Super, 1957, 1984; Super, Thompson, & Lindemann, 1988). But until a few years ago, their focus was on how people choose careers rather than on what happens to them after they enter a given career.

Anne Roe's need model. Career theorist Anne Roe (1956) raised provocative issues about how people's adult career choices relate to their early childhood experiences with their parents. Although Roe's specific hypotheses have not been supported by research findings, her approach helps in understanding many career-management issues from a pragmatic perspective.

Roe looked at people's early childhood experiences and how well their needs were satisfied (using Abraham Maslow's (1970) need hierarchy) and postulated that each need is relevant to later career choices and the resulting degree of comfort in given occupations. According to Roe, our early interactions with our parents result in one of two basic career orientations: (a) occupations that directly involve people or (b) occupations that do not directly involve people. This more or less coincides with the accepted career-counseling practice of sorting occupations into three categories—working with people, working with things, or working with information—but takes this description one step further into its causal childhood antecedents. Roe developed her ideas into a model of occupational choice and an occupational-classification system. This system directly connects career choice to three overlapping continuums of being parented:

- the overprotective or underprotective experience (emotional stance)
- the neglectful or emotionally rejecting experience (avoidant stance)
- the noninvolved or loving experience (accepting stance)

In this model, your primary experience with your parents becomes an internalized beacon that guides your later career selection. It spotlights occupational areas that recreate the feelings and demands you experienced in your early parent–child interactions. Without consciously seeking to do so, you may choose an occupation or a work situation that reflects or recreates the psychological and emotional environment of your early home life.

For example, according to Roe's model, if you were an overprotected child growing up in a warm, accepting family, you are more likely to choose a people-oriented profession like psychology than a nonpeople-oriented profession like accounting. In a service profession, you may work hard to win other's approval to please your constituency, just as you did in childhood. On the other hand, if you were neglected or ignored as a child and your parents were distant or preoccupied, you are more likely to feel comfortable in professions where you work primarily with things or information, rather than people (e.g., conducting research or building technology).

To help people understand how their choices fit actual occupations, Roe separated occupations into eight groups, which were further divided into six levels each. She rank ordered these six levels based on degree of responsibility, motivation, and capacity. Highest in each group is the professional/managerial level, requiring independent responsibility. This is where most jobs in psychology would be expected to fall. Lowest in each group is the unskilled level. You can easily identify the classification of your current job by reading these brief descriptions based on Roe's eight occupational groups.

- *Service*—areas like social work and counseling that emphasize doing something for someone else. Psychotherapists are high level, social service directors are mid level, and psychiatric attendants are low level.
- *Business Contact*—areas like sales and business services, where person-to-person contact centers on persuasion rather than helping. Marketers are

high level, public relations counselors are mid level, and door-to-door sales people are low level.

- *Organization*—areas like management and white-collar work with formalized roles that focus on organizational efficacy. Heads of agencies and consulting firms are high level, human-resource managers are mid level, and staff assistants or "gofers" are low level.
- *Technology*—areas like production, trades, and transportation, where dealing with things takes precedence over dealing with people. Engineers are high level, computer operators are mid level, and laborers are low level.
- *Outdoor*—areas like farming, conserving natural resources, and animal husbandry, where interpersonal relations are often irrelevant. Environmental consultants are high level, farm owners are mid level, and gardeners are low level.
- *Science*—areas like scientific theory, applications, and research. Contributions to knowledge and culture, as well as interpersonal relations, vary. University research professors are high level, psychometricians are mid level, and nontechnical lab assistants are low level.
- *General Culture*—areas like education and the humanities, centered on preserving and transmitting culture, emphasizing macro levels of human interaction, rather than the individual. Scholars are high level, librarians are mid level, and specialized clerks are low level.
- *Arts and Entertainment*—areas like the creative arts and performing arts, involving the individual with a general public or target audience, but that are not directly interactive. Media psychologists are high level, seminar leaders are mid level, and greeting card writers are low level.

Although research has failed to support Roe's specific hypothesis that parental warmth is a direct determinant of occupational choice, the idea that career decisions and career management reflect early parent–child interactions makes sense. Roe's hypotheses regarding the importance of early family experiences require reframing to include other aspects of career management that extend beyond the idea that emotional acceptance or rejection causes the individual to turn toward or away from people.

Let's move beyond occupational selection for a moment and consider your own work experience. Can you identify any attitudes or expectations formed in your early years that continue to operate as an undertow in your work behavior? Are there any areas of hidden sensitivity or disappointments that color your career-management efforts?

For example, consider the experience of psychologist Debbie Cole.

> Debbie worked in the state hospital system for 15 years. She wanted to quit her job and enter private practice. She hated the bureaucracy, the work environment, and eventually herself for her inability to leave. Debbie was capable, accomplished, personable, and immobilized. She had always been a high achiever. But she came from a blue-collar family where security was the most valued need. A job was just a means of obtaining security, not a source of satisfaction. Risk taking, especially for girls, was seen as foolish. Even as a little girl, her overly protective parents discouraged her from taking chances. When Debbie began to examine

the messages her family had given her about risk taking, security, and its consequences, she understood that the roots of her career paralysis were in her early family environment. She was expected to achieve in school and then to find an appropriate *in loco parentis* company or agency that would take care of her in her career. No wonder she felt indecisive.

When you look at your own career management, to what extent are you actualizing your understanding of your parents' expectations about life and work? Also, to what extent are you recreating aspects of your childhood home experience in your current job? If you are a minority, a woman, or from a blue-collar family where you lacked professional parental role models and/or support for pursuing a professional career, you might compare what your parents taught you about approval-seeking, achievement, and self-efficacy with the expectations of your white, middle-class, male colleagues.

Just as Roe found clues to career selection in parental warmth or distance, you may find clues to understanding your own approach to career management in your childhood experiences and in your parents' early expectations for you.

Eli Ginzberg's stage model. Ginzberg, Ginzburg, Axelrod, and Herna (1951) pioneered an interesting developmental model of careers that, unfortunately, stopped at the time of young-adult entry into the labor force. More recently, Ginzberg (1984) revamped his theory to include occupational choice as a life-long process of decision making, particularly for those who consider their careers to be a major source of life satisfaction. Even though Ginzberg's model for adult career management concentrates on issues of early vocational choice rather than career management, it offers something unique to persons at all stages of career development. Ginzberg posited a three-stage developmental model that begins with a *fantasy period* in which career choices considered—like firefighter or zookeeper—have little to do with actual, later career choices and reflect an idealized and constricted view of the world of work. This fantasy period lasts until about age 11, when children move into the *tentative stage* in which their own interests direct them to explore and to look at their own capacities and values. At about age 17, the *realistic stage* begins. This stage involves exploring several occupational options, crystallizing ideas and knowledge, and narrowing down choices, leading to actual career selection and a job.

Throughout this early process, Ginzberg saw people as active, striving agents. Through tentative exploration, they gradually replaced their internalized, fictional ideas with more realistic views tempered by knowledge of their own skills, abilities, and interests. Ideally, only then do people actually make their career choices.

Although Ginzberg's model of occupational selection is centered in childhood and adolescence, its three-stage personal odyssey also applies to managing careers throughout adulthood. Beginning with fantasies and unrealistic views of careers, we can move toward greater awareness of self-interests that culminates in more appropriate and realistic choices. This approach, grounded in gaining data and experience through exploration, adapts well as a model for the ongoing tracking and monitoring of your career issues.

The fact is that personal fantasies continue long after childhood, and these fantasies of adulthood give expression and direction to our innermost longings.

Intentionally staying attuned to your fantasies regarding your idealized career or job can yield valuable information that we, as professionals, may otherwise discount as irrational, nonlegitimate sources of career information.

It is not too late in midcareer to explore new occupations through special projects, volunteer work, professional-association activities, or leisure pursuits. The entire panorama of adult experience provides grist for ongoing career exploration. Too often as adults, we prematurely foreclose on a lackluster career choice because it is the obvious or minimally satisfying solution to a career problem, or because we naively assume that we know enough without checking further. The problem is that insufficient career exploration, even in midcareer, shuts us down too early, shackling us to a career track before we have considered enough alternatives.

The recent career shift of Pat Oliver, a psychologist specializing in family therapy, illustrates the relevance of Ginzberg's approach to adult career exploration.

> Pat had always enjoyed drama and acting, but had let go of that when he decided to become a psychologist. About 5 years ago, he began to dream about being a poet. At first it was a family joke, but then he heeded his need to be creative and joined a writer's support group. At his group's urging, he submitted a satirical movie review to a local, suburban paper. One thing led to another, and he became a guest contributor. He found this satisfying, but clearly considered it a hobby. About 2 years later, Pat experienced serious career anxiety when a local radio station asked him to host a weekly movie review spot. He wondered what his patients and colleagues would think and whether he would like doing it too much. Yet, he found the idea of using his dormant creative and analytic talents appealing. He decided to try it out for a limited period. At last check, Pat was hosting a local, movie-review TV show and spending less than half of his time in private practice. The poet fantasy was replaced with tentative exploration of several related ventures. Reality testing occurred as did gradual crystallization, which lead to a partial, midcareer shift.

This illustrates the relevance of Ginzberg's stages to midstream redefinition of your psychological career.

Donald Super's self-concept model. Why do people work? For some people, it is only to earn a living. Work is not central to defining who they are. But for most people today, work is an important avenue for achieving self-expression and self-development. According to Super (1957, 1984; Super et al., 1988), work life provides a central focus for developing and expressing our personality and self-concept.

Super provides the most conceptually complex, far-reaching model of occupational choice and adult career development. He sees career development as a lifelong process from childhood through old age that is linked to the continuing development and implementation of our self-concept. As he viewed it, the self-concept is a unique, shifting amalgam of inherited factors, experiences, opportunities to play roles and gain feedback, and the ability to evaluate the results of our efforts. Personality and socioeconomic status are important in this schema, but so are the concomitant opportunities to which we are exposed, which stretch and interact with the boundaries of our self-development. If you are capable of changing, it is likely that you will adapt by developing new work tasks, work roles, and perhaps, an altogether new career path. Where you are in your career at any time can be seen as the cumulative sum of your particular past experiences, opportunities, and life decisions.

Careers provide one important arena where we can continually develop, implement, and test our self-concepts. We can test the reality of our personal aspirations and dreams and even choose to start all over again as we gain new skills, abilities, and self-perceptions. However, there is an ongoing, dynamic tension between the phenomenologic self and the social and work realities that we each face. We assume multiple roles in work and leisure to bridge this tension. Some roles fit our self-concept better than others. When we are able to express who we are accurately, we are more likely to be satisfied. Again and again in our work lives, we are faced with that Shakespearean dictum: "Know thyself." When work identity is an important cornerstone of self-definition, tension soars if self-expression is stifled. Unfortunately, as Super recognizes, opportunity structures that foster optimal self-development vary, often depending on factors over which the individual has little control—like sex, race, or socioeconomic class. External factors, like the status of the university that granted you the doctorate or the current favor or disfavor of your mentor's work, can also affect your career potential. The opportunity to develop and be exposed to new environments does not end at adolescence; rather, it continues throughout life.

Super uses a longitudinal, developmental approach to career development rather than snapshot matching like Holland's. Building on the work of Ginzberg and developmental theorists like Robert Havighurst and Charlotte Buehler, Super looked at how people implement self-concepts through predictable, developmental tasks linked to time-ordered stages of career development. He began working on this during the 1950s and 60s when there was little research interest in this area, and only recently has he integrated the various parts of his model, particularly life stage and role theory.

Super's ambitious set of theories incorporates differential psychology, adult life-cycle development, and self-psychology into a stage approach. From the perspective of career management, his more recent focus on adaptability to changing work environments and the handling of career-developmental tasks yields solid dividends. His work reminds us that as situations change, self-concepts and career preferences must change also, and developmental tasks become associated with all phases of careers—not only early occupational selection.

Super placed career development into a five-stage theory. Although these five stages (growth, exploration, establishment, maintenance, and disengagement) were originally conceptualized as a maxi-cycle describing lifelong career development in sequenced, chronological chunks, Super has since revised this idea (1984; Super et al., 1988) to reflect ongoing career changes. He has come up with a faster, condensed version of the maxi-cycle—the mini-cycle. Here, an individual moves through each stage in a matter of weeks, months, or years, rather than decades.

The mini-cycle occurs during career transitions, during transitions from one stage to the next, or during crisis points. Super also used the concept of *recycling* to account for midcareer change involving reexploration, reestablishment, maintenance in a new area, and preretirement disengagement. Although Super noted that recycling is most likely to occur when there are unstable patterns, recycling actually involves a set of skills critical to ongoing career management. Whereas

Super's revised model recognized that more and more normal adults choose not to be trapped by a career choice that they made in their early twenties, before they had substantial knowledge of the world of work, it does not emphasize the major reshuffling of life priorities as does the work of Levinson (1978) and Jung (1974).

Four of Super's five stages are applicable to the adult, postcareer-entry years, although ironically the first one, growth, is not. These stages are described using developmental tasks that a person must master before going on to the next stage. You will recognize stages akin to Ginzberg's among Super's growth, exploration (trial), establishment, maintenance, and disengagement stages. Consider where you are in your career relative to Super's career stages and whether you are maxi- or mini-cycling at this point.

In the *growth stage* (childhood/adolescence) your basic developmental task is to form attitudes and judgments leading to a realistic self-concept. A person moves from having no career interest to using fantasy as the basis of career thinking. Awareness of likes and dislikes later come and then the assessment of abilities and interests required in various careers. When you recycle through this stage, developmental tasks may include getting back in touch with fantasies, preferences, and interests to reenergize and redirect yourself, as well as learning to accept your own limitations.

In the *exploration stage* your developmental task is to learn about career opportunities—finding appealing occupations, work levels, and roles. You will need to decide on training and education leading to career entry or respecialization. This requires narrowing down choices and moving from the general to the specific. In Super's system, this stage normally occurs in the early 20s, but you can recycle through this stage at various life turning points. In evaluating your career paths and choices during career crises, you are likely to recycle through exploration. Then, once you have specified a plan, you are confronted with the pragmatics of implementing it.

Next is the *establishment stage* (25–45 years) in which your developmental task is to get started, achieve independence, and settle into your career—stabilizing your lifestyle and using your credentials and skills. This phase typically occurs in the decade after career entry, although you can mini-cycle through it again after any career change. This is a time for making a name for yourself as a psychologist and as a trusted member of your work organization and for achieving financial security. This is also the time to advance in your career. Ideally, you are doing what you want in a way that expresses who you are.

The next stage, *maintenance* (45–65 years) consists of a period during which you stand your ground and hold your own against competition. Your task is to make your position secure and cope with external threats from the larger world. According to Super, this stage occurs in the mid 40s. But in highly changing technological, informational, and creative fields, holding one's own is hardly enough. You must update and expand skills and knowledge and innovate. This is also a time to become a leader and a mentor.

In the *disengagement stage*, formerly called *decline* (60-onward), deceleration occurs. People want to be more selective about work duties. They want to delegate wherever possible. They opt for reduced pace and quantity of work. Retirement planning becomes a concern, and eventually, retirement from paid activities occurs. A person can experience decline during career-transition periods.

Super also identified seven career patterns based on stability, conventionality, and continuity. He developed a more comprehensive model of adult and life development that he called the Life-Career Rainbow (1984) in which he looked at role salience in work, homemaking, leisure, study, community service, and other activities. This newer model begins to examine the relationship of career change and self-actualization and how people seek life satisfaction when work satisfaction is blocked.

Super's model highlights the importance of finding work that expresses who we are and indirectly suggests that examining and shifting our occupational roles periodically may be one method for better expression of ourselves in our work life, so that we may experience less conflict and greater personal integrity.

Exercise 4.1

Think of a typical day in your current or your last job. Imagine yourself sitting at your desk, performing work-related tasks, and interacting with colleagues. Note how you look and feel. Assess your motivation to succeed. Then answer the following questions related to your own career development.

1. Which of Holland's three-letter codes best decribes the people who dominate this occupational niche? Does it match your own pattern of interests and preferences?
2. How can you tinker with your current job in terms of roles, tasks, and projects to get a better match? What related positions would provide a better fit with your personality?
3. Is your work people-intensive or task-intensive? Using Roe's approach, how do your early childhood experiences relate to your current work situation?
4. What messages did your parents give you about risk taking, achievement, security, independence, or status that are still influencing your expectations or work behavior?
5. What were your first fantasies concerning what you would be when you grew up? What are your fantasies now? Imagine yourself enjoing this fantasy job. What can you learn about yourself and your needs from this exercise?
6. Think of one or more ways that you can explore current fantasies without giving up your profession as a psychologist. How do you feel about pursuing these possibilities?
7. What parts of yourself are not well expressed in your current work?
8. Which of Super's five stages best describes where you are right now in your career in terms of the maxi-cycle? Where are you in the mini-cycle version of these stages?

What Models of Adult Development Predict about Change

Even a cursory reading of research and theories of adult development yields compelling evidence that both major transitions and minor realignments in perceptions, roles, and activites are endemic to adult life. As we juggle our work, family, and personal roles, their boundaries shift and stretch over time. Successfully negotiating predictable, but personally unexpected, life changes requires us to develop new life-planning metaskills to better cope with uncertainty and lack of closure.

Models of adult development give us many different ways to view this panorama of change and its impact upon our work life. We can see the adult years as an organized, somewhat predictable, sequence of developmental stages that provide us with optimal and suboptimal times for resolving lifelong, key conflicts, as did Erik Erikson (1963). We can view adult life as an alternating sequence of structure-building and structure-changing periods in which we have recurring opportunities to evaluate what we have created and to rebuild anew, as did Daniel Levinson (1978). We can see adulthood as a time for developing the less preferred, less salient aspects of ourselves so that we can achieve greater balance and integration in the second half of our lives as did Carl Jung (1974). Finally, we can see our behavior in the adult years as an increasingly complex continuation of the lifelong challenge to adapt and make sense of our lives using Piagetian principles (Piaget & Inhelder, 1969) of assimilation and accommodation to help us align and realign our internal representations of reality with our ever-changing experiences over time.

In the following discussion, we will look at what a few well-known theorists and researchers say about the adult life cycle. Although the adult-development literature focuses on the broader midlife, rather than midcareer, experience, we will look at how career-management issues intertwine with the questioning of previous life decisions and the seeking of new alternatives.

Daniel Levinson's Theory of Stable and Transitional Periods of Adult Life

What Daniel Levinson reported in his book *The Seasons of a Man's Life* (1978) is particularly instructive to understanding how personal changes affect your career. In intensive interviews with 40 men, aged 38 to 52, Levinson found a seemingly ordered ebb and flow of stable and transitional life periods. Put simply, throughout life, people are engaged in either building or changing their life structure. The life structure is the underlying and evolving pattern of a person's roles, relationships, and responsibilities at a given time.

Careers are increasingly important anchors for our adult identity and self-esteem as family and personal ties loosen. Work is a major aspect of the life structure where our personality asserts itself. But what happens at work is not hermetically sealed off from what is happening in family and personal arenas. All interact and spill over. Being fired from a job can adversely affect relationships. A problem with a child or spouse can impede work performance. Both occurring simultaneously can cause self-esteem to plunge. Plus, all this is mediated by whether we happen to be in a stable or transitional period. During transitional structure-changing periods, we are more likely to change jobs, careers, partners, or coping skills. In turn, these changes ripple out, altering other aspects of our self-definition. During stable, structure-building periods, unplanned, large-scale change occurs less frequently. Should it occur, we are likely to see such change as an intrusive, poorly timed occurrence. Therefore, where we are in our own life structure affects our readiness to undertake and implement career change.

Levinson viewed the life cycle as a journey composed of four chronologically linked units, each with its own unique developmental "to do" list. Each of these sequential units or *eras* lasts about 25 years, but overlaps like seasons. We move from one era to the next through change-enabling, transitional, bridge-like periods of 3 to 6 years. Whereas the eras are times to make and develop committed life decisions in occupational, relational, and familial arenas, the transitions are times to search for possibilities fostering greater self-integration.

In early adulthood, there are two stable, structure-building periods—entering the adult world and settling down. The first, entering the adult world, is a time for experimenting with a tentative life structure and testing initial careers and personal choices. The second, settling down, is a time for getting serious and investing effort in advancement. Similarly, middle adulthood has two stable periods in which we can try out a second, more satisfactory, life structure. But Levinson predicted that even during these stable, structure-building periods when we seek to achieve our goals, nearly half of the people going through them will experience the following predictable problems:

- serious professional or personal failure (20%),
- an intolerably flawed life structure requiring breaking out (13%),
- career or personal advancement leading to a new life structure (8%), or
- an unstable life structure that never seems to coalesce (8%).

Only 55% advance with smooth sailing even during these stable periods.

Levinson also identified five transitional bridges that link these stable periods together, creating an opportunity window for change:

- the early-adult transition (approximately age 18–22)
- the age 30 transition (approximately 28–32)
- the midlife transition (approximately 40–45)
- the age 50 transition (approximately 50–55), and
- the late-adult transition (approximately 60–65).

Each of these transitional periods has its own character. Although some can be negotiated smoothly, others are more taxing. For example, think about your own late teens and early adulthood. What was important to you? What was your most pervasive feeling during this transition? Compare this period to a later period like the age 30 transition or midlife transition. The eager excitement you probably experienced during the early-adult transition is less likely to reign during later transitions. In later transitions, you have already invested your energies into specific educational, career, and personal plans. At this point, you may view dissatisfaction with your existing life as a threat to your initial investment. It takes more effort to view your discontent as an opportunity for resumed personal growth. As years pile on, long-standing, unresolved career or personal issues from the past may flare up to exacerbate the normal stresses of change. Whether life and career events have been culturally "on or off time" (Neugarten & Datan, 1973) also seems to matter more at the epicenter of life than when people are first starting out and perceive an unfettered future stretching ahead unbound by time constraints.

Midlife transitions are a special time for major reevaluation. A "now or never" sense of mortality—a shift to thinking about time left to live and what it is still possible to achieve—begins to influence decisions. Midlife is a time for taking inventory of past accomplishments and failures, stripping away illusions, and designing a new future aligned with emergent midlife values. Levinson (1978) borrowing from Carl Jung's (1974) work, noted that a major developmental task of midlife is the integration of polarities within the self. I will highlight a few relevant ideas from Jung's work next.

Questions to address.

1. How has your answer to the question, "What am I capable of becoming?" shifted in the past decade?
2. What are you willing to settle for? How different is that from your answer to the preceding question?
3. Are you currently engaged in building or changing your life structure? What are the key issues and arenas (career, relational, and personal) that you need to build or change?
4. What problems (if any) have you encountered in your career during your stable, structure-building periods? How did they influence your decisions?

Carl Jung's Integration of Polarities

> Ken Jensen began his career as an experimental psychologist working with primates in a medical school learning laboratory. He enjoyed the organization and routine of the laboratory and conducted a series of studies in discrimination learning that won him accolades for design from senior researchers. He published more than 30 articles in 15 years. Ken was well known for spending his weekends in the lab and often would get to work at 5:00 a.m. Some of his graduate assistants said he was driven, others said he was reclusive. But everyone was surprised when at age 41, Ken gained notoriety as an effective mediator between the medical school and an angry local group that was protesting the experimental use of animals. Ken enjoyed interviews with local media and came across as warm and sensible. He began consulting to other medical schools on public perceptions of animal experimentation and served as an expert witness in several hearings. His interest in the issue was undeniable, and he published highly readable articles in the popular press. The changes in Ken's career as a psychologist occurred from the inside out, mirroring changes in his own development.

Ken Jensen's midcareer shift is consistent with Jung's (1974) view of midlife as a time for integrating the internal polarities between our preferred and nonpreferred psychological attitudes and functions.

According to Jung, during the first half of life, we are eager to master the outer realities of the world through goal-directed action and achievement. Therefore, early in our careers, we are performance-driven. We take on jobs and activities that permit us to establish the outer trappings of success in our careers and to produce tangible accomplishments. Like Ken Jensen, we are likely to prioritize and value instrumental, action-based goals, like getting published so many times in a bid for tenure, or taking an appropriate postdoctorate for a research career in health psychology, or working toward a goal that represents success to us.

As we progress in our careers and in our own life cycle, our emphasis shifts. We assess our earlier values. Our raison d'etre is no longer merely getting our career ticket punched in the right ways. Rather, it is to achieve greater personal balance and wholeness. Jung noted that in the transition from morning to afternoon in the middle years of life, we gradually shift from a linear-goal orientation to an orientation in which we look more closely at those aspects of ourselves that we neglected in earlier adulthood. As a young, ambitious researcher working in isolation in the laboratory to perfect his experimental research skills, Ken Jensen set aside his need to be recognized and began to contribute to the community. Eventually, these neglected aspects of self broke out to redirect his efforts.

As decades of our lives pass, we become more internally attuned—turning toward the development of the less preferred traits of our youth. At midlife, these lesser developed functions clamor to be recognized. Therefore, we might find ourselves less performance-driven in our middle adult years and more driven by a quest for meaning.

This has implications for both career development and career management. Not only can we expect change, but the direction of change may be predicated on what we have or have not developed in our earlier years. In any case, the expected shift is toward unity. The analytic researcher develops the more intuitive, creative aspects of the self; the extrovert moves toward a more introverted, reflective attitude; the isolated scientist examines the impact of his or her work upon the larger community; the instrumental achiever becomes more concerned with value and meaning; and the reentry woman embarking on a professional career seeks instrumental achievement in the external world. Based on his clinical work, Jung (1974) suggested that at midlife, people feel an urgent need to examine and appreciate the opposite of their fomer ideals and to move toward greater self-integration. It is as if our neglected functions revolt and demand their own place in the structure of our lives.

Levinson's (1978) viewpoint that the middle adult years are the time for integrating remaining polarities in the self, such as masculine and feminine, old and young, creative and instrumental, fits this Jungian viewpoint. So do Bernice Neugarten's findings (1968) that show an interesting sex-linked crossover at middle age in which men become more nurturing, women become more achievement-driven, and in which members of both sexes become more characterized by introversion. The respective priorities of work and personal roles also may shift at midcareer as issues of balance and meaning become more salient.

Questions to address.

1. In what ways has your approach to your career been performance-driven toward external rewards? What goals are you working toward? Are these changing?

2. In what ways is your career driven by issues of meaning and value? Which values are most salient right now? Are these changing?
3. To what extent have you developed a preference for objective thinking over values or feelings (or vice versa) in making key decisions? To what extent do you prefer facts and details over ideas and hypotheses that have not been proven (or vice versa)? Have these preferences shifted?
4. What polarities are most important for you to integrate in your life right now? How might you begin to develop more integration between your least and most preferred functions in your career?

Being Prepared for Career Changes and Redecisioning

The first step in being prepared for career change is to destigmatize the change process. Change is normal. Change is desirable. Place change in the context of normal professional growth and development. Viewing change as natural makes it easier to examine earlier decisions, assess new directions, and move into a "redecisioning" process without excessive recrimination. By anticipating change as a given, you can often preempt the unexpected and take charge of timing.

If anything, the absence of change is suspect. If nothing is changing in your career, it is time to ask yourself tough questions. The parameters of change and stasis can be defined by two generic questions: "What am I capable of becoming?" and "What am I willing to settle for?" The answer to the first question may require hitting the accelerator, whereas the answer to the second may demand slamming on the brakes. If nothing is happening in your career, you may have inadvertently hit the brake. This is worth exploring further.

On the other hand, when everything is up for grabs, and you have little control over outcomes, it is time to reestablish whatever control you can through investigating, networking, rewriting your vitae, or beginning a job search.

Either situation can signal that your career-management efforts are derailing and that you need to redirect your efforts. Depending on your attitude, times of career redecision can be difficult.

Here are some basic ground rules that I have found helpful when reassessing career directions:

- Make no comparisons with others' situations.
- Assign no hindsight blame to yourself for decisions that you made in another life era.
- See yourself as a student of your own behavior, and impartially gather data about yourself.
- Decide, in advance, to keep your options open even if uncertainty becomes uncomfortable; resist foreclosing on the first easy solution.
- Find a neutral third party with whom to discuss your ideas and get specific feedback.
- Remember that career transition often piggybacks on other life events such as divorce, geographic moves, or termination from a job, so develop effective change-management skills before you need them.

It is generally useful to see change as an opportunity for new development. As psychologists, we use development to describe an unfolding of potential that involves growth. We talk about career development, professional development, adult development, personal development, and organizational development. All are critical to career management. This is a lot to juggle and balance. To be successful requires vigilance—sorting and analyzing incoming data, reevaluating your short- and long-term goals and, simultaneously, readjusting your pace and direction.

Careers are affected by many types of time boundaries. As we gain seniority as psychologists, our occupational and chronological clocks are also ticking. With experience and age, we become more aware of our limits—what we can and can't do and the fact that we only have so many years left to live, achieve, and experiment. We come to understand how time affects our ability to make a meaningful career shift and to reestablish ourselves in a new professional niche.

Midcareer, you may feel trapped where you once felt challenged. Having satisfied the pressing needs that propelled your career a decade earlier, you may be caught unaware by a group of dormant needs that demand their day in the sun.

The timing of work successes and failures and job entries and exits, relative to your life cycle, is also critical. A given event, such as failing to get a research grant, may have different consequences if it occurs during the uncertainty of a structure-questioning period than if it occurs during the security of a structure-building period. During periods of doubt and questioning, small disappointments may be transformed into marker events for a whole period of discontent. Viewing an event as occurring at the right time in our lives (on-time) versus viewing a life event as occurring too early or too late (off-time) may also redefine its subjective significance for us. For example, experiencing an early career failure, such as not receiving tenure, may have a less debilitating impact on self-esteem than experiencing a later career failure, such as not being promoted to a full professor. These are normal reactions that lead people to question their past decisions and to either reaffirm the status quo or move toward a new future with different alternatives.

And remember, organizations change too. You may encounter gentle evolution or major revolution. Even small institutional shifts, such as moving from free-wheeling innovation to greater structure, will affect what the institution recognizes and rewards. If you fail to track these factors, you may find that the evolution in your workplace has left you, your accomplishments, and your values stranded on a side rail.

In difficult periods when change is experienced as a full-blown crisis, commitments made in another period of life that bind us to obsolete structures may now seem foolish. We may look back at our lives and feel that we have come up empty, judging past decisions and behaviors with the wisdom of hindsight and the fear of uncertainty. This is a time for revising our assumptions and corresponding plans, for taking stock of what we have learned, and for setting forth a new course of action aligned with our current values.

For the highly career-invested psychologist who has made many personal sacrifices along the way, all of these changes may precipitate great stress, as well as the opportunity to break out of old patterns. The best antidote for this type of stress is to be prepared in advance. This means developing new metaskills for change management. Useful change-management skills include networking skills, job-search skills, financial-planning skills, crisis-management skills, conflict-negotiation skills, expectation-management skills, and stress-management skills.

Questions to address.

1. Make a list of change-management skills you already possess. Now make a second list of change-management skills you need to develop.
2. How do you answer the question, "what am I capable of becoming?"
3. What is your answer to the question, "what am I willing to settle for?"

Tracking Your Own Preferences

> Don Kasper is a psychologist specializing in marriage and family therapy. He has always characterized himself as a high achiever. He wrote his first mass-market psychology book on divorce only 5 years after receiving his doctorate and earns a solid six-figure income on the national lecture circuit. Audiences rate Don's presentations as brilliant, and colleagues respect his popularization of research. By most professional and cultural standards, Don is a success. Yet, after 3 years of being in the seminar business, he still feels nervous about each talk and compulsively rewrites his material every 2 months. A new opportunity to do a television series on therapy is another feather in his cap, but he is secretly dreading it. Don has prioritized competence and public recognition, but has failed to emphasize the one-on-one work he really enjoys doing. As a result, Don's career is managing him rather than vice versa.

Accurately tracking your own preferences may be the single most important aspect of your career management if long-term satisfaction is what you are seeking. In the quest for professional competence, it is easy to overlook how much your own "psychological set points" regulate your enthusiasm for the work you do. Don loved doing family therapy in private practice, but felt he needed to prove himself in the communications and mass media arenas. Unfortunately, his career choices were at odds with his natural set points, which were introverted, reflective, and empathic. Although he mastered the art of stand-up presentations with anonymous audiences, he never really enjoyed them. He was comfortable solving problems in small groups and pounding out chapters on his word processor. If Don had taken jobs and projects that went with, rather than against, the grain of his own preferences, strengths, and values, he would have felt more at ease in his career.

If you agree with the philosophy that preferences should strongly influence career choices, you will want to conduct regular, ongoing or periodic self-assessments, taking stock of your psychological preferences, strengths and weaknesses, pressing needs, and values. Ask yourself questions pertaining to the meaning of work in your life, and reassess your priorities. Because all of these factors are subject to change with development, experience, and time, keeping yourself updated on your own preferences is critical to your career planning.

Monitoring Your Own "Psychological Pulse"

How do you really feel about your work? What are you most enthusiastic about accomplishing during the rest of your career as a psychologist? What's fun? What can you learn about yourself from analyzing your professional experience in terms of fun versus boredom? Some aspects of your current job or graduate studies have probably put you to sleep. Other aspects are more engaging or at least neutral. Identify that finite list of coveted tasks and projects that you genuinely enjoy doing. You do not have to conceptualize work and play as bipolar opposites. It is all too easy in the course of becoming a psychologist to become so pressured and serious about your work and professional identity that you forget to monitor your reactions to your daily tasks. On some days, getting excited about your work may seem irrelevant. But from a career-management perspective, your enthusiasm is critical. When you stop gathering data about which parts of your work life make your psychological pulse beat faster versus which make you feel brain dead, you are in a one-down, career-management position. You have ceased to be integrally involved in your career.

In this regard, relationships and careers share some commonalities. When you are considering a new job or a new relationship, it helps to assess variables that work initially for both—like attraction, chemistry, and fun. This initial attraction is an obvious clue that the job or career path could have what it takes to generate a serious pursuit or a long-term commitment. Why risk squandering years of your life on an unattractive, incompatible career option?

A coolly rational career methodology may overlook some important quality-of-life considerations. By passing many academic and professional hurdles, you have already established your baseline competence. Now, you must attend to another critical constellation: career excitement, enthusiasm, and satisfaction. Remember your occupational joie de vivre counts: intangibles count; career chemistry counts.

To track this constellation, first make it a priority. Consider it when you evaluate your current work and when you consider other aspects of the profession or other disciplines. Second, evaluate this constellation concretely. Try keeping a weekly log that tracks and rates your feelings of enthusiasm and excitement. Distinguish between activities that prompt a "fast pulse" versus those that prompt a "dead beat." For new positions, specializations, and occupations in which you haven't had experience, obtain data through job descriptions and through interviews with people who hold similar positions.

Exercise 4.2

Imagine yourself at work in your current or last job on a typical day. Envision all of the details (e.g., your desk, your posture, your papers sitting in piles).

- Write down three words that describe how you feel about this job. What do these words tell you about your attitudes and feelings?

- Which work activities energize you? Bore you? Rate these activities on a scale of 1 to 10 (1 = pulse dead; 10 = pulse racing).
- Break down your work activities into Myers-Briggs dimensions of Extroversion–Introversion, Sensing–Intuition, Thinking–Feeling, and Judging–Perceiving. How does your current job match your preferences?
- What would you change about this job? What would you prefer instead?

Questions to address.

1. What do you do for fun outside of work? Examine these activities for patterns that tell you about what you enjoy that is missing from your work life. Think about how you could incorporate these factors into your work.
2. Get job descriptions and university catalogs that list new courses of study that interest you inside or outside of psychology. Highlight with a marker anything and everything to which you feel attracted. Analyze what you have highlighted. What pattern of interests emerges?
3. Which commitments made in another period of your life feel particularly constraining to you now? What steps have you taken to effect change in the desired direction?
4. List five of your strengths and weaknesses as a psychologist and five of your strengths and weaknesses in general. Are there any interesting patterns of differences between your lists?
5. Using 10 index cards, write out what is important for you to accomplish in your career. These are your career-mission statements. Rank these cards from most important to least important. Wait a week and then rerank them.

Developing Career Strategies and Tactics

To plan effectively, you will need to track and compare where you are actually going in your career and where you want to be going. As you near your goals and periodically realign them, you can expect to encounter many difficult career-choice points. Although all career decisions are idiosyncratic to you as an individual, it is helpful to have some decision-making criteria in place well before predictable or unpredictable career crises erupt. This implies developing an enduring strategy keyed to your personality characteristics, values, and mission. A few basic tactics that are easy to implement will help you. Although this results-oriented approach is a far cry from the laissez-faire career-management approach that guides many meandering career paths, it shouldn't feel like a straitjacket either. Setting clear-cut career goals and moving toward them systematically is not for everyone. Some people prefer to allow their professional work life to evolve in a more spontaneous way, reacting to their own intuitive sense of what they need to develop at any given time. But even if you feel this way, a careful look at strategic career management can serve as a useful heuristic and provide an alternative management model that can help you through transitional times.

In the following sections, I will discuss the nuts and bolts of developmental career planning and career decision making, based on the strategical and tactical career-management system, the *Doom Loop* (Hollander, 1991; Jett, 1985; Jett & Hollander, 1986).

The Difference between Career Strategies and Tactics

The first step in developing your career-management schema is to differentiate strategies from tactics. Your failure to do this can lead to a muddled course of action. Although strategies and tactics are originally military terms, they are also applicable to career management. *Strategy* derives its meaning from the overall planning of warfare objectives. It deals with the big picture. *Tactics* are employed in the actual execution of battle maneuvers. They govern day-to-day operations. Military leadership views precise planning in strategies and tactics as critical to winning both the battle and the war. Similarly, using strategies and tactics in managing longer term career objectives and shorter term job decisions enhances your control of your career outcomes.

Confusing strategies with tactics or assuming that they are interchangeable terms related to achieving one's goals has consequences beyond linguistic confusion. Once you make a commitment to managing your own career, the obvious first step is to set goals and move toward them. In fact, this goal-centered approach characterizes high achievers in general. But in careers, setting goals (strategy) is rarely enough to bring about the desired results. You also need a clear framework for deciding the how and when of implementing your goals (tactics) in the workplace. Goals set direction, but provide no automatic pilot for your daily operating plan. For example, choosing the goal of becoming a competent psychologist sets a strategy of striving toward mastery, but provides no step-by-step plan for negotiating your precise postdegree career choices. Therefore, you have no tactical doctrine to guide your actual career maneuvers. You may still achieve success, but it becomes less likely.

Strategy defines macro-level career planning and requires that you set long-term goals and objectives. Tactics define micro-level career action and deal with implementing short-term decisions consistent with your strategy.

The Career Capstone

What is a career capstone? The capstone is an obvious, often overlooked, career-management concept that you may find helpful. I am defining a capstone as any clearly described position that represents success to you, that you are currently not qualified to hold, and that you will not be qualified to hold for another 3 to 8 years. So, by definition, a capstone is developmental. It defines and promotes specific directions for growth and change. Even if structure is inherently aversive to you, identifying a targeted, midrange career objective—the career capstone—is an effective way to set your career course.

A career capstone always has a specific job title, for example, director of organizational development for a large corporation or director of clinical training at a university (Jett, 1985). By identifying the specific job title of your capstone, you operationalize your career goals. This allows you to research the capstone and describe it in terms of the specific set of skills that a person needs to qualify for the capstone and succeed in it. Accurately researching and identifying this set of skills is critical to developing your strategy. Without acquiring these targeted skills, you will not be a qualified contender for the position—no matter how excellent your other professional competencies or academic credentials may be. Therefore, these capstone-related skills define the precise capstone profile that you will need to attain through experience.

An accurate skill analysis of your capstone sets the direction for your career strategy. Simply put, the strategy is to take jobs, projects, training classes, and courses that allow you to develop the skills you currently lack, but need in order to qualify for your capstone. If you are slipshod or misinformed about which skills are required for succeeding in your capstone, you can wind up with an interesting professional-skill profile that fails to lead you anywhere that you want to go. Accuracy in the skill analysis of your capstone is crucial, because the skill analysis specifies the targeted skills that you will need to qualify for the career goal you set.

Selecting the right capstone is important. But it is rarely a one-time, "end-of-problem" choice. Rather, capstone selection and reselection is an ongoing process—another career management metaskill.

Immediately after graduate school, lack of relevant career experience makes choosing the right capstone difficult. For this reason, new graduates are better off taking a series of attractive jobs that engage their psychological pulse and coincide with their psychological set points. Their immediate career objective is to accumulate a wide range of generic work skills, while being exposed to a series of capstones. This step needs to occur before new graduates select their first capstone to help circumvent early career disappointment caused by a common, but dangerous, mix of high hopes and sparse job data. Later in careers, experience clarifies new capstone choices, but the costs of realigning a poor-fitting capstone or series of capstones are higher, and perceived options may narrow. If you land in midcareer, saddled with an outgrown capstone in which you are highly invested and have no alternatives on the horizon, understandably you could feel trapped.

To counteract any natural tendency toward capstone entropy, conceptualize capstone selection as a reusable metaskill that will help you realign or redirect your career when it gets off track. Plan on having several capstones over the course of your professional career. In each case, your capstone should match your career mission. It should fit your current interests, preferences, and goals and leave you ample room for professional development. Although periodically, you will need to reassess your capstone's place in your life and in your career, your capstone should have sufficient staying power to withstand the relentless press of politics, competition, and daily hassles. Once your commitment to your career capstone is forged, the strategy is to move systematically toward achieving it.

Career management without the selection of a capstone is career management by assumption and default. Professionals who fail to set capstones appear to fall into three categories. The first group is made up of those who believe that once they have earned their professional degrees, hard work and competence will suffice to get them someplace. As many people in this group learn, this is a risky strategy. It empowers disinterested others, who do not have the professional's best interest at heart, to recognize, reward, and position the professional's worth to the organization. The second group comprises those who have confused attaining a professional identity through education and training with setting a career capstone. They fail to realize that it is necessary to set clear and realistic postdegree goals. Because academic programs in psychology provide little or no career-management training, psychologists' knowledge of how to negotiate their postdegree careers, typically, depends on their own career savvy or the help of a mentor. The professionals in this second group tend to accept a respectable postdegree job and then go on automatic pilot for a time. Without realizing what they are doing, they are relinquishing control of their career trajectories. The missing piece of information is that gaining a professional identity is the baseline for career startup, not the capstone. The third group are those spontaneous "go with the flow" professionals who follow their evolving interests wherever they lead, optimistically hoping for the best. Even for these free spirits, managing a career without a strategy and a capstone eventually creates distressing confusion. There simply are too many forks in the road.

In fact, even with a capstone securely in tow, your career-management efforts may be error-prone. Career tactics make it easier to decide which fork in the road to take. Tactics are focused on the here and now—on pressing career decisions like taking a job or turning it down or staying with an institution or leaving it. Often, you have no way to duck these decisions, even if you have no idea where you are heading. Still, to make sense, these decisions should fit within the framework of achieving your capstone or you may wind up spinning your wheels.

Consider the case of Gregory Braun.

> Gregory is an educational psychologist currently employed as an assistant professor at a small western college. About 5 years ago, he defined his career capstone to be director of test development for a large national psychological-testing company. To gain appropriate skills, he took a series of seminars to update his test-construction skills and taught an undergraduate testing course. Because there was no graduate division at his college, he began a job search. When his dean heard that Gregory was interviewing for a job with a testing company, he offered Gregory a new job directing an educational grant for developing a new student learning center. This job was considered a plum. It would give Gregory a sizable pay increase, travel monies, and high internal institutional status. Gregory considered these factors and decided to take the job based on increased salary, status, and visibility. It also made his family happy, because they didn't have to move. In the short haul, Gregory won the battle. But from a career-management standpoint, his tactical decision was inconsistent with his overall capstone strategy. Therefore, it was a costly and poor career decision. This new position offered him little opportunity to further develop the skills relevant to his capstone. In fact, it temporarily derailed him from his strategy of taking only jobs, projects, and courses relevant to his capstone of director of testing. In terms of achieving his capstone, he may lose the war.

A career-management rule of thumb is to view career strategy and tactics as highly synergistic. They must support each other and move you toward acquisition of the needed skills.

Questions to address.

1. If you do not have a well-defined capstone, which strategies or assumptions are you using to guide your career-management process?
2. Describe your first career capstone? How did you determine it?
3. If you do not currently have a career capstone, identify and list several attractive options. What are the pros and cons of each one? Which are most appealing?
4. If you were offered an attractive "off-strategy" job, which factors would be important in making the tactical decision to take it or turn it down?

Selecting a Career Capstone

No matter where you are in your career, the next step in implementing an intelligent career-management plan is either to select or reassess your capstone. For every person at various career and life stages, there are many acceptable capstones. So you have many potential choices. Further, there is no single proven way to choose one. But because your capstone sets the strategy from which your job decisions will follow, the more closely you match your capstone with your own unique pattern of preferences, needs, values, and abilities, the more enjoyable daily life will be. And the more attainable your capstone is relative to external economic and work conditions, the better are your chances for achieving it.

People generally choose a capstone based on a subjective assessment of whether or not they have what it takes to perform well in a position and less frequently, on whether or not they believe they will enjoy holding a position. It has been my experience in working with professionals that the most typical error in choosing a capstone lies in basing choices solely on criteria of personal performance and productivity, while ignoring or discounting what they really like and value. High achievers seem particularly driven to discount their own preferences. If you value your competence and achievement over your enthusiastic enjoyment of the work, you may choose the wrong capstone—one that will give you little job satisfaction or one that will bind you in a straitjacket that restricts your professional development. The following is a case in point:

> Ike Kennedy was trained as an industrial/organizational research psychologist in the 1960s and taught for 5 years. His orderliness and organizational skills were so legendary in a loosely run department that he was asked to be department chair early in his career. He excelled. Before long, he was made academic dean. At midcareer, to his amazement, he found himself unhappily contemplating a capstone job offer—president of a small college. This was the very position he had aspired toward. The problem was that Ike found little exciting about his job. He thought about going back to teaching and academic research, but everyone thought he was crazy. Besides, he had been out of his academic specialty for so long that he had lost touch with the field. Asked why he had left teaching for administration to begin with, he said, "Everyone agreed that no one could run a

> department better than I could. One thing led to another, and I became an administrator. I never really asked what I would rather do. I was too busy trying to get to the top—until now."

Ike was in a career crisis termed "doomed at capstone"—when the targeted capstone is reached, but joylessly (Jett & Hollander, 1986). Being doomed at capstone happens for many reasons, but failing to follow one's preferences is probably the most prevalent cause.

The lesson is simple. If you don't enjoy developing and using the skills required by your capstone, you can expect boredom and ennui—not miracles. Expect to ask yourself questions like "Is this all there is?" and "What is wrong with me?" Even though you are good at what you do, you may feel disengaged from your work.

Selecting the right capstone requires the same type of systematic self-assessment and career exploration as did deciding to become a psychologist. You need to choose a capstone congruent with your natural preferences and with what is important for you to accomplish. Your capstone should also satisfy the salient needs (such as achievement, power, and affiliation) that are currently driving your behavior.

The main difference in choosing a capstone rather than an occupation is that you are dealing with a narrower subrange of functional possibilities. And for any capstone, work roles and functions (such as managerial, technical, service, theoretical) are as pivotal as content. Further, to reach any capstone, you must pass through a hierarchy of feeder jobs and positions involving a progression of requisite work roles, tasks, skills, and courses.

Your answers to the questions asked throughout this book will give you insight into how your own patterns fit your current capstone or any future capstone you might be considering. But keep in mind that unless you plan to respecialize or to radically change careers, your capstone should fit your credentialed area of expertise as a psychologist. If not, you must learn what additional schooling or supervised experience you will need.

In summary, no matter where you are in your career, if you don't already know your career capstone, you will need to select one. Even if the idea of a capstone makes you claustrophobic, you will find capstone selection a useful career-management heuristic.

Exercise 4.3

To select a capstone, use some variation of this six-step process as a guide.

1. Analyze your general skill profile in terms of job-related skills in psychology and nonjob-related skills acquired through any life experience.
2. Identify skills you enjoy, but in which you lack expertise, and separate these skills from those you enjoy and already have expertise in.
   Treat this list of preferred skills as a functional, generic job description.
3. Find a job title that fits this functional description by brainstorming and listing positions and projects that use these aforementioned skills.

4. Research these positions and talk to colleagues who hold some of these listed positions about what they do. Ask them about other related positions that may fit your skill profile.
5. Identify any external or internal barriers that might get in the way of your reaching a particular capstone.
6. Select the capstone that gives you the best fit, that feels most intuitively comfortable, and that is a realistic possibility.

Having selected a tangible capstone, you can evaluate it in terms of the subjective costs of reaching it. Identify an optimal series of feeder jobs that create the bridge of experience you need to reach your capstone. Evaluate the pace and stress of these positions, and weigh such issues as the length of time needed to reach your capstone, the lifestyle associated with holding these feeder positions, and the types of additional formal and informal training required. Then, decide if the trade-offs and sacrifices are worth achieving your capstone.

Questions to address.

1. Describe your current capstone position. What needs, interests, preferences, values, and abilities does it satisfy?
2. Go back to the 10 career-mission statements you wrote on index cards at the end of the section in this chapter on "Monitoring your own psychological pulse." Which of the capstones that you are currently considering are most consistent with your career-mission statements?
3. Consider two different capstones that you are interested in pursuing. What are the subjective costs of reaching them? Which factors are most prohibitive?

Translating Capstones into Skills

There are many ways to think about jobs. The career-management system that we have been discussing (Jett, 1985; Hollander, 1986, 1991), the Doom Loop, takes a skill-centered approach, meaning skills are the basic system unit. From this perspective, every career capstone has a profile of specific skills that qualify a person to perform it. In fact, all jobs, including capstones, can be defined in terms of these skill clusters. Identifying those skills associated with your capstone is the first step in developing your plan for acquiring the skills necessary to successfully reach your capstone.

In Figure 4.1, you see a diagram of a hypothetical skill field that depicts the potential universe of skills that define jobs. Each dot represents one subset of possible skills, such as interpersonal skills, communication skills, research skills, teaching skills, or political skills. As you can imagine, the number and type of skills represented in a skill field is nearly endless.

All jobs and all career capstones can be represented with some subsection of this skill field. Once you have identified a potential career capstone, analyze the

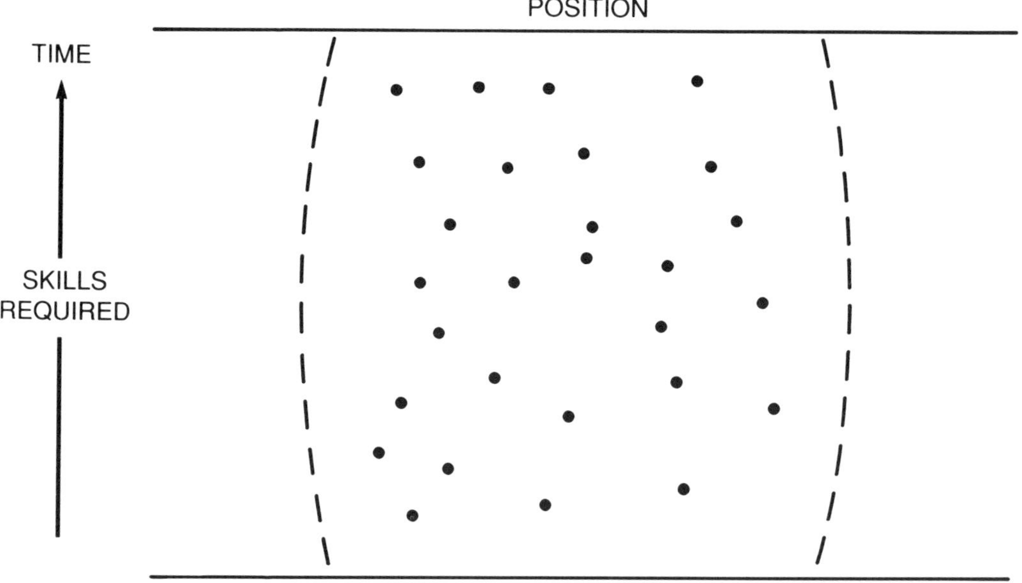

Figure 4.1. A hypothetical skill field.

position for specific skills, abilities, and knowledge required for someone qualified to hold this capstone.

Keep in mind that the target-skill profile that you are constructing is not the same as the job description for this capstone. A job description concentrates more on the requirements of the job itself—tasks and duties—rather than the knowledge, skills, and abilities that you will need to succeed in it. Concentrating on the job description rather than the capstone limits your career management development, because tasks still belong to the job even after you leave it. Because skills are learned, they belong to you once you master them. The skills that define your capstone provide you with a skill curriculum that will rival your academic curriculum in practical importance, because these skills will guide your path through the next 3 to 8 years.

Usually, the best way to find out which skills are required for your capstone position is to interview people who already hold this position. Every capstone can be approached by asking "What skills does someone need to successfully perform the tasks of this job?" During these interviews, go beyind asking which skills are required. Ask which skills are critical to success in this position. Developing these "critical to success skills" gets high priority. The end goal is to construct a target-skill profile that is a blueprint for reaching your capstone intact.

Exercise 4.4

1. Interview someone who already holds a similar position to your career capstone. Determine which required skills are necessary to be selected for

the job. Learn which skills are used on a day-to-day basis. List the skills that are most critical to success for someone holding this capstone.

2. Identify and list the skills you must acquire to perform your next capstone.

Building Your Target Mosaic

If you are using a capstone to set your strategy, you will need to develop a plan for moving toward the capstone. Some capstones require skills so complex that they require many years of postdoctorate training and experience. Others require only a few key jobs to teach you the skills that will make you a qualified contender.

To determine which skills you need, you must develop a *profile* for your capstone, plus a second list that details the skills you have acquired over the course of your graduate training and career. This will be a lengthy list. Some of these skills will relate directly to your capstone; many will not. How and where you got these skills and whether or not you were paid is irrelevant. For our purposes here, only the skills themselves count. This second list, a *career mosaic*, is simply a personal-skill history.

When you compare the capstone profile required by your capstone with your own career mosaic, first focus on the skills that appear on both lists. These skills are directly relevant to reaching your capstone. Although there may not be many of them, use these critical building-block skills to jumpstart your planning.

Because, by definition, you are not yet qualified to hold this capstone, a substantial number of skills on your capstone profile list will not appear on your career mosaic list. Study these skills carefully. They are the precise skills you must obtain through additional experience and training. Each of these targeted skills tailored to your own developmental-career needs must be acquired to form your target mosaic. Then you will be a qualified contender for your career capstone.

Look at Figure 4.2. Whether you are new to psychology or a 30-year veteran of the field, place yourself at "capstone start" at the bottom of the next diagram. This locates you in your current career position relative to the subsets of the skill field that make up your chosen capstone. Although the dots near the capstone-start position are the skill clusters required to succeed in your next jobs and projects, the skills closer to the capstone become more technical and specific to the capstone.

The circles represent experiences that encompass groups of skills you will need to acquire to qualify for your capstone position. Your strategy is to move from capstone start through a graduated series of projects, assignments, jobs, education, and training over a period of 3 to 8 years that enable you to build a qualified skill profile leading to your capstone. With each new career opportunity, you will need to ask, "How does this job, project, or seminar enhance my skill profile relative to my capstone?"

The particular career strategy suggests that your tenure in any job or program should last only so long as that setting contributes to enhancing the skills related to your capstone. Under this plan, with each new job or project undertaken, the list of skills included in your target-skill mosaic will get shorter. Eventually, you will have the right skill profile for your capstone.

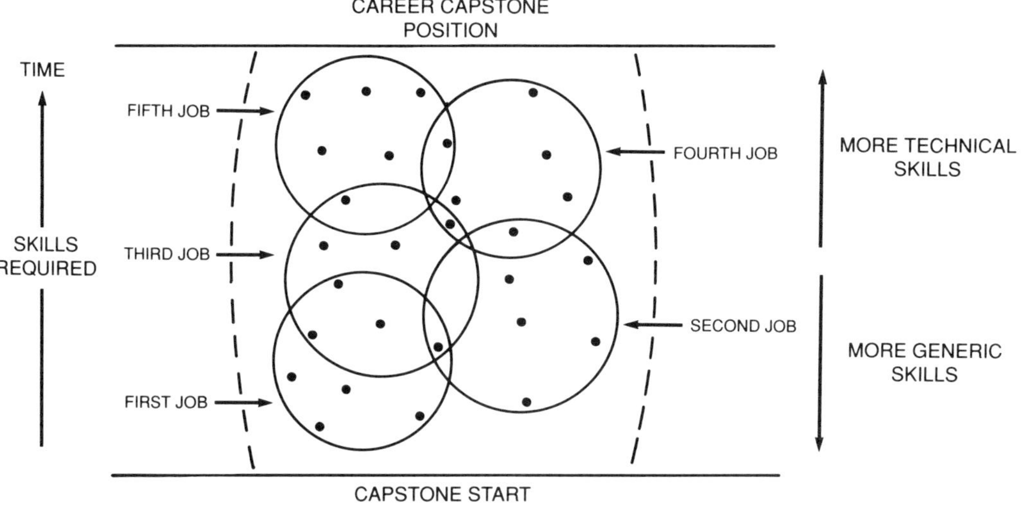

Figure 4.2. A strategy for reaching your capstone.

Because your postdegree skills are enhanced by the content of the work itself, where you work and your actual job title are not as important as the functional skill repertoire you are building. The university, the agency, the hospital, and the company no longer have to take care of you. You are taking care of yourself by building your target mosaic. Although psychologists and other highly trained professionals gravitate toward autonomous career paths, the overall impact of this strategy is to substantially boost your potential to act as a successful free agent.

Another effective career-management strategy is to master generic, all-purpose skills, such as oral and written communication skills and political skills, before tackling more technical, specific skills related to your capstone. A strategy of developing these generic skills first ensures against technical obsolescence and allows you flexibility should you change capstones midstrategy.

The list of skills in Figure 4.3 outlines a few generic and technical skills that will be useful in performing various career capstones in psychology. Use these lists to think about and design target mosaic lists related to your capstone. They are separated into generic work skills, generic skills related to psychology as a profession, and specific technical skills related to specialty areas in psychology. The generic skills are building blocks for career success along many professional career tracks. You can also use the list to rate whether you like (L) or dislike (DL) a specific skill or consider yourself to be good at (G) or not good at (NG) the skill in question.

To become more proficient at the process of identifying and reaching your targeted capstones, consider adding these metaskills to your career-skill mosaic:

- Change-management skills: the art of managing graceful endings, new beginnings, and high uncertainties.
- Capstone-analysis skills: the ability to ascertain which skills constitute a capstone and to plan for acquiring them.
- Job-search skills: the coordinated-skill amalgam of self-presentation, mar-

Figure 4.3. Skills related to career capstones in psychology.

GENERIC WORK SKILLS

Communication Skills

L	DL	G	NG		
______	______	______	______	a	Oral communication skills
______	______	______	______	b	Written communication skills
______	______	______	______	c	Group communication skills
______	______	______	______	d	One-on-one communication skills
______	______	______	______	e	Stand-up presentation skills
______	______	______	______	f	Networking up the organizational chart
______	______	______	______	g	Networking down the organizational chart
______	______	______	______	h	Giving and getting feedback
______	______	______	______	i	Conducting meetings
______	______	______	______	j	Record keeping

Management Skills

L	DL	G	NG		
______	______	______	______	a	Time management
______	______	______	______	b	Setting priorities and goals
______	______	______	______	c	Planning activities
______	______	______	______	d	Supervising activities of subordinates
______	______	______	______	e	Delegating tasks
______	______	______	______	f	Reporting to supervisors
______	______	______	______	g	Demonstrating accountability
______	______	______	______	h	Identifying key problems
______	______	______	______	i	Gathering data
______	______	______	______	j	Problem solving
______	______	______	______	k	Coordinating actions
______	______	______	______	l	Developing personnel
______	______	______	______	m	Organizing meetings

Interpersonal Skills

L	DL	G	NG		
______	______	______	______	a	Providing leadership
______	______	______	______	b	Persuading others within group
______	______	______	______	c	Persuading external community
______	______	______	______	d	Functioning as effective team player
______	______	______	______	e	Negotiating conflicts
______	______	______	______	f	Utilizing negative feedback
______	______	______	______	g	Coping with problem employees
______	______	______	______	h	Dealing with personnel problems
______	______	______	______	i	Showing professional judgment

Political Skills

L	DL	G	NG		
______	______	______	______	a	Positioning accomplishments
______	______	______	______	b	Identifying organizational norms
______	______	______	______	c	Utilizing the informal communication network
______	______	______	______	d	Aligning personal and organizational needs
______	______	______	______	e	Maneuvering through troubled political waters
______	______	______	______	f	Identifying what organization rewards
______	______	______	______	g	Coping with difficult coworkers

Figure 4.3 *cont.*

GENERIC PSYCHOLOGICAL SKILLS

Professional Skills

L	DL	G	NG	
				a Ability to survive graduate academic training
				b Identifying speciality area in psychology
				c Demonstrating required level of professional expertise
				d Exhibiting professional codes of ethical conduct
				e Monitoring professional codes of ethical conduct
				f Acquiring appropriate credentialing or licensure
				g Maintaining expertise/acquiring new knowledge
				h Networking with other professionals

SPECIFIC PSYCHOLOGICAL SKILLS

Research Skills

L	DL	G	NG	
				a Problem identification
				b Hypothesis generation
				c Library research
				d Research design
				e Data management
				f Statistical analysis
				g Data interpretation
				h Computer skills
				i Journal writing
				j Presentation skills

Teaching Skills

L	DL	G	NG	
				a Organizing coursework
				b Reviewing data and theory
				c Lesson planning
				d Classroom skills
				e Leadership
				f Time management
				g Test design
				h Evaluation
				i Reporting
				j Group dynamic skills
				k Peer relations

School Psychology

L	DL	G	NG	
				a Psychological assessment
				b Test interpretation
				c Diagnostic skills
				d Dealing with school culture
				e Child evaluation skills

Figure 4.3 *cont.*

Private Practice Skills

L	DL	G	NG	
______	______	______	______	a Diagnostic skills
______	______	______	______	b Psychological assessment
______	______	______	______	c Therapeutic skills
______	______	______	______	d Listening skills
______	______	______	______	e Crisis intervention
______	______	______	______	f Office management
______	______	______	______	g Treatment record writing
______	______	______	______	h Insurance record keeping
______	______	______	______	i Reporting skills
______	______	______	______	j Small group skills
______	______	______	______	k Workshop leadership skills
______	______	______	______	l Upholding confidentiality
______	______	______	______	m Billing skills
______	______	______	______	n Collection skills
______	______	______	______	o Follow-up skills
______	______	______	______	p Expert witness

Industrial–Organizational Skills

L	DL	G	NG	
______	______	______	______	a Applied evaluative skills
______	______	______	______	b Research design
______	______	______	______	c Systems analysis
______	______	______	______	d Quantitative analysis
______	______	______	______	e Consulting skills
______	______	______	______	f Problem identification
______	______	______	______	g Problem solving
______	______	______	______	h Proposal writing
______	______	______	______	i Report writing
______	______	______	______	j Financial management
______	______	______	______	k Interview skills
______	______	______	______	l Test construction
______	______	______	______	m Public relations

Developmental Skills (QUADRANT ONE SKILLS)

L	DL	G	NG	
______	______	______	______	a Marketing skills
______	______	______	______	b Public relations skills
______	______	______	______	c Consulting skills
______	______	______	______	d Training skills
______	______	______	______	e Expert witness skills
______	______	______	______	f Divorce mediation
______	______	______	______	g Insurance skills
______	______	______	______	h Forensic psychological skills
______	______	______	______	i Entrepreneurial skills

keting, communicating, interviewing, and networking (see chapters 4, 5, and 6).

- Tactical-career, decision-making skills: the sense of knowing which jobs and projects to take, which to leave, and when to do either of these.

This model of career management is completely antithetical to a one-life, one-career modus operandi. Your professional skills, as they currently exist, are hardly "skills for life." The only skills for life are the metaskills for changing jobs systematically, taking on new projects and professional training, and promoting your own learning and development.

The continuing reevaluation of your past skill development as a baseline for future change offers multiple opportunities for realigning identity, values, and interests in the career arena. This is consistent with models of adult development that posit ongoing developmental change and the continuing drive to integrate internal polarities. But this opportunity for growth and development also carries concomitant career risk and uncertainty.

Exercise 4.5

1. Generate your own target mosaic list. Then divide these skills into two lists—a generic, all-purpose-skill list, and a technical-skill list.
2. Identify jobs, projects, seminars, and training sessions that develop skills you need to reach your capstone.

Making Effective Tactical Career Decisions

The career-management model that we have been discussing advocates taking control of your own career, first, by selecting a capstone, and then, by defining the career profile for your current career capstone. The next step is to identify the corresponding target mosaic profile that prescribes a course of varied experiences through a calculated series of jobs, projects, and training sessions. Creating the right situations for obtaining the skills that qualify you for your career capstone may require frequent change, and correspondingly, frequent career decisions. The ongoing challenge is in knowing when it is best to take a job and when it is best to leave it. It is important to have a standard for knowing which jobs to accept and which to reject.

This process requires clear-cut career tactics, which is precisely what most of us lack. By the time most people actually make up their minds to leave an unsatisfying position, strategies and tactics are moot. All they want is to get out quickly—to escape while still semi-intact. Because decision making under siege is often reactive, the results detract from long-term, career-management efforts. Poor tactical decisions undermine even the best capstone-based career strategy. This section describes a tactical career decision-making device, the Doom Loop, which is central to the career-management system conceptualized by Jett (1985) and developed by Hollander (1991). The Doom Loop specifies a career decision-making standard based on a combination of factors, including your own preferences and competencies relative to the skill profile of the job in question, your own personal-skill profile, and the specific target-skill mosaic related to your next career capstone.

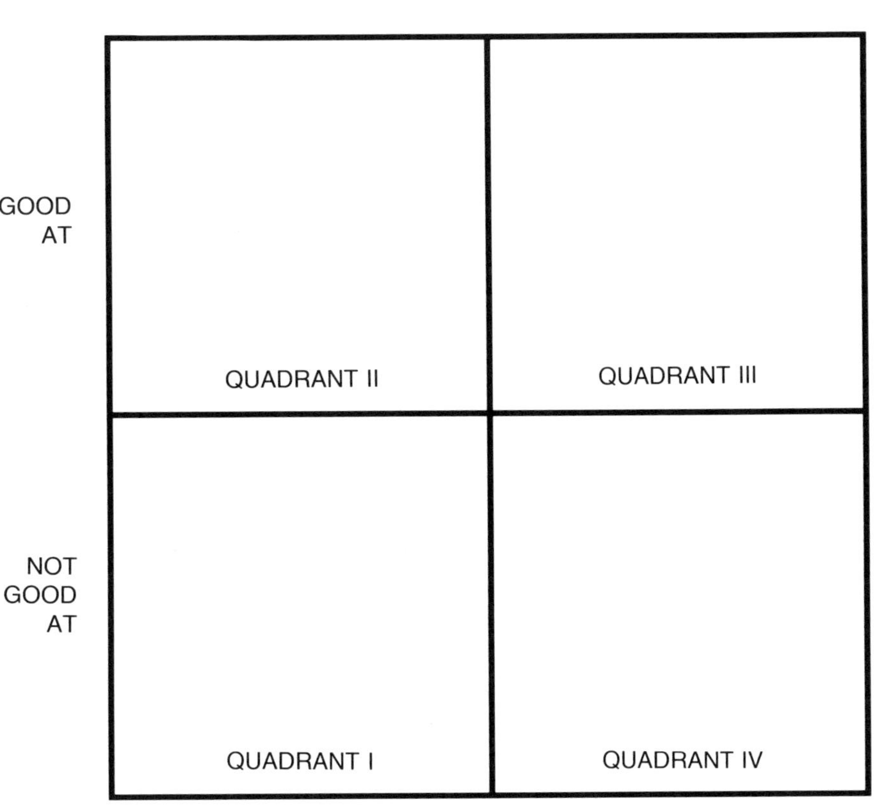

Figure 4.4. Performance/preference matrix.

Skill Mapping: Plotting Preference and Performance

When you think about taking any new job, you are likely to ask a number of questions. Many questions will relate to salary, hours, location, and potential for advancement. But, eventually, you will ask yourself some variation of these two basic questions: (a) Will I be any good at performing this job? (b) Do I really like this job? The first question is a performance question, dealing with competence and expertise. Although your perception of your own competence is subjective, your competence also can be externally verified by performance appraisals, supervisor's reports, and other types of evaluations. You can then rate your performance on a continuum from "not at all good" to "very good" at various work-related skills or tasks.

The second question is a preference question that taps into your attitudes and feelings about your work, the fit between your values and interests and the skills required, and whether this job meets your needs for growth and challenge. You can rate any skills required by a job on a continuum of "not liking" the skills at all to "liking highly" the skills involved. Your response, by definition, is subjective and reflects whatever career and adult-development issues you are facing. But this is okay, because no one can be a better judge of your own preference than you can.

PREFERENCE		PERFORMANCE		SKILL SUBSET
Like	Don't Like	Good at	Not Good at	Private Practice
____	____	____	____	Diagnostic skills
____	____	____	____	Psychological assessment
____	____	____	____	Therapeutic skills
____	____	____	____	Listening skills
____	____	____	____	Crisis intervention
____	____	____	____	Office management
____	____	____	____	Treatment record writing
____	____	____	____	Insurance record keeping
____	____	____	____	Reporting skills
____	____	____	____	Small group skills
____	____	____	____	Leadership skills
____	____	____	____	Reporting skills
____	____	____	____	Collection skills
____	____	____	____	Expert witness

Figure 4.5. Rating skill subsets on performance and preference.

These two factors of performance and preference are critical to developing a simple, but effective tactical approach for deciding whether to leave a job or whether to take a job. First, you will need to construct a simple two-by-two performance/preference matrix with four quadrants as shown in Figure 4.4.

Any job you currently hold or are considering taking, like a capstone, can be viewed as a conglomerate of skill subsets. Once you have determined and listed the skills you will need to perform and to succeed in the job in question, you can then measure these skills according to your actual or anticipated performance (*whether or not you are good at them*) and your actual or anticipated preference (*whether or not you like them*). Figure 4.5 (rating skill subsets on performance and preference) illustrates how to list skill subsets and then rate them for preference and performance.

Once you have rated the skills required by the job that you are considering taking or leaving, you can plot them in the appropriate quadrants of the performance/preference matrix. This is called *skill mapping*. The resulting scatter plot or skill map shows you graphically where the skills for any job will cluster. Because the location of skills in the quadrant is based on your own personal preference-and-performance profile, it is likely that the skills will cluster predominantly in one or more key quadrants as shown in Figure 4.6, rather than scattering randomly. Knowing the quadrant (or quadrants) where the greatest proportion of skills fall, and analyzing carefully which skill subsets are located in which quadrants provide important raw information for using the Doom Loop as a tactical tool for making career decisions.

Exercise 4.6

1. Using Figure 4.6 as a model, list the skills that your current or next job requires and then rate these skills according to whether you like or dislike them (preference) and whether or not you are good at them (performance).

2. Plot these skills as points on the performance/preference matrix.
3. In which quadrant (or quadrants) do the skills tend to cluster? Where does the subset of skills on your target-skill mosaic cluster?

Understanding the Quadrants

The matrix shows four possible skill-based ways for evaluating jobs. In Quadrant I, you will find skills that you generally like, but are not good at. Quadrant II contains skills that you both enjoy and feel competent to perform. Quadrant III skills are ones where you show expertise without enjoyment. And Quadrant IV skills are those you neither like nor perform well. Because your ratings are specific to you, the way these job skills are distributed in each of the four quadrants tells a story that is unique to how you already feel or soon will feel about a position. It is an important story, because your rating of the analyzed job taps into how this position will contribute to your work satisfaction and self-esteem.

For example, consider how a person holding a job that is predominately com-

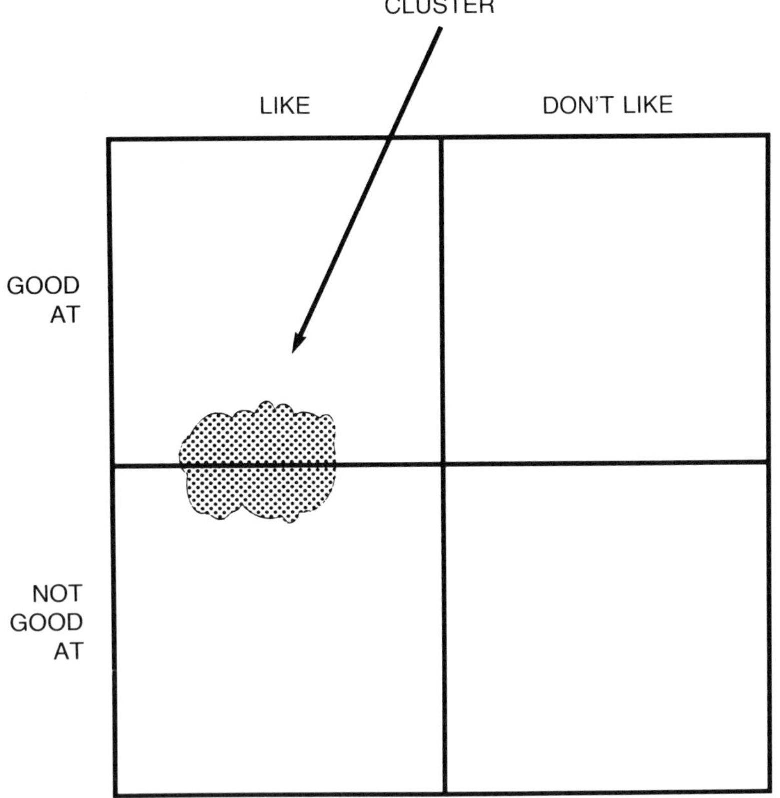

Figure 4.6. A scatter plot.

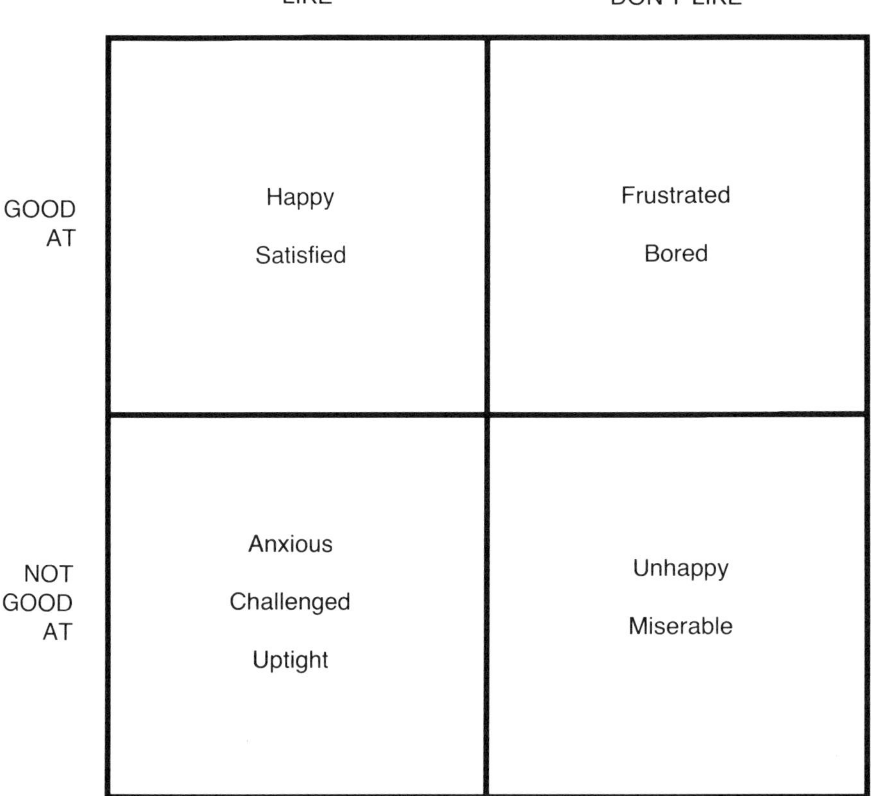

Figure 4.7. Job satisfaction matrix.

posed of skills in any one quadrant might feel. As shown in Figure 4.7, based on interviews and workshop feedback, most people would rather take jobs with skills clustered in Quadrants I and II, where they feel hopeful or good about themselves, than in Quadrants III and IV, where they are more likely to feel trapped, lethargic, and depressed. In fact, most people, when asked, say that their ideal job clusters skills in Quadrant II, where they expect to feel happy and satisfied.

But that might be a mistake. The matrix, as we have discussed it so far, is like a time-frozen snapshot. It shows how you subjectively rate and plot the skills of any particular job at the present moment. Although this provides an interesting framework for organizing information about any job you are considering, it fails to account for the passage of time and the unique mix of experience and learning that spurs development.

Let's trace what might happen if we make the matrix more dynamic by adding dimensions of time and learning. Imagine yourself holding the same professional position over a period of years. Let's suppose that when you took this position, it required skills that fell mostly in Quadrant I (like/not good at) of the matrix. Typically, people enter Quadrant I jobs with some performance anxiety, because they have no proven track record. But, so long as you have the ability and motivation to learn, a reasonably sound base of knowledge as a psychologist, and a job in which the tasks remain relatively stable, we can predict that over time, your competence at the required Quadrant I skills will increase.

When this happens, your concentration of skills progresses up the matrix from Quadrant I to Quadrant II. You move up the slope of a learning curve to Quadrant II, where you now hold a job that you both like and feel good at. Even though you didn't enter this job in Quadrant II, you have managed to land there anyway.

Most people would like this duo of high job satisfaction and high competence, characteristic of the Quadrant II job, to endure. They would like to stay in Quadrant II from career start to career finish. However, the reality is that time and learning will continue to interact to produce additional changes in your performance and your feelings about your work. If the job undergoes no major structural change or enrichment, the daily grind may begin to wear you down. Despite professional expertise as a psychologist and competence in the skills required by your job, you may find that you no longer love your work. You may feel more stagnant than challenged. As this happens, your personal rating of the skills required by the job changes, insidiously moving to the upper right part of the matrix, to Quadrant III. You may need more perks and external rewards to keep yourself interested. When this happens, you have peaked and slid over the top of your own personal learning curve, relative to the skills necessary for this job. You have gone over the top of the Doom Loop. As you can see in Figure 4.8, the Doom Loop is simply an individual's learning curve over time, set against the backdrop of the performance/preference matrix.

Staying in a quadrant-three position for any length of time without a viable alternative plan is a high-risk career-management strategy. But many professionals

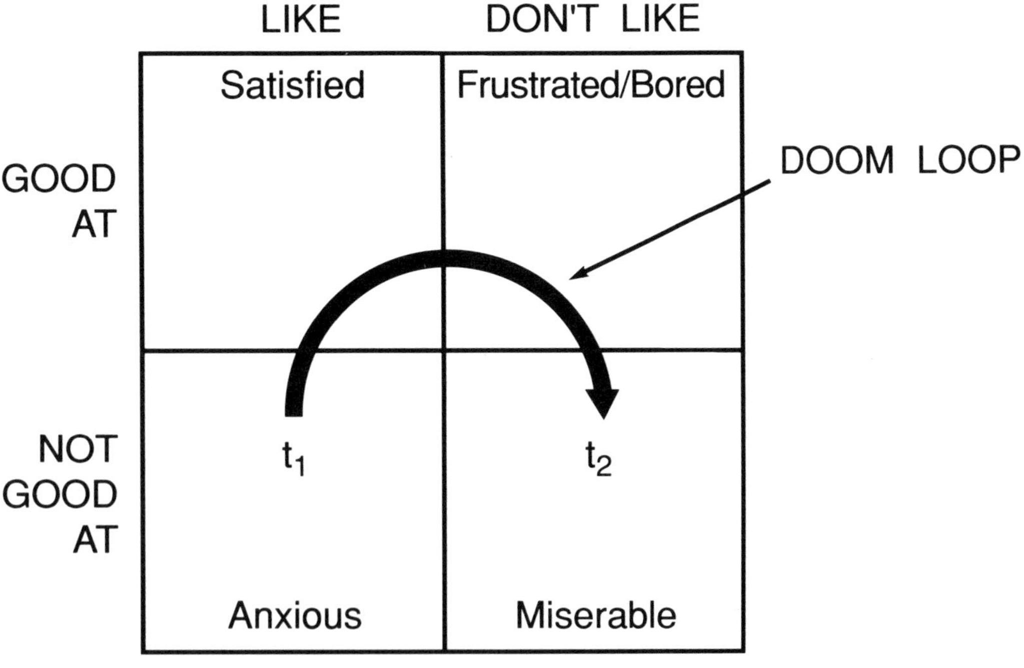

Figure 4.8. The Doom Loop.

do it anyway. Often, they don't even recognize what has happened to them. People who have conceptualized their career choice as a one-time life sentence are particularly subject to permanent entrapment in Quadrant III. You may face a personal crisis of generativity versus stagnation (Erikson, 1963). For a person caught in a Quadrant III or Quadrant IV career slot, it is a major struggle to maintain an ongoing sense of making a meaningful and productive contribution to society and future generations—at least through one's paid work. It is easy to slide into a laissez-faire stance of boredom and futility, leading to stagnation and loss of hope.

But the story doesn't end here. Without sustaining interest in your work, it is easy to lose interest in staying up to date on those apsects of psychology that relate to your job. Unless you remain rigorously vigilant, your general performance is likely to drop. Missed deadlines and sloppy work become the transitional norm as people slide from Quadrant III to IV. When you are no longer good at a job you don't like, you have landed in Quadrant IV, at the bottom right corner of the matrix. Insofar as your identity is linked to your career achievement, any length of time in this quadrant can erode your sense of self-worth, plunging you into doubt concerning the career or life structure that you have built. In Erik Erikson's (1963) terms, you may encounter a premature crisis of integrity versus despair. You may feel despair over the way you have chosen to live and work, rather than a sense of having made choices that you can stand behind with acceptance. When this is the case, if a significant part of your self-identity depends on career success, the result may be a bitter self-disempowerment and an inability to come to terms with the past or change the future.

Questions to address.

1. Which quadrant of the performance/preference matrix best describes your current or last job? In which quadrant did you begin? In which did you end?
2. Think of a job or project in which you moved through two or more quadrants of the matrix. How did your feelings and attitudes about your performance and the job itself change?
3. If you have ever gone over the top of a Doom Loop, to what did you attribute the changes? What impact, if any, did this experience have on your view of yourself?

The Doom Loop and Career Satisfaction

The Doom Loop predicts that unless there is some job redesign, change, or intervention, a person will progress sequentially through the quadrants over time. By taking a job with stable work demands, while demonstrating a basic ability to learn and seek challenge, you can expect to move up a learning curve, eventually peak, and then move down its slope into Quadrants III and IV.

Based on my interviews with more than 300 people, it appears that a person's location in any particular Doom Loop quadrant tells a story about how that person is likely to feel currently about his or her job. Of course, individual factors like personality and values also influence how a person feels in each quadrant. A highly security-minded professional is likely to feel more at ease in Quadrant III if the pay and fringe benefits are solid, whereas an achievement-driven professional may begin to feel trapped soon after entering Quadrant II. Risk-takers may be comfortable contemplating the same Quadrant I jobs that create performance anxieties among perfectionists.

Job satisfaction is often defined as the outcome of the interaction of competence and motivation. This interaction corresponds roughly to the interaction of performance/preference matrix variables in Quadrants I and II. Among my clients who have sought career coaching, those holding Quadrant-II jobs generally report high job satisfaction. Their career problems usually deal with external changes in their work field, such as a new supervisor or an organizational restructuring.

All of this has powerful implications for career management. If you have been attending solely to competence and have failed to adequately identify and track your preferences, you may be prone to five common, but costly, career-management mistakes. For example, you may do one or more of the following:

- seek and take low-risk, competence-intensive, Quadrant III jobs
- stay too long in a Quadrant-II job, and go over the top of "the Loop"
- avoid Quadrant-I jobs, because being seen as an expert is what counts
- take short-range satisfaction, Quadrant II and "top of the Loop" jobs
- take Quadrant-IV jobs, because they are available or a challenge

When things begin to go wrong in that once perfect job, people often wind up blaming themselves. This is unfortunate, because they simply may have drifted into Quadrant III by failing to understand this dynamic and by having no alternative career tactics.

Exercise 4.7

At one time or another most people have held a Quadrant-III job. Think about a time when you held a Quadrant-III job.

1. How did you feel when you were at work? Why did you stay as long as you did? How important a factor was job security in keeping you there? How uncomfortable were you with job risk? What caused you to leave?
2. Look at the five career-management mistakes listed in this section and consider which you have already made. Which do you feel most likely to make again?

Riding the Upside of the Learning Curve to your Capstone

Tactical career management helps. Any time you are faced with a job opportunity or need to evaluate your current work situation, you can use the concept of the Doom Loop and your rating of job skills on the performance/preference matrix as two of your tactical decision-making devices. The tactical rule implied by this model is simple: Take only those jobs that fit your capstone's target mosaic and that have a high concentration of Quadrant-I and Quadrant-II skills. This rule is graphically illustrated in Figure 4.9. Remember that your capstone sets your strategy, and tactics and strategy must work synergistically. If you have selected a capstone, this tactical model fits your career strategy, because you are already evaluating job offers on whether or not they provide the new skills you need to qualify for your capstone.

The key is to search for Quadrant-I jobs, projects, and tasks that allow you to develop professional skills that you like, but in which you lack expertise, while avoiding positions primarily composed of less preferred skills, on the backslope of the Doom Loop in Quadrants III and IV. Quadrant-I jobs maximize your motivation to learn, because they match your preferences, needs, and values.

For the professional who is used to assuming an expert role that may land near the top of the loop or in Quadrant III, this tactic implies intentional trade-offs between assuming a well-earned senior slot and the need to be challenged by learning in new areas. This means weighing each new career opportunity in terms of the relative costs and benefits of retaining an expert role in a job involving little new learning versus the costs and benefits of assuming a novice role in a job fostering challenge.

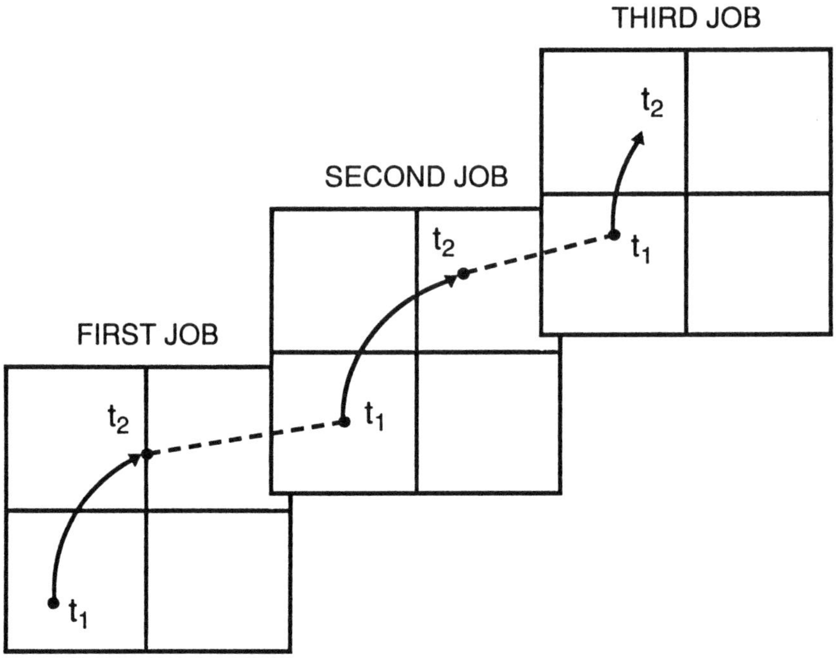

Figure 4.9. Staying on the up side of the Doom Loop.

Sometimes, this dilemma can be resolved by combining both elements. Analyze positions in terms of potential for job enrichment consistent with your targeted-skill development. Consider specific projects, grants, or sabbaticals involving new skill development related to more distant capstones as ways to enhance your skill profile. Ask whether your job can be redesigned to include new areas of responsibility. Or more informally, assume a mentor role for less senior colleagues. If none of these alternatives seem viable, and you still want the position, the solution may be to target personal-development capstones and find Quadrant-I activities outside the job that move you toward these personal capstones. For example, if you are at a point in your life when your priorities have shifted, or you are attempting to integrate your own psychological polarities and analyze your needs, you may decide to look for activities outside of your job. If affiliation needs are stronger now, this may be an optimal time to become more active in state or local psychological associations or other professional groups. Or you may opt to develop and use your networking skills in your own work organization. Having identified the problem, you will find many possibilities for riding the upside of a learning curve toward professional and personal capstones at every stage of career and adult development.

Questions to address.

1. What are the specific skills that you will acquire in the next two jobs or projects that are most relevant to your career capstone?
2. How can you enrich or redesign your current job to provide you with quadrant-one skills that fit your target mosaic for your capstone?

After Capstone?

What happens after you have successfully reached your capstone? Because your capstone sets your strategy, no matter how happy and satisfied you feel in your ultimate career position, you have to resist the temptation to let plans slide. The key is to formulate new growth-oriented postcapstone capstones that foster your development and guide your career path through the years ahead. If working toward a new capstone is not feasible, you will need some alternative career-management strategy, such as restructuring your full professorship to include a specific series of Quadrant-I objectives or enlarging your sphere of operation as director of clinical intake to meet some newly evolving preferences. In any case, it is wise to be researching and selecting your next capstone (or capstones) and developing a plan for achieving new Quadrant-I challenges well before you reach your current capstone. For most people, there are many opportunities for reaching postcapstone capstones—even after retirement.

But sometimes people find themselves in an unanticipated postcapstone crisis. They feel "doomed at capstone." This happens for many reasons—developmental, environmental, and interactive. By the time you reach the capstone of your choice, your priorities, values, preferences, and enthusiasms are likely to have shifted. Perhaps you have experienced career burn-out under the pressure of your own drive for success and workplace demands. Perhaps your specialty area has undergone major change, or your organization has restructured, truncating or even eliminating your capstone. Or you may find that you overlooked factors needed to make the right capstone choice "way back when."

In any case, you may find yourself unhappily at work in your capstone—without enthusiasm and feeling depressed, disappointed and trapped. Often, when you find yourself doomed at capstone, you are also in Quadrant III or IV of the performance/preference matrix. This is illustrated in the following example.

> After getting her degree in school psychology and working in the public school system of a Chicago suburb for 6 years, Sandy Goldfarb was tired of living with bureaucracy. She wanted autonomy. She decided to start her own educational consulting firm working with institutions and families on problems of special students, including the gifted. Having identified her capstone, Sandy developed a target mosaic for heading a consulting practice, and over a period of 5 years, she took three different administrative positions in the school district to acquire management skills. She developed networking skills with school administrators through national and local organizations and attended and gave nearly 100 workshops to develop the remaining targeted skills. She founded her own consulting firm. Now, 4 years later, the firm was thriving, whereas Sandy was not.
>
> She hated dealing with the firm's accountant, lawyer, and public relations firm. Her travel schedule kept her on the road 2 weeks a month, and she had developed an aversion to airports and airplane food. She was supporting eight employees and a healthy payroll. She was undercapitalized, and cash-flow problems fueled her anxiety. Exactly where she wanted to be, Sandy felt more exhausted than successful. She didn't like what she was doing. To her horror, she prepared a seminar in Pittsburgh on the wrong topic and was nearly an hour into it before a participant called the error to her attention. Sandy was doomed at capstone in Quadrant IV (don't like/not good at) of the matrix. When asked what she wanted to do next, her single-word response was "retire."

Sandy had chosen a capstone that had met her needs for autonomy and independence. In the early stages, the creative, marketing, management, and organizational skills required to establish a consulting firm matched Sandy's preference profile and kept her in Quadrants I and II of the matrix. Eventually, time and learning interacted to push many of these administrative skills into Quadrant III. As the business developed, she felt obligated to take on more, without letting go of earlier responsibilities. Many of these tasks required Sandy to use Quadrant IV skills (e.g., accounting and finance, seminar travel, and interfacing with hired consultants in other fields). Because there were so many perks, Sandy's disenchantment with her job was gradual and insidious. She didn't anticipate it.

Yet, she could have. Being doomed at capstone is a highly predictable career crisis. Because it seems counterproductive to anticipate an unhappy ending to your career dreams, it is easy to ignore this crisis until faced with it. By anticipating that it will happen, you have time to conceive and implement one or more alternative plans. Had Sandy been networking with people and gaining skills related to a new capstone, she could have cut her losses earlier, selling her firm and moving on. Postcapstone reselection is another career-management metaskill that you need to master during the course of your career.

But what if you experience disappointment and distress after reaching your capstone position and see no acceptable alternative strategy? First, confront and accept your feelings. Then, organize a program for reclaiming your energy through stress reduction, counseling, putting small pleasures back into your life, and so forth. Develop new competencies that are altogether unrelated to your capstone. Consider how you can salvage your capstone by restoring Quadrant-I and Quadrant-II skills, while trimming and delegating Quadrant-III and Quadrant-IV skills. Reassess your preferences and values to see which critical shifts have occurred. Perhaps, as Jung suggested (1974), this is the right time to develop your less salient functions. If your identity is no longer centered in this particular career or in work in general, you will be facing tough decisions related to cutting your losses and developing new professional and personal capstones. Getting professional career consultation is a valuable shortcut to resolving the crisis when you are "doomed at capstone."

Sandy did get professional counseling and didn't retire. She sold her consulting practice and took a nonadministrative job as a consultant for a prestigious, multicity consulting firm. Her new capstone of becoming a senior research consultant in the development of programs for gifted students minimized her Quadrant-III administrative skills. By returning to Quadrant I, she regained her enthusiasm for work. She also repositioned her capstone within a personal framework of achieving greater balance in her personal, professional, and family life.

No one has to settle for being doomed at capstone.

Questions to address.

1. Do you have one or more postcapstone capstones? If not, what might they be?
2. Have you ever experienced the career crisis of being doomed at capstone? How did you feel? What actions were helpful?

The Role of Organizational Politics in Career Management

To reach your career capstone and assure continued career success, you will have to do what no one told you about in graduate school. In addition to being professionally competent, you will have to survive diverse organizational cultures, decipher conflicting hidden agendas and mixed messages, and confront unanticipated external forces in your work environment. Politics, like mountains, command your attention just because they are there, and there are few ways to get around them easily. Politics, in fact, are part of the complex ecological system in need of management that Kilburg discussed in chapters 2 and 3. Even the best laid strategy and tactics can derail when they crash into organizational politics. Whether or not you like politics is irrelevant. As an intentional career manager, you dare not omit mastery of organizational politics from your skill portfolio. Consider these two situations:

- Helene Harris has been teaching, conducting research in, and consulting in human factors for 8 years. She loves her work and has won awards for innovative design. Now, having just lost a messy tenure battle, which seemed to be centered around personality issues, she is suing the university. How, she wonders, could her colleagues have done this to her?

- Andy Cassidy served as a planned-change agent, heading a team effort to move his community mental health agency toward interdisciplinary management. Six months after achieving a successful outcome, the agency director says they are restructuring again. But this time, Andy's job has been eliminated. Andy feels betrayed.

Both of these psychologists shared a common error—they sincerely believed that the high caliber of their work was sufficient for success. They thought they had their eye on the ball—professional competence. But they also needed to track a less obvious ball—organizational politics. Being bright and competent didn't keep them from being blindsided.

As a professional, you have invested too much in your career identity to risk naively political derailment. The price is too high. It is no wonder that politics makes many psychologists anxious. No career-management plan should trivialize the role that politics plays in achieving desired career outcomes.

Developing Political Skills

Your career as a psychologist will be more predictable if you meet these three baseline conditions:

1. Attain a reasonable level of competence as a psychologist.
2. Design an intentional career-management strategy, setting capstones and developing a tactical plan.
3. Become aware of and master organizational politics.

For psychologists, competence is rarely a primary career problem, although where mediocrity is the work norm, too much drive occasionally creates unexpected career fallout. A more typical barrier to success is lack of career-management strategies and tactics. But when careers run amuck, despite competence and planning, institutional politics is often the culprit.

Earlier in this chapter, I identified politics as a primary generic skill cluster that psychologists must master. Recognizing and weathering struggles for control of limited institutional resources is at the heart of much political infighting. And when your personal needs don't match organizational needs, your accomplishments may be invisible to key power brokers. These conditions can shorten your job longevity.

Viewing political game playing as dirty, trivial, and beneath one's dignity is a sure formula for being tripped up by them. The political context of jobs is a variable that is critical to your career success.

If we pragmatically reframe politics as competing sets of needs and interests that underlie the positions of individuals and groups in the organization (Culbert & McDonough, 1980), it is easy to surmise that power and politics are basic to any interactive system. Kotter's power/dependence analysis, discussed in chapter 3, offers valuable cues for identifying and reducing your workplace dependencies, while increasing your power. The challenge is to be politically vigilant before a crisis demands it.

A visual mnemonic for remembering how performance and political issues interact is the familiar gestalt chalice/faces illustration (see Figure 4.10). The chalice represents the figure, and the faces represents the ground. The figure is easier to spot at first than the ground. Imagine that the figure (the chalice) represents your job performance, while the ground (the faces) represents organizational politics, norms, and hidden sets of competing needs in your work environment.

If you concentrate only on your performance (the figure), you will attend exclusively to the performance/hard work cluster and the strategy of task-oriented achievement. Unfortunately, whether or not you notice, the context (ground), (e.g., organizational needs and goals and coworkers' self-interest) is still influencing, if not igniting, outcomes.

A survivor's rule of thumb: Treat performance and political issues like the figure and ground in the gestalt drawing. Shift your focus back and forth until job performance and contextual organizational factors oscillate. Both interact to determine your career schema.

Professional Socialization as a Barrier to Political Savvy

The professional role itself may be a serious liability in developing political savoir-faire. The professional role expectations that graduate school education fosters may be at odds with postgraduate school institutional values in nonacademic settings. Autonomous achievement, individualism, and independent problem solving often conflict with work norms like networking, placing a premium on team and committee work, and other affiliative values. In our earlier example, Helene Harris didn't pay enough attention to networking. The thorough scholarship that is rewarded in doctoral studies may be seen by time-pressured administrators as stalling

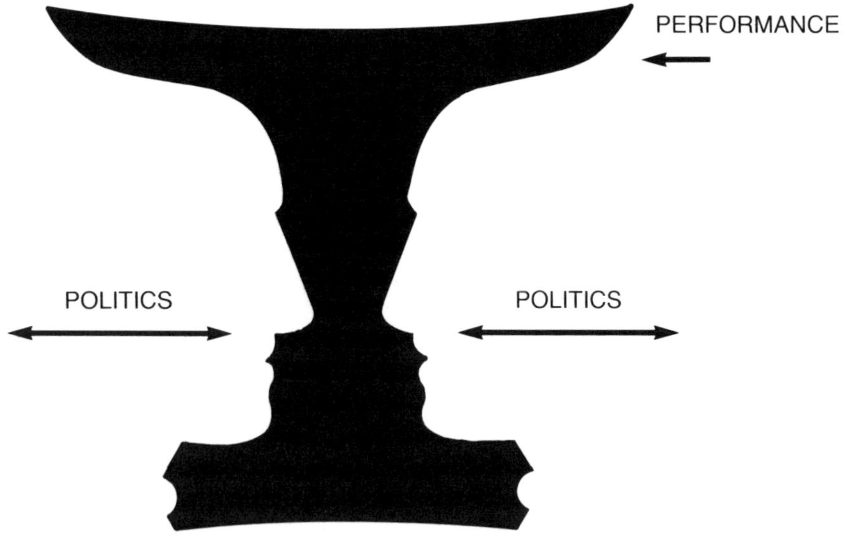

Figure 4.10. Gestalt figure/ground drawing.

or obfuscating and will win kicks, not kudos. Program directors may perceive your erudite qualifying statements as elitist waffling. Your bias toward scientific objectivity may blind you to the subjective, irrational nature of much organizational decision making. Hanging onto the expert role, or demanding to be addressed as "Dr." may push you into an outsider's marginal role—particularly in nonprofessional institutions. In some organizations, your identification and commitment to professional reference groups, like the American Psychological Association, may even cause key people to question your loyalty.

If your specific training in psychology has inculcated humanistic values like openness, trust, and authenticity, you may encounter another level of political aftershock. Information freely given may be freely used by creative adversaries to advance their own agendas at your expense. Remember the earlier example of Andy Cassidy, whose job was eliminated after he took on the role of organizational-change agent? Andy's colleagues used the information that he freely gave them to undermine his projects and eventually his job security.

Recognizing the liabilities and assets of your role as a psychologist is important in protecting yourself from unanticipated political problems. Nonpsychologists may exaggerate how different you are from them, particularly if there are only a few psychologists at your workplace. An "us against them" mentality undermines organizational support for your accomplishments. To counteract this, identify commonalities between yourself and your coworkers to better align your needs with theirs and with those of your organization.

A second issue that creates political misfiring for professionals is that of *performance-orientation* versus *norm-orientation*. Professionals are hatched and touted as high-performance experts. Both professional socialization and the work ethic coincidentally prescribe that hard work and accomplishment pay off. Professional success is more frequently defined by achievement than by external status trappings such as "dress for success." Proving competence is paramount, particularly for the new professional or the professional in a Quadrant-I job. But as most old-timers eventually learn, performance is only a small part of what it takes to be effective in organizational work life. Recognizing and fitting in with the norms is paramount. Most professionals could benefit from a crash course in norm-orientation before tackling the workplace.

No matter how excellent your performance is, there must be a perceived organizational need for your contributions, or they are likely to go unnoticed. Part of your unwritten job description is to create this perceived need for your contributions. To do this, you must first identify the informal norms that govern the organizational culture in which you are working. Then, you must fit your efforts to this system.

Norms are "the way things are done around here." *Normative roles*—how people are expected to look and act in a particular organization—are also important. Norms are to organizational politics what capstones are to career planning. They set the standard for success. It is easier to be recognized in organizations when your style, behavior, and performance output approximate the norms. Like it or not, organizational culture generally prefers clones to mavericks. Excellence pays off most in organizations that recognize excellence as a normative standard.

It is important to promote visibly your accomplishments to highly valued organizational reference groups. To achieve the recognition that your accomplishments deserve, identify and talk to key persons about your projects, aspirations, and how your goals mesh with the organization's and their own. Without the support of these gatekeepers and sponsors, your projects will languish. The more your style and contributions fit valued norms, the more receptive these key people will be to your achievements.

If the rift between your values and the organizational norms is too great, consider cutting your career losses and finding a closer fit with a new organization. The closer the fit, the more natural and less Machiavellian it will feel to master the politics.

The knack of deciphering and matching what the organization actually rewards is a third common political blindspot for many psychologists. This knowledge, together with your target mosaic, allows you to compare the general skills required in your current position with the much narrower subset of critical skills that the organization actually rewards. This second subset of matched skills is requisite to your success.

Discovering what an organization actually rewards requires skills already familiar to psychologists—unobtrusive observation, hypotheses generation and testing, and data collection and interpretation. The challenge is in applying these familiar skills to understanding organizational reward systems in the service of your own career. It is tempting to trust at face value what people say the organization rewards. Some professionals regard a job description, a performance evaluation, or a supervisor's directive as a career road map. Unfortunately, this map often lands you in the wrong part of town. Misreading reward cues can lead to wasted energy, ineffective positioning of achievements, and unnecessary failure. If you find a large discrepancy between the skills that your organization actually rewards and the skills that you need to develop for your capstone, you might want to look for an organizational context that better fits your strategy.

The last political pitfall we will discuss is the danger inherent in hidden assumptions of homogeneity. Most of us grew up in relatively homogeneous environments. As college students, we temporarily accommodated to a greater variety of ethnicity, socioeconomic class, and so on. But as we specialized in graduate school, the range of differences narrowed again to like-minded sorts of people with similar professional interests. Powerful professors stamping their imprimatur on the department and its graduates narrows this range even further. On the whole, graduate programs in psychology provide a rarefied, homogeneous cohort relative to the broader spectrum of people in postdegree jobs.

Unfortunately, subtle baseline assumptions of homogeneous interests and values operate long after the graduate school cloning experience is a distant memory trace. Assumptions of similar needs, values, and goals are often abetted by unwritten organizational norms governing professional conduct. If your coworkers adopt a standardized "dress for professional success" mode (whatever it may look like), speak a common jargon, and have similar ambitions, it is easy to believe that they also share similar values. You let your guard down and relax only to find yourself unexpectedly sabotaged or blocked by your coworkers. Underestimating individual and group variances in the workplace can have a high career cost.

The fall-out from assumptions of homogeneity is high also. If you don't agree with key peers and supervisors and don't fathom the extent of the differences, you could waste effort on dead-ended projects and work groups with interactions more reminiscent of parallel play than collegiality.

When you slam into unexpected opposition, the work environment suddenly feels hostile and nonsupportive. This leads to *rust-out*—career dysfunctionality due to corrosive forces in the workplace that eat away at self-esteem. Competent people experiencing rust-out wonder what is wrong with them.

A good rule of thumb for counteracting these assumptions of homogeneity in the workplace is to consider yourself a stranger in a strange land. From the first day that you step into a new work environment until the day that you leave, view yourself as a cultural exchange student whose foremost task is to learn the host country's customs. Refuse to be lulled into spurious assumptions of homogeneity, knowing that heterogeneity is a hidden land mine in your career-management terrain. Competing interests are a fact of life in organizations, so add conflict-management skills to your political survival gear.

Questions to address.

1. When you think of the word *politics*, are your associations positive or negative?
2. What words describe "the way things are done around here" in your organization? What actions or performances are not acceptable? How do these norms match your own needs and values?
3. What does your organization reward? Is this compatible with your own expectations? Is it compatible with what they say they reward and with the ethics of the profession? What behavior does your organization punish?
4. Which assumptions about your professional role are liabilities to your career management?

What Helps: Integrating Politics and Career Management

A sound career-management strategy must include consideration of the impact of organizational politics on your career outcomes. You must track your own needs and how they mesh with those of your coworkers and organization. To do otherwise is to put yourself in professional jeopardy. Starting with awareness of your own needs, you will also want answers to these two questions: (a) Which goals are professionally and personally most important to accomplish in this job? (b) What trade offs are you willing and not willing to make to achieve them? Developing organizational awareness is tricky. This requires that you move outside your own frame of reference to identify certain political trigger points hidden in your organization's culture. Remember that these trigger points are there whether you identify them or not! Knowing an organization's norms, role expectations, and actual rewards is always to your benefit, but because covert rules are by definition hidden, you need to plan to spend time sleuthing, observing, and talking to people. In organizational life, what you don't know can hurt you. Reading the norms is the first step. Because there is great power in being seen as "one of us," the second step is locating any confluence where these norms match your own style, goals, and ethics. These confluences tell you where to focus your political efforts and dictate your strategy for positioning your accomplishments. If there are no naturally occurring alignments, and the trade-offs for fitting this organizational culture are unacceptable, it is probably wise to move on. In these situations, hindsight dictates that the pain of leaving is often less if done sooner rather than later.

You will also need to tune into how information gets passed around, by whom, and how to access the informal information network so that you are privy to what is happening. This requires that you conduct a communications-network analysis, so you can identify the town criers, the bottlenecks, the power brokers and gatekeepers, the protectors of the crown, and which hidden agendas are being harbored by which colleagues. Should you find this process distasteful, try regarding it as the unobtrusive collection of observational data.

Summary

In summary, you are the principal actor in your own continuing career-management schema. No one is waiting in the wings to coach or rescue you. You will need to understand and appreciate your own complexities and needs for ongoing growth in order to express yourself optimally in multiple life contexts—work, family, and personal. You will need to know yourself and the world of careers to get and maintain the best fit. Because change is endemic to career and personal life, you will need to remain vigilant in tracking all kinds of internal and external changes affecting your mission, your preferences, and your motivation on the one hand, and changes in your work context, the field of psychology, and the larger culture on the other. A clear understanding of career and adult development will help you to make sense of your own career and personal transformations and crises, and periodically, to redirect and realign your career path to better match inevitable shifts in your values and priorities.

Most critical to successful career management is the ability to design your own well-planned and executed career-management strategy, along with precisely calibrated career tactics that emphasize your continuing professional development. To make all these approaches viable in the real world of organizations, you will also need to accept, understand, and master the social context of careers, commonly referred to as organizational politics. Successful career management requires a complete portfolio of skills that extend well beyond acquiring and implementing technical and professional credentials and competence. Don't leave home without them.

References

Culbert, S. A., & McDonough, J. J. (1980). *The invisible war.* New York: John Wiley & Sons.

Erikson, E. H. (1963). *Childhood and society* (2nd ed.). New York: W. W. Norton.

Ginzberg, E. (1984). Career development. In D. Brown & L. Brooks (Eds.), *Career choice and development* (pp. 169–191). San Francisco: Jossey Bass.

Ginzberg, E., Ginzburg, S. W., Axelrod, S., & Herna, J. I. (1951). *Occupational choices: An approach to general theory.* New York: Columbia University Press.

Holland, J. L. (1973). *Making vocational choices: A theory of vocational personalities and work environments.* Englewood Cliffs, NJ: Prentice-Hall.

Holland, J. L. (1985a). *The self-directed search.* Odessa, FL: Psychological Assessment Resources.

Holland, J. L. (1985b). *The occupation finder.* Odessa, FL: Psychological Assessment Resources.

Holland, J. L. (1985c). *Making vocational choices: A theory of vocational personalities and work environments* (2nd ed.). Englewood Cliffs, NJ: Prentice-Hall.

Hollander, D. (1986, August). *The politics of thriving: Identifying doom loops and external barriers to success—a report from the trenches.* Paper presented at the meeting of the American Psychological Association, Washington, DC.

Hollander, D. (1991). *The doom loop: Overcoming the doom loop and taking control of your career.* New York: Viking-Penguin, Inc.

Jett, C. J. (1985, August). *The doom loop.* Paper presented at the meeting of the American Psychological Association, Los Angeles.

Jett, C. J., & Hollander, D. (1986, March). *Riding the doom loop to success: Strategies for impostors, achievers and managers.* Workshop presented at the meeting of the Society for Psychologists in Management, Tampa, FL.

Jung, C. G. (1974). *Psychological types.* New Haven, CT: Princeton University Press.

Levinson, D. (1978). *Seasons of man's life.* New York: Ballantine Books.

Maslow, A. H. (1970). *Motivation and personality* (2nd ed.). New York: Harper & Row.

Neugarten, B. L. (1968). *Adult personality: Toward a psychology of the life-cycle.* Chicago: University of Chicago Press.

Neugarten, B. L., & Datan, N. (1973). Sociological perspectives on the life-cycle. In P. B. Bates & K. W. Schaie (Eds.), *Life-span developmental psychology: Personality and socialization.* New York: Academic Press.

Piaget, J., & Inhelder, B. (1969). *The psychology of the child.* New York: Basic Books.

Roe, A. (1956). *The psychology of occupations.* New York: Wiley.

Roe, A., & Lunneborg, P. W. (1984). Personality development and career choice. In D. Brown & L. Brooks (Eds.), *Career choice and development* (pp. 31–45). San Francisco: Jossey Bass.

Super, D. E. (1957). *The psychology of careers.* New York: Harper & Row.

Super, D. E. (1984). Career and life development. In D. Brown & L. Brooks (Eds.), *Career choice and development* (pp. 192–216). San Francisco: Jossey Bass.

Super, D., Thompson, A. S., & Lindeman, R. H. (1988). *Adult career concerns inventory.* Palo Alto, CA: Consulting Psychologists Press.

Part III

Applying Concepts and Skills

5

Elliot Blass

Professionalism and Academia

My own research interests have focused on the biological bases of behavior in general and on motivational processes in particular. This focus has led to studies on the physiology of thirst and for the past decade, on the development of motivational processes and their underlying neural and chemical mechanisms in newborn rats and humans. I have been blessed with many outstanding graduate and postdoctoral students over the years and their training has provided the same satisfaction and joy as the research itself. Although I am considered to be a good undergraduate lecturer, the classroom is not a particular source of satisfaction to me. A much richer source has been the presence, at any given time, of a coterie of 8 to 12 undergraduates in the laboratory. Finally, I recently (1982–1983) have had clinical training and am a licensed psychologist.

I include this biographical sketch so that you, the reader, by knowing the source of what follows, will better be able to judge its appropriateness for you. So let's start at the beginning.

Career Choice

An academic career in psychology is a difficult way to make a living. Safer and more lucrative jobs abound and other careers may be equally rewarding. However, if your interests, skills, and disposition are such that they can best be nurtured in an academic setting, then follow the course. First, though, ask yourself a few questions and be ruthless in your answers. Discuss these issues with a good and knowledgeable friend or with an advisor or colleague who will not flinch at providing an honest answer.

1. Are you interested in the area of psychology, broadly defined, that you have chosen to pursue at present?
2. How do you know? Is your answer to Question 1 based on experience, reading, discussions, and so forth?
3. Why are you interested in this area of psychology?
4. Are you good at this area of psychology? Do you have an intuition for psychological research, for example, or a clinician's naturalness as a listener, or do you have a flair in front of an audience?
5. Are any or all of the above sources of excitement and satisfaction?

If your answers to these questions seem noncommittal or half-hearted, you might consider some other career. Academia's rewards are largely internal. They are neither financial nor institutional.

If, after answering these questions (and they should be reasked periodically), you choose to continue an academic career, then two parallel preparations must be followed. One is professional; it entails mastering the literature (or literatures) relevant to your professional discipline and establishing a professional program, for example, in research. This preparation also entails reflecting on the types of courses and seminars that you want to teach and the level (or levels) of discourse at which you can be most effective.

The second preparation is pragmatic and concerns finding and attaining a position. The doctoral candidate must consider whether he or she is better off with a postdoctoral position or with going directly into the job market. The postdoctoral issue is tricky. In certain fields (e.g., psychobiology), postdoctoral experience is currently thought to be absolutely necessary to allow the individual to further hone his or her technical skills in the chosen area of concentration and to develop new techniques. I can safely say that, for people interested in research careers in psychobiology, it is a strategic error not to undertake postdoctoral training.

This is decidedly not true for all experimental disciplines. In perception and cognitive psychology, for example, the postdoctoral experience often falls to those who did not compete successfully for the available jobs that year. Things may change, however. In any event, the person with a legitimate professional basis for choosing the postdoctoral option (i.e., becoming steeped in a new discipline, field, or technique) should maintain his or her professional integrity and take the additional training. At some point, however, you must enter the job market—a prospect that is simultaneously exhilarating and demeaning, challenging and anxiety producing. However, it need not be overwhelming.

Employment

There are a number of ways to discover job opportunities. Institutions must advertise the availability of positions in order to meet affirmative action requirements. This may simply be a pro forma gesture if they have the candidate in hand. Alternatively, the advertisement may be legitimate. These advertisements appear in standard society outlets like the American Psychological Association *Monitor*. They also appear in journals such as *Science* and *Chronicles of Higher Education*. The updated job file that your department should have is a less formal, but effective means of job announcement. Department chairs and other senior faculty members routinely receive announcements of job openings that many departments collect in a central file.

An important service provided by national and major regional conventions is a job-placement center where individuals meet prospective employers. This represents a good, although a somewhat harrowing, opportunity for establishing contacts. Interviewers are almost always potential employers—the process is too time consuming and intense for them to undertake without a firm institutional commitment. In this regard, they might be interviewing dozens of individuals. You can gain an advantage by establishing contact before the convention by calling and setting a time at the convention for a meeting, or by having a faculty member who knows an interviewer contact that person and alert him or her to the possibility of contact by you.

This is the first time that I have raised the issue of personal contacts. Its importance can not be overemphasized. Although the "old boy" network of informal contacts is, fortunately, not as dominant today as it was when I first entered the job market, it remains the case that doors open more easily through personal introduction. It is important to understand the limits of the contact. The contact serves to get you in the door; the rest is entirely up to you.

This raises the last means of discovering job opportunities—informal contacts through advisors, colleagues, and friends. This actually becomes increasingly more important with time and seniority. Again, this must be placed in its proper perspective. No one hires on the basis of letters of recommendation or phone calls. The best that the informal system can do is provide entry for an interview. This should not be minimized, however. In short, there are a number of formal and informal means through which one finds out about job opportunities. They should all be fully used.

Establishing Contact

With the exception of convention interviews, all other interviews are through invitation. By definition, a search committee has only three sources of information: (a) letters or calls of recommendation, (b) your curriculum vita (CV) or resume, which includes reprints or preprints, and (c) your personal letter to the search committee. Let me address each in turn.

References. References should be selected with care. Each person you choose should be familiar with your ability to fulfill the particular job requirements. Thus, if the job description calls for teaching and administrative skills, your references should be familiar with your talents in those areas.

You need to make your reference's task as simple as possible. Writing letters of recommendation is an important professional responsibility. It is also time consuming and, in general, a nuisance. Be sure that your reference has complete information for each position, including the job description and contact person. The reference can be more effective if a letter can be tailored to a particular institution or individual. This becomes relatively simple through the magic of word processing. As a rule, you want the "best possible witness" to write on your behalf. At the beginning, this must include your major thesis advisor. Later, colleagues and people at other institutions are appropriate. Regardless, the same rule holds—the writer must know to whom and why he or she is writing. Finally, never list someone as a reference without first obtaining explicit (and hopefully enthusiastic) consent from that person for each situation.

Curriculum vita or resume. Books have been written on this topic and courses are offered. There are experts in this area, and I am not one of them. I can tell you, however, what I look for—clarity of presentation, a sense of perspective, and accuracy. Each discipline has its own accepted format and list of things to include. Thus, CVs of M.D.s include a listing of papers presented at conferences. Academic CVs almost never do—it is considered gilding the lily. Things to include are the date of the current CV, your name, phone number, mailing address, educational background (including postdoctoral experiences), internships and residencies when appropriate, and positions you have held with the dates of occupancy and title (or titles). Honors and professional experiences beyond education should also be listed. This includes serving on editorial boards, grant review committees, and special service positions at your university. Things change. Thus, while it is appropriate upon leaving graduate school to list that you were on a student–faculty search committee, it is no longer appropriate once you are an assistant professor.

The publication record is the core of an academic psychologist's CV. There are a number of ways of presenting this record. My own preference is to list publications according to year. First, I list books that I have edited or written. To me, at least, these were important contributions to the field that extend beyond my own more restricted scientific contributions. My preference is to list everything published during the course of a year, including book chapters as well as original articles. I have even included some contributions that I made to a science encyclopedia. This format for publications allows the reader to trace my career—he can see the shift in interests, the pattern of publication, the breadth of journals and their quality, and the culs-de-sac that I have sometimes entered.

The next CV section documents all grant support that I have received by title, agency, and dollar amount of the award, starting from my predoctoral fellowship through present funding. The penultimate section lists courses and seminars that I have taught. The final section, not always included, lists references.

Again, this format is not for everyone. It is not appropriate, for example, for someone whose major focus is teaching. In this situation, course offerings would be featured more prominently, possibly including a statement of goals for each course recently taught and teacher ratings if available. The CV of someone with a more administrative bent would look different yet again, and so on.

It is fair to say that your CV is your most important professional document. It tells the professional world who you are and what you think of yourself. Do not make it too fancy with a variety of type faces and fonts. To me, at least, this conveys too great an emphasis on form over substance.

Personal statement. Once again, be guided by the situation. If a statement is not requested by an advertisement, do not offer one—a simple cover letter will do. If a statement is requested, however, see it as an opportunity to impress the committee with your sense of perspective. Why have you chosen the research problem (or problems) that you are investigating? What have you achieved? Others might emphasize why they chose a clinical or industrial career, what their fundamental career objectives are, and how these objectives have already been and will continue to be met. Speak about interests, skills, and limitations as a teacher if appropriate. Be both honest in what you say and comfortable in how you say it. On my CV, I point out what I feel have been important contributions and tell why. In the same spirit, I also acknowledge areas of less complete satisfaction.

Thus, at the end, the reader should emerge with a clear picture of who you are and what you have accomplished. Your own self-evaluation can be checked against you record of achievement and validated through the letters of recommendation. A final note in this regard: Your competition is also at your level. Thus, although the publication record is an important validation of an individual's ability to deliver, it is not a substitute for the quality of thought and sense of time and perspective you can provide in a letter.

The Interview

The above process, if successful, garners an initial interview that will become part of your growing application file. This file will blossom to incorporate notes on your application, informal and formal conversations, and the interview (or interviews) itself. The initial interview can take at least three forms: A conference call, a meeting with one or more members of the search committee in a neutral location, or the actual institutional interview. The first two interviews serve as a culling process. They are a relatively inexpensive way of reducing the finalists candidate pool to 4 to 6 applicants. These interviews are usually brief. Their major purpose is to establish if there is a basis for a match between the interests of the department, or a subgroup therein, and that of a particular candidate. It is also an opportunity to assess the candidate's perspective and understanding of the scope of the research problem in which she or he is engaged.

Generally, you are given a week or so notice of the call or interview. Do not try to second guess the committee's desires, because they are situational. A major concern, for example, might be that the budget allotted by the dean for start-up funds is $50,000 and your absolute, bare-bones start-up needs are $70,000. Either you will be eliminated from the competition or the committee might successfully petition the dean for the additional funds. The point here, as in any interview, is to remain open and forthright. Be realistic in your needs and do not back down from the minimum amount of space or support needed to do your work. It is not in anyone's interest for an individual to accept a position that offers inadequate facilities or funds to support the research enterprise.

Institutional interviews and interview processes vary widely reflecting, among other things, institutions, positions and levels, department sizes and needs, and, of course, the personalities involved and their individual needs and expectations. With all of these variables, it is clear that there is no single interview strategy. There are, however, a number of factors that cut across all interview situations. These include (a) preparation, (b) personal conduct, (c) knowledge of technical issues, (d) avoiding fatal flaws, and (e) finding a friend.

Preparation. There are two major components of interview preparation that capture the essence of the interview process. They are (a) preparation to be evaluated by the faculty and (b) preparation to evaluate the faculty members. They, as much as you, must make an impression that will ensure that your first choice is their offer. By definition, the person to whom the offer is being made to is the first choice.

A lot of preparation is technical and should be completed in advance to allow you to prepare at your own pace for the substantive aspects of the interview. Some things are sufficiently routine and obvious that they warrant mention only in passing (eg., travel arrangements should be made at the lowest cost possible). Make sure that the clothes that you wear fit and that you are comfortable in them. You don't want these trivial things to get in the way. It is worth mentioning in this context that although universities like to project a liberal image, the fact is that they are generally very conservative institutions. Their annual budgets can run in the hundreds of millions of dollars, and they are beholden to state legislatures and governors or to well-established boards of trustees, the members of which are often selected because of their fiscal abilities. Moreover, in general, universities have lagged far behind industries in establishing opportunities for women and minorities. University operated day-care programs are scarce. All of this is to indicate that you should rid yourself of the idea of universities as forward thinking, relaxed institutions that encourage a laissez-faire attitude, and that this casualness trickles down to hiring practices.

A more important technical aspect of your preparation concerns your presentation (or presentations). Be sure that slides are clear and to the point. Do not overload a slide with data. Try to avoid the use of tables. Make sure that slides are placed properly so as not to project either upside down or backward. Be sure that they are in the proper order and that you convey that order to the projectionist if you are not the one loading the slides into the projector. Be sure to indicate your audiovisual needs—keep them simple. The same rules hold for transparencies. In my view, the only reason to use transparencies is if you actually need to write on them to make a point. They don't project nearly as well as slides and the overhead almost always gets in somebody's way.

The job talk generally represents the most important, single event of the interview process. It provides the opportunity to demonstrate your understanding of the conceptual issues concerning your research, how this translates into your research enterprise, how your work has advanced the field, the limits of your work, and your future plans. Do not be afraid to be critical of your studies, especially if the inherent limitations are nontechnical. Also, be prepared to answer very technical questions. Any serious department will bring in a colleague from a different department to evaluate your expertise in areas that extend beyond the department's limits. I have always seen this as an opportunity and not as something to be afraid of.

Another aspect of preparation is to become familiar with the faculty and their research interests. This especially holds true for people in one's general area. You want to be able to explore or evaluate the possible interfaces for collaboration and so does the department. Also, you want to know the best perspective to bring to your presentation. This does not mean to be anything less than scrupulously honest. It does mean that your address should be geared to your audience. My own presentations at meetings, colloquia, etc., using the same data and slides, will vary substantially if I am addressing a convention of psychiatrists–pharmacologists, a psychology department, or a group of pediatricians and nurses. As it turns out, my research bears on areas that are relevant to all of these groups, and each presentation is tailored to allow the greatest interface with each particular group.

Familiarization with department members, of course, helps prepare you for evaluating the department. You can get a roster from the university catalogue, which should be in your university library, and even look up a few published articles of select members. You will not be starting each interview anew, rather you will have the appropriate context for each individual. This form of preparation allows meetings to proceed more smoothly and expands the range of topics that you can deal with comfortably.

Finally, rehearse your presentation—not with the idea of memorizing it, but with the idea of presenting the material in the allotted time, anticipating questions and interruptions, and doing justice to your ideas and to the individual slides. Ask your practice audience to bring to your attention things that they do not like, as well as those that they are really enamored of.

Prepare a budget. This should include a rock-bottom estimate (allow 10% for inflation and error) of minimum needs, space, and equipment necessary for you to create a laboratory. Also, prepare a budget that will allow you to sustain the laboratory for 2 to 3 years without funding. Do not be concerned about the costs. The department must be prepared to provide the appropriate level of support to its members when they arrive. If your legitimate needs exceed their budget, then either there will be no match, or they will petition the central administration for additional funds. It is a fatal mistake to omit necessary items from budgetary considerations.

Personal conduct. There is little to say here. Be yourself. Don't try to do things that do not feel right. If you are not naturally gregarious, do not try to be extroverted for the interview. If you have a sense of humor, don't be afraid to use it. Feel free to enter into open discussions of ideas and data, but do not attack an individual. Use good judgment. You are going to be tested in a variety of ways. Do not try to second guess an individual or evaluate his or her motives. Remain unflappable through what might seem like provocation or stupidity. If you are asked an esoteric question or a question with an esoteric frame of reference, feel free to ask for clarification. At the end, you may simply say that you don't have an answer. Don't worry about it. If the question seemed exotic to you, then it surely did to others.

People have varied opinions concerning what I am about to say. For me, the interview starts when I leave home and ends when I get home. It has been my and others' experience that in traveling to and from a university, especially one situated in a college town, one often meets someone relevant to the decision-making process.

I recall a situation in an airport in which my connecting flight to a job talk was delayed for about 2 hours. The flight was finally boarded with everyone complaining in no uncertain terms. My neighbor complained mildly about the inconvenience, and then we both shrugged it off as not being a big deal. Each of us turned to our reading after some talk about the purpose of our travel, especially mine. As it turned out, my neighbor was the president of the university to which I was traveling, which I found out the next day when I was ushered into his office.

Would I have been offered the job if I had groused like others on the flight? I don't know. This was a high-level position that included meeting with the public. Would I have complained more under other circumstances—probably, although I am not much of a complainer. The frequency of such incidents is not trivial. The lesson is obvious. When you are going on an interview, the whole process from start to finish must be managed professionally.

Technical issues. Don't be the one to raise them. They will be raised by your host, department chair, dean, or some other official. If not raised on your initial visit, they will be on subsequent ones or in follow-up conversations. Once an issue is raised, however, be sure to get all of the relevant information. Either the interviewer will provide you with it or will ask if you have any questions. For example, you may be shown the library, told about the number of volumes, shown the psychology area, holdings in relevant disciplines, and the reserve system. At some point, it will be clear that your host is through, and then you can ask, for example, about mechanisms for ordering texts or journals for the library. Is there a university budget? Is each department allotted a limited budget? This holds true for any general issue concerning institutional facilities and policies.

There are a number of standard technical matters that you will be informed about in your meeting with the university's representative, generally the chair. They are salary and fringe benefits; teaching responsibilities, including possible release time during the first year; department and university responsibilities; space; start-up funds; promotion; and tenure.

In all likelihood, you will be given a tour of "your" space by your host. It is appropriate to find out about space shared with other members of the department, such as computer facilities, animal-housing areas, surgical rooms, experimental rooms, etc. This will allow you to assess the adequacy of the proposed space. This is also important in terms of possible renovations that may have to be undertaken in order to make the space work for you. In this regard, find out what lies between the walls. Is there a central computer facility that can be wired from lab to office? Are there shielded rooms or cables? Are there air pressure and vacuum lines in place? At all times, you must be aware of your minimum requirements as well as your deluxe, yet reasonable, wishes for space and equipment.

During the course of your interview with the chair, you may be asked what you need in the way of start-up funds. Be prepared to discuss this issue from the perspective of minimum and maximum needs and to present a detailed budget. Actual dollars are not the issue at an interview. The legitimacy of your needs is. Certain areas of biopsychology research are very expensive with standard equipment costing $25,000 to $50,000. A department seeking a person in that area must be prepared to spend what it takes to allow the person to get started.

On the other hand, if your research is not expensive, do not show poor judgment by asking for more than what is needed to start. If you are being courted as a distinguished research professor, a computer at home with a laser printer is small potatoes. If you are seeking an entry-level position, however, the department might look askance at such a request.

The initial interview is not the time for negotiation over salary or over other things for that matter. You should have an idea as to what salaries are in that institution (the American Psychological Association can be helpful), and what the cost of living in that area is so that, if asked about salary, you can present an informed, reasonable, but somewhat elevated figure. If you are presented with a salary figure and then asked how it sounds, use your judgment. If it is the same as or more than what you expected, all to the good. If it is somewhat less, you can say that it is in the "ballpark." If, however, the figure is substantially below what you anticipated, and you are asked, then be honest. You might say that you may have overestimated things, etc., but that you had expected something in the range of so and so. Remember, although negotiations almost always come after the offer is made, if the question is asked early, be forthcoming.

Fatal flaws. The idea of a fatal flaw is introduced here and will be raised in other contexts. It refers to mistakes made or personality characteristics that either predict or guarantee failure. In the job-seeking process, actions that demonstrate a lack of judgment will "do in" a candidate. A sloppy or badly out of date CV will give people pause. Markedly inappropriate dress or looseness of tongue will also cause problems. Remember, among other things, faculty members are considered role models for students. Although one can seriously debate the notion of "in loco parentis" on the college campus, our role as models, whether we like it or not, is a given.

Concerning the interview itself, the major fatal flaw is to not show up. The only legitimate excuse is the tragedy of death of an immediate family member or the joyful event of a birth. A major illness might also do, but it better be very serious. Broken-down automobiles and missed flights are not excuses. If caught in a snowstorm that messes up your flight schedule, be sure to have alternate schedules in hand prior to calling and giving the news.

It is certainly the case that universities make bad mistakes by rejecting diamonds in the rough. As I have indicated, universities are conservative institutions with an obligation to students, parents, and alumni. Also, an interview crams a lot into a very short period of time and people make judgments based on superficial, as well as meaningful, characteristics. The system is less than perfect, so know well its limitations.

Make a friend. During the course of the process, there will invariably be one individual with whom you will connect personally. It may not necessarily be on the first interview. This person can be an enormous help to you and to his or her institution by allowing discussions to be very open, frank, and honest. You can get the inside news from this individual concerning the chairperson, departmental policies, and true quality of graduate and undergraduate students. This is not idle talk, for all of these issues are important contributions to your decision-making process. By gently probing individual faculty members and graduate students, you should have independently reached some tentative judgment about these issues. Verification or lack thereof is crucial.

Evaluating the institution. It is important to find out about the institution's professional evaluation process. When is tenure? On what basis is the decision made?[1] This will give you some information concerning institutional and depart-

[1] My own feeling about tenure (and I have always held it) is that it is a terrible system that is harmful to all facets of the enterprise. The university can be stuck with someone after 3 to 6 years of his or her being on the job. That may mean 30 to 50 years of expensive nonproductivity, while occupying a slot that could be better filled by others. The individual suffers too by not fulfilling his or her potential and not attaining the aspirations and hopes of an optimistic youth. Students suffer most of all by being placed in forced contact with people who have essentially quit and are simply going through the motions. There are a number of alternatives that require integrity on the part of administration and faculty. The one that I favor is a series of contracts of increasing length. Contract termination must be for due cause and with due process. This will eliminate capricious behavior on the university's part. The negative side of this is that it will add yet another set of bureaucratic layers and will place demands on faculty time. It will go a long way, however, toward eliminating much of the flotsam and jetsam that bounce in the academic waters.

mental expectancies. Ask explicitly what the expectations are. Are there hidden agendas? I once received a faculty position offer from a university. After careful discussions with several administration officials, it became clear to me that the organization had several very different ideas about the nature of the job. One person thought I should concentrate on junior faculty development. Another was concerned about grant funding, and a third thought I would become the department chair in a year or two. I did not accept this position.

This section ends as it began with an exhortation of critical self-assessment. What are your skills and weaknesses? What do you enjoy professionally, and what do you dislike? Are you ready for new challenges, or are you happy where you are and in what you are doing? Shed as much light on yourself as possible from spouse, friends, colleagues, and students. (Chapter 6 also has some useful information for conducting yourself in the job search process.)

Getting Started

Well, you made it. The prize is yours—what now? The arriving faculty member has four major professional tasks, three of which can be started in advance. They are (a) laboratory establishment, (b) grant application, (c) course preparation, and (d) department and university responsibilities.

Before starting the job, as much time as possible should be devoted to the first three activities. Establish a mechanism for ordering the equipment that you need so that much of it can be there upon your arrival. If possible, have someone check the invoice against your purchase order. Start a grant application before leaving your present position. This has a number of advantages (e.g., it provides you with an informed critic—your present advisor). If funded, there will be a smooth transition to your new research project with little lost time or dependence upon intramural funds. Also, you can start to collect summer salary—no small consideration. Start preparing your courses as early as possible. Get a sense of the students that you will be teaching as well as the class sizes. Contact the bookstore.

In the event that your space is being renovated, be prepared for the absolute worst. It is the rare (I actually do not know of any) university that has a plant operations department that can catch all of the errors that occur in each phase of construction. You should be on the scene as much as possible to catch technical errors that you might recognize. The general rule of thumb is that it takes as much time for a renovated space to become functional after construction as it did to make the renovations themselves. One always hears horror stories about renovations; all are true. Do your best to move into slightly used space. Avoid renovations, if you can help it.

Establishing a Laboratory

On this matter, I write from personal experience. The laboratory should reflect your own style and needs. For me, the emphasis has always been on flexibility. Thus, nothing was fixed in place in my lab except for two high wall cabinets and two sinks. Everything else was on wheels or could be lifted for rearranging or discarding if there was no longer an experimental need. Others might seek greater stability.

I found it enormously useful to gain facility with scale rules. This helped my communication with architects and allowed me to plan equipment location without having to move things about. The need for a well-planned physical layout cannot be overemphasized. It makes data collection easier and facilitates movement of people within the laboratory. Space is invariably at a premium, so use it well.

Given the nature of construction schedules, your space may not be ready for occupancy when you arrive. Don't consider this a total loss. It will allow you to keep a closer eye on the construction. Do not be intimidated by the powers that be if you find a mistake. It is your chairperson's responsibility, or that of a senior faculty member, to make these problems known to the appropriate parties.

Plan to start an experiment that requires minimal equipment. It could even be one that you have run before. This will give you the satisfaction of starting in your new space, shaking out the bugs, and replicating (with luck) a previous finding.

Keep track of your budget. In most places, you are held personally responsible for any overexpenditures. The university will not bail you out of an overspent budget—appropriately so.

Teaching

Teaching loads, arrangements, and other factors vary enormously among and within institutions. An important part of your university responsibility is in the classroom, even if a university does not consider it sufficiently important to include it in the tenure-making decision. Once past your initial trepidation, teaching can be fun, and many find it enormously rewarding. It takes place in many settings (e.g., lecture halls, classrooms, seminars, lab meetings, at the workbench, in the corridors, and over lunches or beers).

The preparations for all of these different forms of teaching will vary. For seminars, classes, and lectures, syllabi should be made available prior to your arrival. Texts should be ordered, and articles should be made available through the appropriate mechanisms. The particulars of procedures are going to reflect your own style. Some teachers write out all lectures, others depend on index cards or notes. Do what works best for you. Prepare as much of the course in advance; read all the material. Above all (this is particularly important at first, when developing your classroom style), know the material cold and understand it thoroughly. Be honest if you don't have a good answer to a question; students are quick to pick up and tear apart the bluff.

In my experience, students are also forgiving. I remember an occasion about 10 years ago when a lecture of mine on Freud was not coming out well. I stopped about halfway through the class, announced that it was the worst lecture that I had ever given, apologized for it, and said that I wanted to try it again at the next class meeting. The class, heaving a collective sigh of relief, agreed, and the next lecture was a hit.

Collegial Relationships

These relationships are a potential source of joy and should be cultivated from the outset. Some of your colleagues will invite you to lunches or to coffee breaks and will genuinely offer whatever services, bits of advice, or helpful hints that they can to make yours a softer landing. Helpful senior colleagues will assist you with grant proposals, provide you with information about available intramural funds, and instruct you on how to apply for them. Explore opportunities for collaborative research and team teaching. Again, there is a great deal of variability among and within institutions and even within the same department, reflecting the style and temperament of the individuals within a subsection.

Students can be a wonderful blessing when they are good (I have been incredibly fortunate in this regard), but the bane of your life when they are not. At first, especially as you are feeling your way around, students can be an enormous time and energy sink. It is vital to be clear with them and to convey your expectations for them and for your relationship with them. Try to leave as few things as possible ambiguous. Graduate school is already anxiety-producing for students, and they deserve all of the support and clarity that you can provide. As always, develop a style that suits your personality. In my case, I have tried to be clear, supportive especially at first, directive at first, honest, and enthusiastic. On the whole, this has worked for me as students welcomed the early support, were not intimidated by the honesty, and matched my enthusiasm with their own. There are other styles, of course, that are at least as successful.

Fatal Flaws

A fatal flaw that raises its head here is disorganization to the point of immobility. If you are disorganized by nature, and you find yourself losing a lot of time, redoing things, missing deadlines, driving secretaries to distraction, and encountering classroom difficulties, seek help. One of the great advantages of academia is the ability to savor and utilize time. You will lose this advantage through extreme disorganization and the franticness involved in catching up. You don't have to be a compulsive, clean-desk type of person—just don't get yourself into a bind.

Another fatal flaw is laziness. I am astonished at how much laziness I have seen—even in research-oriented universities. Lazy academics do not stay the course.

Grants

The seeking of funds, during the 2 decades of my own career, has undergone changes of revolutionary proportion. The changes are both superficial and deep and reflect technological improvements (e.g., word processing), the demands upon funding agencies in terms of number of grant applications, and, especially, federal cutbacks and increased private-sector funding.

Other things have not changed in grantsmanship. The quality of the document must be high, the research problem must be articulated with clarity and brevity, the importance of the issue must be presented in its appropriate perspective, preliminary data must be provided in support of the feasibility of the enterprise, and the document must follow meticulously the forms of the granting agency. Let's start at the beginning.

Funding sources. Today, any university with a research commitment must have a grant development office that can provide information concerning public and private agencies that have funded projects related to individual interests. There are encyclopedia-like volumes that list all registered public and private agencies, their general interests, and their anticipated funding levels. There are at least two national services, the Illinois Research Information Service (IRIS), at the University of Illinois, and the Sponsored Projects Information Network (SPIN), at the State University of New York, that provide booklets with code words that allow your funding officials access to grant titles (and sometimes abstracts), agencies, and dollar amounts of grants funded under each code.

Contact the most promising agencies. Your grants office may already have some of the literature concerning application deadlines, preliminary statements, lengths and styles of applications, and other types of vital technical information. When applying for a federal grant, it is often helpful to discuss the application with the study section secretary. These people are knowledgeable and, within limits, can provide information. The range of cooperation you may receive from these officials is breathtaking. Some return calls the same day and will meet with you personally. Others don't even have the courtesy to return a call and will communicate with you via form letter. On the whole, the contact is worth pursuing.

The process. Read the instructions carefully and be sure that the agency is appropriate for your general research problem. Each private agency has its own charter, the essence of which is publicly available. Your grant proposal should reflect a sensitivity to these goals.

Although applications vary from agency to agency in terms of format, length, etc., all grants have three core features—a broad statement of the problem and its particular significance, proposed research addressed to the critical aspect of the problem, and a budget. There may also be an abstract and a report of progress.

Let me digress here for a moment to provide the perspective of someone sitting on a review panel. This will help you, as a grant applicant, to better appreciate the decision-making process. I can speak from first-hand experience as a member of the National Science Foundation (NSF) study section in psychobiology. The panel of seven reviewers met three times a year. Each meeting lasted 2 days, during which time, 60 to 70 proposals were discussed and evaluated. Each proposal was read by at least three panel members and generally three to six outside reviewers who submitted evaluations for the panel's consideration. On average, each proposal was discussed for only 20 minutes, including discussion on the budget, and a score was given by each panel member. This is pretty much the style of the National Institutes of Health (NIH) and National Institute of Mental Health (NIMH), although they rely less on outside reviewers. Each NSF panel member read between 15 and 30 grant applications for each study section and was prepared to discuss each one in detail.

This boils down to the following: Your application is one of many that is studied and discussed by your peers, who volunteer their time and undertake a tremendous responsibility to maintain high-quality science for the funding institution, for the individual investigator, and especially for the starting scientist. It is our responsibility as applicants to make their task as easy as possible and to present the work in such a way that the reviewers will serve as our advocates. One wants to strive for a proposal that will garner a review starting with, "This is a wonderful proposal by . . ." Technically, this is achieved through the use of precise language and thought, adherence to format and pagination guidelines, and by making sure that the document is structurally perfect. Check for typos, quality of printer problems, and other flaws. Seek the opinion and critique of your best informed and most knowledgeable colleagues.

The research problem should be placed in its broadest and most meaningful perspective. The area does not have to be hot; it has to be fundamental and important, and you must convince the reader of this. Try to approach the issue not only technically, but also broadly and with perspective.

Given that this has been achieved, you want to demonstrate that you are an excellent person by virtue of your background and current and past achievements in order to advance the issue. This can take the form of submitting a progress report or preliminary data. The applicant should demonstrate that the proposed research effectively translates data- or theory-based issues into an experimental research program. That is the essence of the grant. It should demonstrate to the overburdened reader the importance of the work and the individual's capacity to carry it out. The proposed research should be programmatic and cohesive. The budget amount proposed should be appropriate to the scope of the problem and to the amount of time requested.

Budgets

The budget should accurately reflect the research needs of the grant. It is expected that the applicant will seek summer salary, support a graduate student (or students), and attend at least one professional meeting. Other line items are questionable. Are technical support staff needed for relatively small research enterprises? What about a secretary?

My feeling has always been to ask for staff and support lines that will clearly improve the productivity and quality of the proposed research endeavor. Budgetary decisions almost never influence priority ratings except when the requests are so out of line that the individual's judgment is questioned. Thus, if the request is legitimate, it may be granted. At worst, a line item will be declined or the dollar amount reduced.

All requests must carry with them clear documentation. Specify the meetings that you will attend. Justify the need for a specialized item. Identify how a technician will help the research and how a secretary can free up your time to make your research more effective.

The application procedure need not be overwhelming. Remember that essentially the same application can be sent to various agencies and this, of course, can be simplified by word processing. Also, remember that it takes 1 to 2 weeks for a proposal to go through the university bureaucracy, so leave enough time. This raises the final point. Take enough time to really reflect upon the grant and on what your short- and long-term professional aspirations are. Decide if the grant will fulfill these aspirations. I generally take 2 to 3 months to write a proposal. This allows leisurely, reflective thought and unhurried, unpressured conversations with colleagues and students as to the goals of each proposed experiment, their possible outcomes, and what possible benefits will be learned from them.

Other Issues

Research Fluidity and Burnout

Although I have written this chapter for individuals about to embark on an academic career, several issues remain central throughout one's career. The validity of one's research program should be routinely assessed and evaluated to determine if it is the best one possible for the issues that are being addressed. Do these issues continue to excite you, or with time, have they become stale? Are you open to new approaches and new scientific issues? My own path has been to follow my scientific muse, provided she steered an interesting course. I have tried to avoid culs-de-sac through honest and critical discussions with colleagues and graduate students. This has allowed me to be involved in a number of separate, yet related, experimental projects at any given time and to shift major fields at least twice.

Research fluidity relates reciprocally with teaching fluidity. Teaching interesting and bright undergraduate and graduate students has forced me to come to grips with scientific and intellectual issues that might otherwise have gone unexplored. Out of these challenges have arisen new projects and broader perspectives. Taken together, change in my laboratory and course work has prevented, so far at least, academic burnout.

Again, I add that this path is not for everyone. Some see this flexible approach as being the antithesis of science and simply a dalliance. Their position is that scientific issues are sufficiently complex to require a lifetime to really make headway on any particular problem of scientific or psychological import.

This, too, (except the dalliance part) represents a legitimate concern and approach that works for some people. Again, there is no hard and fast rule for staying with a topic, switching areas, or avoiding academic burnout. For me and for many others whom I know that have remained vigorous, the best strategy has been to hold multiple interests.

In this regard, the number of psychobiologists who have taken clinical training and maintained a clinical interest is impressive. Perhaps it resolves an asymmetry between an original desire to have a career in psychology (i.e., in human behavior) and the actual career choice of studying mechanisms, often in animals, that underlie behavior. Rather recently, I completed a clinical residency and am now licensed in Maryland. I spend a small percentage of my time as a therapist, but this might expand in the future.

I have never wanted to be a department chair in an institution in which the chair rotates. It would be exciting, however, to start a program from the beginning or come into a situation that demands radical change, thereby leaving my own mark on the processes.

Sabbaticals

I believe it to be a mistake not to leave your home institution for a full sabbatical year. Location choice is obviously determined by professional and personal considerations. The two 1-year sabbaticals that I took (one in Toronto and one in Jerusalem) were remarkably different, and each satisfied different personal and professional needs. In each case, I embarked on new research pathways.

There are many sources of support for sabbaticals, including postdoctoral fellowships. Incidentally, especially for senior placements, leaves of absence and sabbaticals become bargaining chips that the university is often willing to concede.

Final Fatal Flaws

In addition to some of the fatal flaws mentioned during the course of this chapter, it is appropriate now to highlight some others.

Inability to bring experiments or projects to a close. Some scientists pursue every little question that arises from their research at the expense of not completing, in a formal way, the major experiment at hand. Often, there is nothing substantial to show for their very considerable efforts, just a flurry of hints.

Tendentious personality. This especially becomes a problem in cases where talented and overly frank people find themselves in departments inhabited by people of lesser ability. The fatal flaw resides in a person's inability to distinguish between discussion of ideas and attacks on individuals. This will often lead to termination of a nontenured faculty member.

Lack of perspective. This is a difficult problem to pin down. It concerns the absence of the ability to place particular experiments in a broader context. This individual does have the discipline to complete major experiments, but, in fact, may publish an extraordinary number of short studies, each differing along a single parameter. This individual is similar to the person who does not complete a single study in that both reveal a lack of appreciation of what the basic enterprise is about.

This raises the issue of publish or perish and what it takes to get tenure. As indicated earlier, I think the system is awful. For those who already are intrinsically motivated, no additional pressure is necessary, and the system is not much more than a nuisance. For those whose performance is motivated primarily by the security of tenure, a guarantee is built into the system of anxiety, resentment, and reluctance to perform seriously once tenure has been secured. Thus, what started as a system to allow freedom of expression and exploration without fear of job loss has often turned into a license for "publish to tenure and then perish."

Would I recommend an academic career to the average undergraduate? Definitely not! There are many research psychologists now, and by definition, departments are top heavy with senior faculty because tenure is generally granted after 3 to 6 years on the job. After you finish your training, you may be competing with upward of 200 to 300 individuals for a position in a first-rate department. Things are bound to get worse for federal support in an economy that bears the current national debt.

On the other hand, if an undergraduate was brimming with enthusiasm, had a talent for the laboratory, and for good measure, was creative and persisted through my objections, then she or he just might be individualistic enough to withstand the uncertainties, eccentric enough to doggedly pursue questions about behavior that are valued by only a few, and determined enough to stay the course. In such a case, I would do everything in my power to place this individual in the best program that I could, for it would be hard for him or her, like me, to imagine doing anything else.

6

Richard R. Kilburg

Managing Practitioner Careers

Introduction

In previous chapters, you have seen that careers in psychology share a number of major elements and that success depends on the application of a wide array of practical skills and concepts. Thus far, we have emphasized the commonalities between the various subfields within psychology. Yet, we know there are major differences between academic- and practice-focused psychological careers. The following discussion will briefly describe some of the major stages of practitioner careers, the critical themes and issues that practitioners confront across each of the stages, the practical matters that are so important to success in the different stages, and the strategies that you can use to your advantage as you develop professionally. Chapter 5 did the same for academic careers. As in the previous chapters, I will illustrate the material with examples and suggest exercises that will help you to develop specific skills and explore some of the material in more depth.

Stages in Practitioners' Lives

This could hardly be a book by, for, and about psychologists without some discussion of ages, stages, or some other schemata to organize and describe human lives. As in most situations involving humans, it is fairly easy and safe to say that psychological careers have three general stages: a beginning, a middle, and an end. Of course, this rather simplistic notion becomes much more complicated as you delve into each stage. However, it serves our purposes well if you start to think about these three major epochs in your career.

Stage I—Training and Choicemaking

The opening phase of a practitioner's career usually starts in the junior or senior year of the undergraduate experience. By then, you have selected the field of psychology to study and have established that you are able to understand the material. If you are practical, favor concrete tasks, or enjoy helping others, you will probably gravitate to the subareas of psychology that provide services—clinical, educational, counseling, industrial–organizational, and so forth. Assuming that you successfully complete all of the usual undergraduate requirements, you apply and are accepted into a graduate program in your chosen subarea of psychology. The first stage intensifies here.

In graduate school, we are both trained and socialized as psychologists. We learn about the field in depth, develop specific skills, and improve on our natural abilities. The graduate years are elaborately subdivided into subsets of specific courses, training experiences, and personal events. However, even at this early time, the importance of strategy and choice begin to be felt. As a psychologist, you will be defined by the choices that you make. The materials that you read and master, the skills that you practice and refine, and the colleagues that you develop and cherish will significantly determine what you do in your psychological career. Strategy consists largely of thinking carefully about what you want to say yes to and creating the opportunities to do so.

Major Themes

In the context of each of the stages of your career, a series of major themes will recur. As you read through them, think about the points mentioned above about choice and strategy.

First, you confront the question, "what do I know?" This is a simple, four-word question; however, it defines you as a practitioner of psychology. What you know consists of everything you read, see, hear, and experience. In graduate school, you discover that you can learn what there is to know of importance in psychology. You can decide what you need to know. This knowledge then begins to help define who you are as a psychologist.

Second, you ask, "what can I do and what do I want to do?" More than anything else, the practice of psychology means doing something about behavior. This involves the application of your knowledge through the specific skills and abilities that you have mastered. During graduate school, faculty members usually define the skills that you are expected to develop. Through courses and field work, you are presented with a continuum of increasingly complex tasks that require you to do things with your psychological knowledge. Increasingly, as the training years pass, you begin to feel a sense of mastery. You demonstrate that there are skills that you can use. You also become able to make choices about which new skills to acquire.

This developing ability to do what you want to do and learn what you want to learn begins to define you as a practitioner in psychology. If you emphasize psychotherapeutic skills, your career begins to move in a particular direction. If you find yourself fascinated and drawn to how organizations develop, you will move in a different way. Emphasis on specific populations (e.g., children or the elderly), specific skills (e.g., test construction or community consultation), or unique settings (e.g., private practice or large, organizational-development firms) increasingly define who you are as a psychologist.

These decisions should come naturally as a consequence of participating and learning in areas that interest you. It is vitally important that you realize that this natural and spontaneous process is also one that you have control over and responsibility for. Once you focus on this point, you begin to understand that you are the master of your own destiny. You write your own history as a psychologist by what you decide to do and learn.

Third, as you near the end of your training, you begin to confront a new and critical issue. You know a lot about psychology. You have even learned how to apply some of your knowledge to very practical problems. If you are fortunate, you also understand that you can regulate who you are as a practicing psychologist. However, now you face the question, "what will people pay me for?" This is a somewhat crass but very pragmatic issue. It is all well and good to know a lot of psychology and to be able to do things that you enjoy. But reality dictates that you must begin to make a living through the application of what you know and do. This represents your first concrete brush with the marketplace.

Someone must want to buy the applications of knowledge and skill you possess in order for you to practice and to earn a living. In the United States and other market-oriented countries, there are consumers with problems, issues, and needs for your services. Your job is to find these potential consumers and convince them that they should pay you to help them. In countries that are not market-driven, consumers of psychological services are directed to agencies of the government that provide what they need. Even here, you still face the issue, because you must find an agency that will pay you to practice for them. In the United States, with its emphasis on the private-practice model of service delivery, finding a job with an agency of government or some other corporate organization is still the most frequent way that psychologists practice. As you finish your graduate years, you realize that the bottom line is the financial reality that you must earn a living through what you know and know how to do.

This leads us naturally and spontaneously to the fourth major issue. "How do I present what I know and can do, so that I can get paid?" In other words, how do I market myself. Marketing has become an area of specialization in human activity. It can be made very complicated. At its roots, there are several deceptively simple issues:

1. *What do people need or want?* For the psychologist, this means what do people need in the way of psychological skills or knowledge? It gets complicated because, usually, people do not define what they need in ways that make an easy connection to practitioners in psychology. When you need transportation, it's easy to look for a car. When your organization is not reaching its goals or you feel that something is wrong in your life, you do not automatically go and shop for a psychologist. The fact that people do go shopping for us now reflects a lot of successful marketing by past generations of psychologists.
2. *What do you want to provide by way of services?* This goes back to the first three issues. You are responsible for developing a strategy for getting your knowledge and skills to the people that need them. Your decisions about what you like and want to do constitute the core of your strategy. These are the services you want to provide.
3. *Where is your target population?* Who are they? Are they individuals with problems such as eating disorders, depression, or anxiety? Are they parents with children that they are worried about? Are they unproductive orga-

nizations with a need for competent executives or work groups? Are they schools that need to assess and serve children? These are all audiences, populations, and markets for psychological services. Again, you must decide what population or market you want to serve and how you want to serve them.

4. *What is the message that you want to give to this population, and how are you going to deliver it?* This is also a complicated proposition. In its most simple version, you send a letter and résumé to an organization that has advertised the availability of a job for a psychologist. Increasingly, however, psychological companies spend a great deal of money conceiving and implementing massive advertising and sales campaigns to reach potential customers that they have identified. Hospitals now advertise their services on television. Private practitioners purchase display ads in the yellow pages. Publishers use direct mail to tell psychologists about their books. These ads give a message to potential clients. These are the services you will obtain from me. The more carefully crafted messages also say something about how you will treat the people who come to you. Words like competence, quality, satisfaction, and solutions are slowly creeping into professional marketing messages.

Increasingly, practitioners are becoming conscious of these explicit marketing problems. Psychologists must determine what people need, what services they will provide, where their potential clients are, how to reach them, and what messages to send them. This will also be a central focus of your professional life.

The last major issue that psychologists face in each of the stages of their career involves the question, "how can I do some good in this life?" During your graduate years, you spend a great deal of time reading and talking about the human condition and how psychology can help. A central part of this process focuses on becoming an ethical practitioner. Your course work and introduction to practical ethical questions through field experience begin to emphasize the "doing good" aspects of your work.

As you move into a full-time practice, the question tends to submerge itself in the daily pressures and decisions that you make. Yet, as you serve individuals, families, groups, and organizations, you are doing good. More broadly, when you speak to an audience for free, serve on the board of an organization, or decide to provide services to someone on a pro bono basis, you are doing good. The notion of balance that was introduced in chapter 2 is useful to reconsider here.

Making decisions about whom to serve and how to make a decent living frequently leads us to submerge the humanitarian aspects of the practice of psychology. It is easy to forget that our practice is equated with helping people and not just with making a dollar. As you discipline yourself to compete in the increasingly tough markets in psychology, keep in mind that you are also in the field to do some good for other people.

These five themes repeatedly play themselves out in our lives. In Stage I, we find them operating with simplicity. The courses and practicums define what we know and can do. The training programs market our services. We grope for a way to do good in a halting but spontaneous fashion by serving our first clients and learning about ethics. Eventually, we graduate and move into the end of Stage I by taking our first jobs in the field.

The First Job

Finding your initial job is a real challenge. Be aware that this is your first major career transition. In chapter 7, I describe transitions and job-search strategies in much more detail. The principles and techniques are always the same regardless of when you look for work. The steps include deciding what you want to do; pulling together your résumé and other support materials; searching for opportunities through newspapers, trade papers, telephone connections, and discussions with friends and colleagues; applying; waiting; interviewing and marketing yourself; and winning and losing competitions for positions and dealing with the emotional consequences. You need to apply all of the knowledge and skills presented in chapters 2 and 3. As Georgine Pion describes in chapter 10, the market for psychologists is still fairly strong. Practitioners in particular are usually able to find work in areas close to their training.

In your first job, you may not be able to dictate terms to your employer. The position may also not be exactly what you want—it rarely is. When you accept the job, you take the second major step toward defining who you are as a psychologist. You begin to practice, and you get your license.

The details of licensure and regulation have been covered thoroughly in Sales's (1983) handbook. Suffice it to say that the procedures vary from state to state. The national exam is another hurdle to get over. The vast majority of psychologists with solid graduate preparation have little difficulty passing the exams.

Once you start to work in the job, the processes of behavioral transformation and self-management described in chapter 2 begin to assert themselves. Even if you do not intentionally guide the process, the job and your adaptation to it will change you. This is where the concepts and skills presented by Dory Hollander in chapter 4 can be applied. You must remember the Doom Loop and begin to think creatively about possible career capstones. These ideas can guide the choices that you make in your job about the activities you undertake, the people you cultivate as friends and colleagues, and the new skills and knowledge that you develop.

Work Characteristics

Our awareness of what our day-to-day lives as psychological practitioners will be expands slowly during our training. As we slog through each year of study and work experience, we are exposed to the wonderful, challenging, wacky, harsh, and sometimes bitter world of practice. I think it might be helpful to review briefly the characteristics of your work as a professional psychologist. Mintzberg (1973) presented six sets of work characteristics that we will describe here along with four additional problems.

Pace. Psychological practice is very demanding. Workweeks of 50 to 60 hours are the norm, and, for many, 80 to 100-hour weeks are routine. Weekends and evenings are seldom completely free of professional intrusions. Client contacts, telephone work, work-group meetings, record-keeping tasks, handling of the mail, business details of a practice, liaisons and monitoring work, report writing, and continuing education all consume vast amounts of time. In my experience, a rule of thumb is that it will take you anywhere from 33% to 200% longer to do a task than you originally anticipated. The ability to conserve energy and manage time become increasingly important under such conditions.

Patterns of activities: action vs. reflection. Mintzberg (1973) stated that the chief characteristics of managerial work are brevity, variety, and fragmentation. In graduate school, papers and reports are drafted and redrafted as facts, impressions, and metaphors are honed to a fine point of communication. In full-time practice, one often has time to say things once and then in an abbreviated form. The typical pattern involves shifting one's mood, energy, and attention to the constant tumult of the environment. Spending quality time with each of your clients becomes difficult as the next person waits in line, the telephone rings, a colleague stops by to talk about a problem, and the mail threatens to overwhelm you. The emphasis shifts to action in practice and away from reflection. You frequently have little time to second guess yourself, because there is always something else to deal with coming along. Retreats, planning meetings, and organized respites to take care of paperwork, telephone calls, and other chores become crucial parts of a successful practice.

Types of media. Mintzberg said, "The manager uses five basic media: The mail (documented communication), the telephone (purely verbal), the unscheduled meeting (informal face-to-face), the scheduled meeting (formal face-to-face) and the tour (visual)" (1973, p. 38). In psychological practice, we can add testing sessions, therapy or consultation hours, report writing, court visits, case conferences, negotiation sessions, and so forth, typical in the various subareas of the field. Most of these latter activities are modifications of formal managerial decision, communication, and strategy meetings.

The hardest part of the transition from graduate school to practice is the shift from written to verbal exchanges. The verbal media improve efficiency even as they create problems with accuracy and quality. Knowing when and where to document things in writing and how to create good written products are still useful skills. However, verbal and auditory skills are of premier importance in psychological practice, with the capacity to persuade and argue articulately and with understanding, empathy, and sensitivity being critical to success.

Contacts. This attribute of work emphasizes the boundary-spanning functions described in chapters 2 and 3. We have discussed the information and dissemination roles psychologists must play to maximize their adaptation to work life. In your work as a practitioner, you will be as dependent on information as any other psychologist.

The key to obtaining information is developing a network of people and a pool of written sources of information that you can consult frequently. The network should have people with access to critical information about the performance of your organization in marketing, production, finance, administration, personnel, and research. It should include your competitors from other organizations, government officials, and other advisors such as lawyers, accountants, supervisors, friends, and colleagues. A carefully selected sample of written material should be scanned routinely from newspapers, magazines, trade publications, and academic journals. Professional associations such as the American Psychological Association (APA), APA's various divisions, and state psychological associations should also be included.

This kind of network gives you an ongoing stream of information. Your job is to sort through the constant flow, find the most important pieces, and act on this information wisely.

Rights and duties. During the final year or so of your training as a psychologist, you tend to grow tired of all of the supervision and constraints. You long for a time when you can practice as you see fit. As you move out on your own, you soon recognize that the choices are now yours. You can make your own commitments and take advantage of them (Mintzberg, 1973). This gives you a true sense of elation.

However, as you make commitments, you also accumulate responsibilities. It is your right to decide what you will do, but it is also your duty to perform well. You now realize that you have traded the regulatory system of the training institution for the one that guides us as we operate independently. It includes the policies, procedures, norms, and values of any organization for which you work, including your own practice, and the legal and ethical frameworks erected around the profession of psychology during the past 40 years. Miller and Sales review these regulatory issues in more detail in chapter 8.

The real world of psychological practice is a complicated existence full of the ambiguous shaded meanings and events of life. Often, you will practice at the limit of your knowledge, skill, and ability and at the very edge of legal restriction. Maintaining a sense of propriety about your rights and duties, using your support networks wisely, and knowing who you are and where you are going will enable you to make prudent decisions.

In addition to Mintzberg's (1973) characteristics of work, there are four additional factors that are equally important to consider in your work as a practitioner.

The pressure to perform. From the moment you enter graduate training, you are engulfed by an environment that demands achievement. Academic and practice requirements are stiff. You quickly lose sight of your personal life. Competition for grades is intense and encouraged by the faculty. The environment provides a steady stream of criticism in the form of grades, supervisor's remarks, fellow students' comments, and the overall questions of what and how you are doing. You adjust to the pressure psychologically, physically, and socially. It is an intense, demanding, and stressful experience, which produces a significant number of casualties. You cannot escape from this experience unchanged.

As you leave the training environment, you feel that a major burden is being lifted from you physically and emotionally. You have a real and deserved sense of accomplishment and a glowing sense of anticipation about the possibilities ahead. In many ways, you are not prepared for an intensification of the graduate school process. Yet, in a very real way, this is exactly what happens in the world of professional practice.

Most often, you trade the school environment for a full- or part-time job in an organization. Your practice will be limited by the policies, procedures, and management structure of the enterprise. Managerial supervision and support replace faculty oversight. Your goals may be established for you. The only real latitude that you may have is to accept the job or not. The pressure of graded performance continues in the form of the annual performance and salary review. The pressure to perform increases, because criticism from clients, colleagues, and supervisors can directly affect your take-home pay and whether you will continue to have a job.

You may leave an organization to establish your own business. Usually, the major motive is to gain a sense of control over your own life. Although you do gain more control, if anything, the pressures to perform increase. You must rebuild all of the confining and supporting structures of an organization. You need to establish financial and management systems and set policies and procedures.

Beyond these pressures lies the ominous and sometimes excruciating experience of marketing your services. Gone are the organization's visibility and marketing muscle. These are replaced by your own time, energy, and savvy. Making enough money for the payroll depends on having satisfied, paying customers. There is no more critical group in the world. All of the legal, regulatory, competitive, and financial pressures are faced alone without the support of other team members in independent practice.

To be sure, there are very real pleasures in professional life. However, it is important to recognize that the pressure to perform will continue throughout your career.

Professional isolation and the need for support systems. The work characteristics described thus far can be overwhelming to any one of us. Most of us adapt well to our niches. However, one of the problems that frequently arises because of the characteristics of professional work is a feeling of isolation and a consequent need for sources of external support.

For independent practitioners, the experience of isolation is easy to identify and describe. The work life of an independent practitioner consists of sitting alone in an office, which may or may not be well appointed, and seeing a (hopefully) never-ending stream of clients. There are fleeting contacts with colleagues who support or collaborate on specific cases, but the pressure to perform with each client continues unabated. External regulatory and market pressures affect everything. Frequently, you will have a profound sense of loneliness and isolation.

The problem of isolation in institutional and consulting practices is less visible and, frequently, less intense. In a sense, organizations were created to solve many of the problems of the cottage industry through proliferation of support structures and specialization by colleagues. However, in some cases organizations produce cold, sterile, and even hostile climates that are far more difficult to manage than a quiet private practice. Hypercompetitive colleagues, pathological supervision structures, and the day-to-day bombardment from multiple sources can leave you feeling hopelessly alone and looking for shelter.

The answer lies in developing your own support network. Colleagues can give you a safe place to talk about the pounding from clients and supervisors. They can provide intellectual support and stimulation, helping to fill the gaps in your own knowledge, skill, and ability. The network can provide avenues of emotional and physical escape, because you can leave the job and go to a professional meeting or convention. It can help you cope with the stresses associated with dealing with the unknown. Research has clearly demonstrated that humans and other animals are more daring, inquisitive, and courageous when they move into new environments if they feel that they are strongly and warmly supported. The absence of such support can be a recipe for professional disaster. The importance of these collegial networks cannot be overemphasized.

Staying technically current. We live in an era of information overload. "Infoglut" is real. We practice psychology based on the knowledge and skill obtained in school, yet, the research and development base for psychology has expanded enormously. *Psychological Abstracts* incorporates articles from over 10,000 sources relevant to psychology. This data must be integrated into your day-to-day practice despite the pressures described earlier. You have little time to stay abreast, but the risks of failing your clients, malpractice litigation, and potential censure of other ethical and legal systems makes this a real and critical problem.

Managing this integration is difficult. You must begin with the certain awareness that your information foundations are eroding continuously. The awareness leads you, in turn, to develop a cautious approach to decision making and an anxiety- and curiosity-based commitment to shore up the foundation constantly. Again, your support network becomes a central resource in handling this problem. Careful shaping of your network should enable you to keep abreast of most of the critical developments in psychology that are relevant to your chosen area of practice.

Joys and satisfactions. Most of the discussion so far has emphasized the more difficult and somewhat negative aspects of professional work. It is absolutely essential to realize that everyday, you should reap an enormous harvest of joy and pleasure from what you do in psychology. This joy springs from four basic sources.

First, there is the true and honest delight in helping people. For the most part, the practice of psychology consists of assisting people and organizations with their problems. Watching clients grow as they use the resources you help them to develop is deeply gratifying.

Second, performing competently can help you to be happy. Like the well-trained athlete after a particularly difficult game or practice, you know when your knowledge and abilities have been put to the test. Using your abilities effectively can provide a lasting and intense source of well-deserved pride about your work and yourself.

Third, professional work can facilitate a profound strengthening and deepening of the characteristics of the heart. Maccoby (1976) described this as follows:

> Considered as not separate from but integrated with the head (and the rest of the body), the development of the heart determines not only compassion and generosity, but also one's perception–experience, the quality of knowledge, capacity for affirmation (of truth or sham, beauty or ugliness), and the will to action (courage).

> The quality of perception depends on our openness to experience. We can see that another person is sad or happy, but if our hearts are open to him, we also experience with him. Empathy and compassion, or experiencing together with another person, are activities of an open, listening heart. (pp. 179–180)

Finally, the economic rewards for working in a profession are well known and appreciated. Despite the changes in the marketplace, the difficulties with competition, and the problems associated with practice in psychology, the vast majority of psychologists are able to find or create jobs that pay well. This might be the most visible reward. Being able to climb out of debt, provide for yourself and your family, and execute a financial-security package are all part of a successful practice in psychology. (Financial issues are discussed further in chapter 9.)

Exercise 6.1 Strengths and Weaknesses

The goals of this exercise are first, to help you discover how hard you can work and, second, to assist you in looking at some of your professional strengths and weaknesses.

1. How hard can you work? Try to answer the following questions as truthfully as you can.
   a. What is the longest number of hours that you have worked without a substantial rest period?
   b. What is the longest number of days in succession that you have worked without a full day off?
   c. What is the longest period of time that you have gone without at least a full week of vacation?
   d. How many hours of sleep do you typically need per night? Per week?
   e. How many hours per week do you need for eating, chores, recreation, relationships, rest, and so forth?
   f. How many hours per week do you like to work?
   The answers to these questions will give you some idea about how you can and do handle the pace of your life and what, if any, spare capacity you have to handle an additional load if you want or need to do so.
2. What are your professional strengths and weaknesses? Again, try to answer the following questions as truthfully as you can.
   a. Rank order your skills in the following areas: direct services such as psychotherapy, testing, consultation; administration; research design and methodology; writing; speaking; obtaining grants; teaching; working with groups; evaluating programs, and so forth.
   b. Using Mintzberg's (1973) forms of media identified earlier, pick out those which you feel you are particularly skilled at and those which you feel could use some work.
   c. How do you learn best? What is your own style of mastering a new concept or skill?

These answers should give you a pretty good idea of where you are and some notion of where to start to try to change things if necessary.

Transitions. Sometime during the first year or two in your first job, you are going to feel the first nagging tugs of boredom. It may happen the third or sixth time you see a client presenting a problem that you have already come to understand thoroughly. It may be when you go to a conference and realize that your own knowledge and experience in an area exceeds that of a presenter. It may also occur the umpteenth time you try to persuade an administrator that your ideas deserve financial and political support. You will not realize it at the time, but this signals a growing sense of dissatisfaction and the beginning of the end of the first stage of your career in psychology.

If you are savvy, you will heed these signals and begin to think seriously about what you want to do next. You will manage your transition into the middle stage of your career wisely if you use the material provided in this book, especially in the last three chapters. As you simultaneously reflect on what you have accomplished and look forward to what you might do next, you will understand how the adaptation process works. You can see clearly how your efforts applied through time have led you to sustained achievement. You can be confident that you can continue to grow. You should also see that it takes large chunks of time to make major progress. The decision to take your next position or to change your present one must be guided both by what you believe you want to do and by what you believe is the next best step to move you toward the capstone you have tentatively selected.

Exercise 6.2 Initiating a Transition

1. If you are in graduate school, sit down with a pen and a sheet of paper and make two lists.
   a. Head the first list "What I Know in Psychology." Write down the topics and issues that you could talk spontaneously about for 10 or 15 minutes. Also include the areas that you could do a formal presentation on with a few hours of preparation. You might find yourself including such things as the major categories of psychopathology, key elements in the social organization of schools, research design, test construction, what makes a group tick, or the normal stages of human development. The list should be at least half a page in length.
   b. Now head the second one "What I Can Do to Apply What I Know." Write down the specific skills that you believe you have mastered. Your list might include designing a test, interviewing a client, taking a history, doing systematic desensitization, consulting with a teacher about a child,

programming a computer, writing a psychological report, or teaching a class. Exhaust the possibilities.

c. Review your lists. This represents your definition of who you are as a psychologist. Are there glaring areas of weakness in your knowledge or skills that you think should be strengthened? Don't be surprised if there are. Also, are there islands of strength, subject and skill areas about which you feel confident? You can use your list to select other courses you could take or practicum experiences that would be useful. The lists will be helpful when you go to construct your first résumé.

2. If you are finishing graduate school or are in your first job, take some time and start thinking about the idea of potential capstones for your career (see Hollander's explanation in chapter 4). It may seem stupid to spend time considering the end of your 40 or 50 years in psychology, but I promise you that the time will be well spent. If one or more ideas strikes you as fun or interesting, or if you have the notion that it would be very satisfying to look back on your career at some time and say "I did that!", jot them down. Next, try to find someone in psychology who is doing something similar. Talk to your friends, colleagues, or supervisors. Identify some prospects. Then call them and offer to take one or more of them to lunch. At lunch, explain that you are doing some career planning and are considering moving in directions in which you believe they have some experience and expertise. Tell them that you would like to seek some advice from them. Most psychologists will make time for a colleague. When you sit down over lunch (pay for it), tell him or her that you are considering positions like the one he or she has and want to get an idea about what steps you will need to take in order to get there. Review the issues and themes identified earlier, and ask the person to describe what he or she does, how he or she got the position, what knowledge one needs to function well, what ethical and personal problems are involved in the position, and so fourth. At the end of the lunch, you will have a much better idea about that particular direction of your career. You can base some of your present plans on real information rather than speculation.

Stage II—The Experienced Psychologist

If you are an experienced psychologist, about a decade ago you began concrete steps to enter the field. After 6 or 7 years of education and 2 or 3 years or more of practical experience, you now can legitimately call yourself a practitioner. You have a sense of pride and feel relief about your achievement.

In a way, you are very much like the early settlers of our country. They decided that they did not like it where they were and organized themselves to come to a new land. The journey was long and arduous. However, on arrival, they faced a new and very complicated question, "Now that I'm here, what should I do?"

This is the central issue of the second stage of your practitioner career. You can now practice psychology. You have 3 or 4 decades of productive time and energy ahead of you. How are you going to use that time? You have energy, knowledge, skills, abilities, and about 35 years to use them for yourself, your family, and the good of the world. Let's begin to examine this issue through an example.

Example 6.1 So Now What?

Pat Brown is a young clinical psychologist. Pat graduated from a major university with a PhD in clinical psychology 3 years ago. Pat's first job has been in the psychology department of a Veterans Administration (VA) hospital. Pat has been licensed to practice in the state for 18 months.

After working under supervision during the internship and first year and a half at the hospital, Pat has become increasingly more independent with the aid and support of the department director. Pat's years of training and experience have led to the development of substantial expertise in rehabilitation, crisis intervention, psychological evaluation, various forms of psychotherapeutic intervention, and program evaluation. For the most part, Pat has been reasonably happy and productive.

Recently, Pat got married to another professional person. The two of them are committed to raising a family of at least two children and supporting each other in their careers. They both have good salaries in their positions. They have purchased a house and are slowly putting the pieces of their life together. However, they realize that, shortly, they will have a number of crucial decisions to make concerning where they will settle down, the comparative investments of time and energy in career and family, and the type of lifestyle they wish to lead. They have agreed to explore their options both as individuals and as a couple.

Without realizing it, Pat quickly stumbles onto the capstone issue. Pondering the question, "What do I want to do?" Pat devises the following list of possibilities:

1. Stay at the VA hospital—routine promotions, good family life.
2. Stay at the VA hospital—pursue directorship.
3. Pursue directorship at another VA hospital.
4. Start a private practice—full- or part-time.
5. Move into the rehabilitation field full-time.
6. Full-time research or evaluation.
7. Obtain additional credentials (law, administration, research, professional practice of health psychology, or psychotherapy).

Pat's spouse comes up with a similar list. They see that they have a wide assortment of career paths and lifestyles from which to choose. They also understand that they need to collect a lot more information on each before they can make an informed decision.

The problem for Pat or for any of the rest of us in the field is that rational decision making is only part of the solution. The other part comes from our psychological, physical, and social responses to our decisions. We can identify and explore options, collect information, and make the best choices given the alternatives. However, we must always live with the consequences.

The process of adaptation to the niches we select is both exciting and painful. At times, our decision is correct, and we find that we can create a wonderful fit for ourselves. At other times, we find that we have made a mistake and that the job/niche is simply unsuitable. Remember, 35 years is a long time. Decisions and positions that work for us at the age of 30 may not succeed at the ages of 40 or 50. Stage II is a lifetime for each of us.

Stage-II strategies. There are several major types of strategies that you can use in the pursuit of your capstone or simply in chasing personal and professional goals. The following treatment of strategies does not exhaust the possibilities nor deal with some of the explicit tactics I will discuss later. Figure 6.1 presents a chart of the principal strategies and some example niches in each of the categories.

There are four basic strategies or courses that you can pursue in your career. In the *specialist* category, you stay close to a particular area of expertise through most of your career, although you might exercise your skills in a variety of ways. In the *generalist* category, you continually branch off into new areas of practice and different jobs. You take the knowledge and skills you've gained in each position with you to the next; however, some technical information and specific skills will not apply in each new job. As a *beachcomber*, you meander from position to position without any true sense of capstone or career plan. You let yourself be open to opportunities for new growth, or you simply move on out of boredom when the situation demands. As a *climber*, you are the type of person who has an idea about what you want to pursue in your career, and you move systematically to obtain it as the environment permits. Each of these is a valid career strategy for practitioners.

Figure 6.1 also provides a series of example niches that a psychologist might occupy as he or she uses a particular strategy. In the specialist/beachcomber cell, we see a clinician who prefers to do work providing direct services. The individual moves from organization to organization accumulating experience with different client populations and settings, but always in the role of a direct service provider. A climber/specialist is exemplified by someone who goes to work in a testing and measurement company and seeks to advance to a senior management position in the technical and administrative sides of the business. Different jobs are obtained within the company, but they are all tied together through the provision of test design, construction, and delivery. Eventually, the person reaches a senior management position in the firm.

Similarly, a climbing/generalist who starts to work as a school psychologist in an educational system might move naturally and easily into program-evaluation services and from there into curriculum-design responsibilities. Consultation to schools and a program directorship ultimately lead the individual to a position as assistant superintendent of schools in the district. In the capstone, all of the knowledge and skills acquired in the previous positions can be applied with good effect.

The final example is an applied social psychologist who starts out doing research. Soon, he or she moves into an administrative position that allows for the application of research expertise. The growing visibility and knowledge makes this a valuable consultation experience. Eventually, an agency recruits him or her as a director. Contacts acquired lead to positions in the federal and state bureaucracies. Again, the individual can construct a successful career without a detailed blueprint.

Peters (1987) offered a series of 45 specific recommendations grouped into five major prescriptions for developing business and professional strategies in the mod-

	Beachcombing	Climbing
Specialist	Niches CMHC Clinician Corrections Clinician State Hospitel Clinician Private Hospital Clinician Independent Practitioner Public School Superintendent	Niches Test Design Product Manager Sales Consultant Unit Manager Company Vice President Company President
Generalist	Niches Survey Research Program Director Consultant Agency Director NIMH Staff State Government	Niches Psychological Testing Program Evaluation Curriculum Designer Administrative Consultant Director of Evaluation Services Assistant School Superintendent

Figure 6.1. Strategies for career advancement.

ern era. These include (a) creating total customer responsiveness; (b) pursuing fast-paced innovation; (c) achieving flexibility by empowering people; (d) learning to love change: a new view of leadership at all levels; and (e) building systems for a world turned upside down. These suggestions are thought provoking even for individual psychologists pursuing careers, because they flow out of an understanding of the world as an increasingly competitive and chaotic place in which to do business. Reading this material will reinforce the basic approach to career development advocated in this book.

However, you must understand that *there is no one true path to success in psychology* or any other profession. You must make choices based on your knowledge, skills, abilities, interests, and other restraining or supportive forces. You may also find yourself blending different strategies during Stage II of your career. You might begin with a firm notion of a capstone, but run into a roadblock or burnout as described by Dory Hollander in chapter 4 of this book. In this situation, you could relax a little, take a meaningful but less ladder-oriented position and wait to catch your breath. After you catch your breath, you could look for a more exciting opportunity. Similarly, you may start with no particular idea of what you want and take a series of interesting jobs for 10 years or more before you discover or decide what you really want to pursue. Regardless of the path you choose, you can find fulfillment and achievement in your career if you know how to manage it.

Exercise 6.3 Your Perfect Job

Assume that you are in the early or middle phase of Stage II and that you have had at least two different jobs in psychology. You are a little bored with what you are doing, but at the moment, you do not have a burning desire to push yourself in any particular direction. You may also have constraints such as geography, children, or your spouse's career to consider. Do the following and take notes as you go through the steps:

1. Go back to Exercise 2 and try to define who you are as a psychologist at the present time. Be as honest in your appraisal as possible.
2. Now, think about the jobs that you have had. What did you like and dislike about them? What tasks did you perform that gave you satisfaction? What working conditions did you relish or hate? Which colleagues did you enjoy the most?
3. Next, think about what your true interests are now. This will be reflected in many subtle ways in the daily activities of your life. What are you reading that excites you? As you sort through the junk mail that offers books, conferences, and educational programs, which of the advertisements do you read all the way through? What conferences have you attended recently, and what did you enjoy about them? This exercise should give you some idea about possible areas that you would like to explore further.
4. Sit down with any lists or notes you have and design your next perfect job. Make sure that your blueprint includes the following details:
   a. Geographic location
   b. Organizational setting
   c. General area in psychology (or other field)
   d. Job title
   e. Description of duties (include percentages of time you want to spend in various activities each week)
   f. Salary desired
   g. Fringe benefits desired (include vacations, time you must put into the

job to be successful, office space, furniture, travel benefits, professional-development support, child care, growth potential in the job, pension plans, insurances, etc.)

   h. Organizational climate (colleagues, attitudes about work, communication, goal setting, reward systems, problem solving, and decision-making styles)
   i. When would you be ready to assume the position?

5. Now make a list of all the people you know who live in the geographic area that you have selected and who practice in the subarea of psychology which you have chosen who might know about jobs like the one you have designed. Set aside a 1/2 hour each week to start calling these people to discuss your dream job and to find out if they know of any possibilities that are reasonably close matches.

Stage III—The Mature Psychologist

The final stage of your career does not arrive with the clarity of your initial introduction into the field. Rather, it dawns slowly like a lazy fall sunrise. One of my colleagues summarized it best when he said to me, "I'm pretty well set now financially, and I figure that I have about 10 more years of vigorous professional activity in me. My problem now is to decide how I want to best use that time." I cannot think of a more succinct description of the major task of the final stage of a professional career.

Having spent several decades working in psychology, you now have an excellent idea about what you can do and what you like to do. You know how much time projects take and how much energy you have. The closing years of practice are increasingly concerned with making sure that you are on firm financial ground and selecting some activities that let you finish off with good, positive feelings about what you have accomplished. These end-game activities will vary widely according to your strategy, needs, previous accomplishments, and goals.

For climbers, the last decade of professional activity usually offers the best opportunities to reach those long-sought capstones. With the accumulation of experience, visible achievement, and connections, bigger jobs with greater responsibility and authority become more possible. For beachcombers, the last decade is about filling in the gaps, trying to do those activities that you always thought would be interesting and stimulating, but never could quite get around to doing. Some psychologists choose not to retire at all and merely reduce the number of hours they work to allow for a greater amount of leisure time to pursue other activities. Whatever you choose to do, remember that the transition to retirement can be quite difficult for many people. Retirement planning is essential to the maintenance of your health and well-being throughout the rest of your life.

Practical Matters

No matter what stage of your career you are in, and regardless of which strategy you choose to pursue, you are going to be in the real world with real people. There are a variety of very practical issues that you will face as a result of these daily pressures. What follows is a discussion of several of the most important concerns.

Politics and Power

As discussed in chapters 2 through 4 of this book, politics and power are central features of life. We cannot escape them. Even with all of our training in psychology, we are still subject to them as they operate in and around the organizations to which we belong and through which we work.

In every organization, there are multiple cultures operating with their own norms and rules. Each of these cultures generates a political life that centers on the distribution of power, money, influence, information, positions, staff, buildings and space, and so forth. The major cultures include administration, information services, finance, public affairs, production/services, achievement (marketing, sales, research, and design), and social life. Most often, psychologists find themselves in the professional worlds of the achievement or service cultures. It is here, in the interplay of ideas, the production of research, or the provision of services that we typically spend the majority of our careers.

All of the issues and techniques described in chapters 2, 3, and 4 apply to psychologists in practice. You must be able to diagnose the type of organization in which you work or design the type of organization through which you wish to practice. In the service organizations in which you will usually find yourselves, there are several important points to keep in mind.

First, there is real power in practice excellence. Having the knowledge and skill to help others with their problems and developing a reputation for doing so are the easiest ways for most practitioners to begin to build a base of power. Remember, each satisfied client probably has a family and a network of friends, and some have an organization with other potential clients in it. Do not be afraid to promote yourself within the bounds of professional propriety. Letting your clients know that you are available to consult with others, asking them for a reference or a letter of satisfaction to the director of the agency or president of the company, and providing them with a copy of your card or brochure are all helpful and easy steps in building a power base for practice.

Second, if you work in a medical institution, remember that the medical culture has different rules and norms than the psychological culture in which you were socialized. Medical cultures vary widely on how authoritarian they are and on how accepting of other types of providers they are. Psychologists are every bit as intelligent as physicians, but our knowledge and practice bases vary significantly. Careful assessment of the medical culture is necessary as you enter any of these organizations. Thousands of psychologists practice safely and successfully in them. Similar issues are important when working in educational systems or any other organization with a dedicated purpose, rigorous traditions, and a separate professional-development ladder.

Finally, no matter how much you wish it were not true, every organization has its own brand of politics. Decisions are made and resources are allocated for rational reasons, because of relationships, and for less desirable purposes such as to curry favor, repay debts, and gain control. Guiding your own career through political water requires an acknowledgment that politics are important, good assessment skills, and the ability to design and implement a strategy that will both protect and advance your interests. Your information network, negotiation skills, and communication ability will be crucial in helping you to do this.

Let us illustrate these points with a brief example.

Example 6.2 The Reality of Power

Chris Matthews worked as a clinician in a moderate-sized private practice in a suburban area. Chris had joined the practice after finishing an internship in the same city. Chris's strengths were in individual psychotherapy, diagnostic testing, and biofeedback. Marriage and family therapy, hypnosis, public speaking, consultation, and education services were of no interest to Chris.

The owner of the practice had commented on several occasions that skills in these latter areas were vitally important to achieving success in that organization. The majority of referrals the practice received were for marital and family problems, and every member of the clinical staff was expected to do his or her share of this work. In addition, the staff members were required to market their own services through the development of consultation contracts, creation of public speaking opportunities, and development of new types of clients. Chris had steadfastly refused to do these activities for some time, repeatedly pointing out that his lack of interest and skill put clients at risk if Chris was forced to provide the services.

During the past 2 months, Chris had noticed a sharp drop in the number of referrals that the organization was providing to him. Initially, Chris enjoyed the respite. However, because Chris's salary was solely dependent on the number of clients that received services, it soon became a matter of some importance.

Chris first checked with several colleagues in the practice to see if their referrals were also down. They reported that they had not experienced any unusual decline. Chris now understood that the organization was sending him a message, but he was unclear about exactly what the message was. Chris decided to talk to the clinical director, an amiable and talented psychologist who ran the practice for the owner.

The director confirmed that the referrals to Chris had been down during the past 2 months. He reassured Chris that he would do all that he could to increase the number, but he pointed out that the substantial majority of referrals received during that time were requests for marital counseling. The director offered to supervise him if Chris would be willing to take on several marital cases. Chris thought it over quickly and agreed to accept the referrals and the supervision.

In this example, we see a straightforward case of someone refusing to understand the structure of the organization in which she or he works and deciding not to play by the rules. When informal communication failed to change Chris's behavior, financial sanctions were applied and were immediately successful. The costs of the sanctions to Chris's self-respect and loyalty to the organization are not dealt with in this example, but are none the less real components of the exchange. The owner of the practice obviously believed that Chris had to change and used financial leverage to accomplish the task. These tactics are common in many organizations. Failure to diagnose and engage in power-development strategy, combined with poor negotiation skills, can easily lead to outcomes like this one.

The Role of Social Support

To begin with, there is now ample evidence that individuals with good social-support systems are better able to tolerate the normal stresses and strains of life. Having a spouse and children, a significant other, or a network of close friends to whom you can turn when you have a lousy day or when your career takes a turn for the worse significantly improves your chances to weather these storms without major damage.

Social networks permit and, at times, force us to grow in ways that are different from what the adaptation to professional life demands. If we are open to opportunities, families and friends can expand our spiritual selves. We cannot be immune to the miracle of childbirth. We must stand in awe of the process of physical and emotional maturation as our children grow before our eyes. We are humbled in the face of trying to support the human development of a spouse, a lover, or very close friends. These lessons cannot be recreated in the classroom or office. They must be lived. Through this living process, we are enriched beyond imagining. This stretching and expanding of our own experiences often works to our advantage in our practices as we come to understand many of the difficulties that clients are troubled by through what happens in our own lives.

Families, lovers, and friends are people with whom we can invest our time, energy, and talent. When our careers hit natural low spots, the people who are close to us can absorb our energy and investment and return them with interest. Through the expansion of ourselves in the roles of spouse, lover, friend, and parent, we become different people, often more capable, loving, and understanding.

Families and friends can also have negative influences on us. If our relationship with our spouse or lover is not supportive, it creates additional stress and tension in our lives. Rather than offering a safe haven from the natural storms of our professional lives, we can have the experience of leaving a thunderstorm at work and entering a hurricane at home. Similarly, if there are problems with a child, friend, or other family member, it can worry us continuously, interfering with every aspect of our professional lives. When times are tough at work and at home, there is no such thing as a safe harbor.

As I described earlier, professional life is draining. It will take as much time as you have and more to create success for yourself. Families and friends demand attention just as intensely as careers and even more righteously. The requirements of maintaining a home, supporting a spouse or lover in his or her own life and career, and investing in the lives of our children and friends can burden already-busy practitioners. The time and energy invested are real. The resources are not available to see other clients, develop new skills or areas of knowledge, or find new colleagues. In economic terms, these are the opportunity costs of having social support. In other words, it is difficult if not impossible to have it all. When there are limited resources, something must give.

The majority of psychologists decide at some time in their lives to get married, and a majority of those also decide to have children. These decisions are made in a variety of ways. At times, individuals simply do what seems right at the moment. Others agonize over the decision, trying to foresee all of the unintended consequences that might occur in the future. No matter how you make the choice, having a family will have several major effects on your career.

Families create complex financial pressures for us. On the positive side, many psychologists are in two-career marriages that dramatically expand the financial resources available. On the negative side, with a family, there appears to be an infinite variety of places for money to be invested. Children and homes are expensive to support. These needs drive us to invest more time into practice to increase our income. However, the social and emotional pressure to be available to our families and friends continues unabated. The net result can be a sort of subtle, emotional frenzy as we struggle constantly to maintain our balance against the variable and conflicting pressures. Chapter 9 discusses financial issues in more detail.

Most of us learn to cope successfully with the conflicting demands of career and social-support systems, and most of us grow in the process and are better people because of it. Nevertheless, some of us are permanently injured or scarred by the experience. Facing up to the important role of families and other sources of social support in our lives, consequently, is a matter of intense practical concern for all of us.

Establishing Your Own Business

At some time in your career as a practitioner, you are going to start thinking about the issue of creating your own business. Despite the support and benefits of working in an organization, you will be naturally drawn to the question of whether you can make it on your own initiative. The allure of independence and increased financial reward will result in a sort of mental experiment. The central question in this experiment is, "what would it take to succeed in my own company?"

There is not sufficient space in this book to do justice to the complexities of establishing and maintaining your own business. A number of excellent references are available that cover small business, private practice, and consulting (Kaye, 1986; Pressman, 1979; Rachman, 1988; Silvester, 1984). The reference list at the end of this chapter provides information on these for you. However, there are several key issues that you will confront if you embark on the challenging journey of creating your own company.

Market analysis. Most of us know intuitively that businesses start with an idea. You have a product or service to offer, and your job is to figure out how to let people know about it and how to convince them to use it.

The reality is that good ideas are easy, but building a successful business is hard. Before you do anything else, you must do a market analysis to determine if your service or product has potential customers; if it does, you must find out where these customers are, and what it will take to reach them. This is the core of a market analysis. The main tasks are as follows:

1. *Define your products and services.* What kinds of psychological products and services do you want to provide to your customers? Most clinically oriented practitioners naturally think of evaluations, therapeutic services, consultation and education, training, and supervision—in other words, the models in which you were trained. Industrial/organizational practitioners will lean to consultation, test design and construction, organizational development, training, selection, etc. Associated with this issue is the complex question of specialization. Should you narrow the focus of what you will offer potential customers? Or should you try to be all things to all people? You cannot answer this central question by yourself. In a sense, it is not up to you alone to define your services.
2. *Explore your environment.* Your business cannot be built in isolation. You must look at where the customers for your services are, who your competitors are, and what it will take to get your share of the market. As you explore, the issues of competition, niche, and location will become prominent. You must position yourself in the general business environment and pitch against the opposition providing similar products and services. We have discussed the issue of defining your niche in chapter 2 and earlier in this chapter as well. The success of your business venture depends on how well you choose your niche and implement your business strategy. Also, keep in mind that the geographic location of your business is a key part of your niche. Location is defined mainly by customers, access, and competition. Questions of cost are secondary.
3. *Write a business plan.* Even if you do not need to solicit the financial support of a bank, a written business plan will force you to clarify your thinking about your company. The more questions and answers you identify in advance, the fewer nasty surprises you will have along the way.

Capitalization. Most businesses, particularly small businesses, fail in the first 3 years because of a lack of working capital. Before you offer a service or sell a product, you will spend a lot of money. To be sure, you can reduce and minimize your up-front costs in a wide variety of ways. Your business plan should address this. However, you are going to need a lot of money to make your business succeed. Business cards, announcements, brochures, office space, furniture, forms, supplies, equipment, office staff and secretarial support, and the costs involved with production require money to get started and to keep operating.

You must try to calculate how much money you will need and then figure out how to get it. Business and personal loans, second mortgages, personal savings, venture capital firms, and wealthy partners must all be considered. If you calculate how much money you need to operate for 5 years independent of any income from your business, you will have a fairly good idea of the underlying capital base your business will demand.

Cash flow. Another problem that kills a lot of businesses is cash flow. You must establish policies and procedures that ensure that you are paid in time to pay your own bills. The worries over uncollected receivables in business can produce extraordinary problems for you.

Many professionals resolve this problem with a cash on delivery policy. Customers receive the service and pay immediately. Others bill monthly or quarterly depending on the customer, the type of service or product delivered, and the desire for the business. The core issue here is that your own creditors can force you out of business if they are not paid in a timely fashion. Also, the emotional stress of being unable to pay your bills and dealing with collection agents and policies should not be underestimated. Managing cash flow so that you can pay yourself and your creditors requires a special brand of toughness that you must acquire quickly if your business is to survive.

Risk and dedication. When you decide to establish your own business, you take a risk. If your business is a part-time practice that you work on in the evening after your full-time job, the risk will be low. If you decide to invest yourself full-time along with major amounts of your own or some other person's capital, the risk is very high. Regardless of the size of the risk, your reputation, self-esteem, and the future course of your career will be affected by the outcome of your decision. The rewards of owning and operating your own business are well known and much ballyhooed. Financial, emotional, and professional freedom are mentioned most frequently. In my view, the reality of business ownership involves trading one set of constraints for another. The policies, procedures, job descriptions, and work flows of an employer are replaced by those you create for yourself.

This raises a last crucial point. No one works less when they start their own business. Almost uniformly, professionals in practice end up working longer hours than their counterparts who work in institutions or organizations. This is a natural consequence of trying to succeed, save money, and avoid failure. You tend to say *yes* very often because you keep an eye on the future. Even if your caseload is full or several contracts are lined up, you always need to worry about where the cash to operate will come from tomorrow. This requires dedication; the desire to succeed must be matched by equal parts of talent and investment of time and energy. The true financial payoffs usually come after years of hard work. The professional and personal rewards are usually more immediate. If they are not, you will probably not be in business for long. Let us explore these issues a little further through an example.

Example 6.3 Building a Private Practice

We left Pat Brown in Example 6.1 having completed an analysis of potential career directions. Let's assume that, with the concurrence of the spouse, Pat decides to stay at the VA hospital and open a part-time private practice. This is the most common way for psychologists to start their own businesses.

Pat knows that the practice will focus on psychotherapeutic interventions. Pat has developed real expertise in helping veterans with their marital and emotional problems. Pat knows that these are central issues for a large number of veterans and for the population in general. The VA hospital policies permit part-time practice for certain classes of employees, and Pat fits into this category.

Pat goes to the department director and tells him about the plan to start a business. The director encourages Pat, gives some instruction on the VA hospital policy, and provides the names of several others in the VA hospital who have gone this route. Pat contacts several of them, arranges meetings, and comes away with a flood of information and a couple of offers of part-time space rental and potential referrals. The major conclusion Pat draws is that it will take more time and thought to put together a coherent plan than Pat had initially believed.

Pat makes other contacts—with an accountant and an attorney familiar with psychological practices—and learns a great deal more about incorporation, legal liability, tax requirements, accounting systems, and the need for good professional help to start a business. On a suggestion from the accountant, Pat gathers information on the distribution of practitioners and population growth in the metropolitan area. Pat identifies several possible regions in the area where a practice might flourish and begins to explore them, looking for potential office locations, referral sources, and competitors.

After evaluating a number of possible sites, Pat settles on the one offering the most promise. A new medical arts building in a burgeoning suburb offers initial financial incentives to sign a lease. A number of other health-care practitioners are moving into the building and are potential referral sources. Pat looks at business cards, stationary, announcements, brochures, office furniture, telephones and other types of business equipment and starts to add up the costs before a client is even seen. The obligations seem overwhelming.

Pat goes back to two of the colleagues who had offered to sublet space to determine what the costs would be and what arrangements could be made. One offers an hourly fee to be paid on a month-to-month basis depending on usage. The second wants a commitment of several evenings per week, a formal sublease for a year, and offers to share some referrals if an appropriate arrangement can be made for the marketing and overhead costs to be reimbursed to him.

After further discussions with the attorney, accountant, several colleagues, and Pat's spouse, an initial commitment is made to rent the one office on an hourly basis, to print business cards and announcements, and to start a very limited part-time practice that can grow along with referrals. Pat is now much more sophisticated about the business of practice. The exploration has taken 9 months. The new venture is launched with an attitude of cautious optimism.

Preventing Burnout and Impairment

Regardless of which subarea of the field you work in, the practice of psychology is challenging and at times, very stressful. As psychologists, we are not immune to the very real threats of burnout and impairment (Kilburg, Nathan, & Thoreson, 1986). You must accept that you are vulnerable. It is likely that you will experience burnout during your career, and it is possible that burnout will develop into a more serious form of impairment. We are all at risk.

Now you'll ask yourself, "So what can I do about it?" In a sense, this whole book has been constructed around the theme of preventing burnout and impairment. The lessons embedded in the material, exercises, and examples describe and illustrate many of the ways that you can get into and out of trouble throughout your career. In my own mind, successful prevention has several components. They are

(a) awareness of risk factors, (b) planning prevention strategies, (c) developing coping skills, and (d) periodic assessments of risk and status.

In previous chapters of this book, a number of the risks attendant to work in the field of psychology have been discussed. Adaptation to work life is a constant challenge that must be met with knowledge, skill, and determination. The demands of the different phases of your career, the people you work with and are related to, and the structure of your personality will determine the exact nature of your own challenge.

If you begin to think systematically about yourself as a professional psychologist and about your career in the field, you must, by definition, develop prevention strategies. Knowing what you face, planning to address problems in advance, and implementing your strategies with technical competence and interpersonal skill should help to keep your ship afloat in even the stormiest of seas.

By now you should realize that my approach to the development of coping skills goes far beyond what you will usually find in books about stress management. Managing your career effectively will enable you to manage the stress that comes with it. No amount of exercise, healthy foods, or meditation will help you to negotiate a good deal for yourself as you enter a new job. Support systems are enormously useful, but you also must be prepared to handle the pace and performance demands of your work. Good managers balance opportunities, demands, pressures, abilities, weaknesses, threats, and strengths to create a wonderful performance. You can prevent burnout and impairment by learning to manage yourself effectively.

References

Kaye, H. (1986). *Inside the technical consulting business: Launching and building your independent practice.* New York: Wiley.

Kilburg, R., Nathan, P., & Thoreson, R. (1986). *Professionals in distress: Issues, syndromes, and solutions in psychology.* Washington, DC: American Psychological Association.

Maccoby, M. (1976). *The gamesman: The new corporate leaders.* New York: Simon and Schuster.

Mintzberg, H. (1973). *The nature of managerial work.* New York: Harper and Row.

Peters, T. (1987). *Thriving on chaos: Handbook for a management revolution.* New York: Alfred A. Knopf.

Pressman, R. M. (1979). *Private practice: A handbook for the independent mental health practitioner.* New York: Gardner Press.

Rachman, D. L. (1988). *Marketing Today (2nd ed.).* Chicago: Dryden Press.

Sales, B. D. (Ed.). (1983). *The professional psychologist's handbook.* New York: Plenum.

Silvester, J. L. (1984). *How to start, finance and operate your own business.* Secaucus, NJ: Lyle Stuart Inc.

7

Richard R. Kilburg

Successfully Managing Career Transitions

Introduction

Robin Martin was a fourth-year graduate student in developmental psychology at a prestigious midwestern university. Robin had completed all course requirements for the doctoral degree and was beginning to work on the prospectus for a dissertation. Although Robin felt a measure of deep satisfaction about finishing most of the program, overall anxiety actually increased as the work on the dissertation was initiated.

The tension was experienced in two related but quite different ways. First, there was the dissertation. Choosing a committee, finding an acceptable topic, and completing the project were complicated and difficult tasks. A great deal depended on making wise choices and following through on them. Second, and even more anxiety arousing, Robin had begun to consider in depth what would happen when the dissertation was finished. A complex array of options and choices had to be confronted.

Robin had to decide if a career in research was suitable. If so, would an academic position or a job with an independent research firm be best? If not research, then psychological practice in consultation or direct services was a possibility. But that would mean more training and the problems of licensure. Another option was a career in management. Robin had met several psychologists who were full-time administrators in research or service organizations. However, Robin had no clue as to the necessary steps to move in that direction.

For the present, Robin believed that an academic position would be best, but the competition was quite stiff. A great deal would depend on establishing a research program. The dissertation would be crucial, and a post doc to further establish the research was probably necessary. Robin frequently felt overwhelmed when considering these issues. When they came up, Robin found the surest cure for the associated anxiety was to read something that might be relevant to her dissertation.

Robin's dilemma is typical for psychologists in the opening phase of their careers. As we have discussed in earlier chapters, the change from graduate student to practicing psychologist is a difficult and challenging transition. However, it is only one of many transitions that confront all of us at different points in our careers.

Successfully managing such transitions is one of the major guarantors of career satisfaction.

The material presented thus far has discussed transitions from a variety of perspectives. We have reviewed the generic issues that confront psychologists in their careers, the skills and concepts needed to understand and survive as a psychologist, the general approaches taken in career management, the Doom Loop, and the specifics of practitioner and scientific pathways. The purposes of this chapter are to review the reasons for career transitions, the process and methods for managing career change, the mechanics of conducting a job search, and several specific issues that transitions force psychologists to confront.

Major Reasons for the Initiation of Transitions

The following is a list of the principal reasons why most psychologists either choose to or are forced to initiate changes in their careers.

1. Burnout
2. Rust out/Boredom
3. Kicked out
4. Life Crises/Life Changes
5. Problems of Fit
6. Better Opportunities

As you can see, there are a variety of potential causes for transitions. We will examine each of them briefly to get a better idea of what is involved.

Burnout

I discussed briefly the phenomenon of burnout in chapter 3, and Dory Hollander described it in chapter 4. As initially described by Freudenberger and Richelson (1980) and further refined by Maslach (1982) and Pines and Aronson (1988), burnout has three primary characteristics: emotional exhaustion, depersonalization, and reduced personal accomplishment. When psychologists develop burnout, they feel emotionally depleted and unable to respond to the demands of clients, colleagues, or students. They distance themselves emotionally from what they are doing and seem to experience life in a cold and harsh way. They often become callous and even cruel to those whom they are supposed to serve or educate. They also begin to feel intensely that they are incompetent and unsuccessful.

These symptoms seem to arise from a complex interaction of forces that pressure professionals. The amount and type of client or student contact plays a major role. As the number of hours and difficult clients and students increases, the likelihood of burnout goes up. Collegial and supervisory contact can also play a significant role in burnout when it is prolonged and negative. Organizational conditions such as lack of positive feedback, role ambiguity and strain, and lack of autonomy and control increase the potential for burnout. Finally, your expectations of a job and of personal achievement, a low sense of self-worth, an inability to be assertive, a greater hostility than average, a strong need for approval from others, and an inability to set personal or professional limits can dramatically increase the probability that you will have problems (Maslach, 1986).

When these symptoms increase in frequency and intensity, you begin to look for what could be making you feel so bad. Eventually, you realize that your job is a key contributor to the problem. At this time, you are likely to think about changing jobs. Depending on your individual situation, these thoughts may or may not lead you to take action.

Rust out/Boredom

As Dory Hollander described in chapter 4, eventually, in almost every job, you reach a plateau. Once you have mastered the basic skills and tasks of a particular position, the job consists of applying what you have learned repeatedly. At some point, the number of variations decreases and you start to see the same situation or pattern over and over. Although there are positive aspects to this experience, such as a feeling of mastery, this repetition can also lead to decreased interest and motivation.

There is ample experimental evidence documenting the effects that task repetition has on motivation (Carver & Scheir, 1981). The important point is that you will gradually become aware that you are bored with a job. In some instances, the boredom can be easily corrected with a change in tasks or responsibilities. In other cases, nothing works, even, as Hollander pointed out, when you are in your capstone position. Over time, there is a slow increase in anger, resentment, and depression. Often, you know what is wrong, but feel absolutely stuck, either because of a lack of other opportunities or because of external factors such as family commitments.

If you stay in a position that has become boring and repetitive, eventually, you begin to "rust out." The decreasing motivation, unwillingness to develop new skills or knowledge, and increasing sense of distance from what you are doing will reach a point at which you start to become incompetent. Your knowledge base is old. You haven't had a new idea or done anything different in years. Your colleagues cease to consult you. Your professional isolation increases. You become a rusted wreck. If you do not take steps to rectify the situation, it is likely that environmental pressure will mount from supervisors and colleagues for you to change. In the worst case, you are fired. In every case, some sort of transition is necessary.

Kicked Out

The most difficult transition for anyone to face comes when your boss tells you, "You're fired!" Sometimes the language is a little more gentle: "We must let you go." "There will be a reduction in force." "It's just not working out." "We need to cut back." "The Committee decided that it would be best not to send your nomination for tenure forward." No matter how the message is transmitted, the results are the same. You are out on the street and must find another job.

The reasons for firing people vary widely. Most often, significant problems arise either with the financial condition of an organization or with how you "fit" into the enterprise. We will talk more about fit later.

Being kicked out of a job is by far the most difficult career transition to make. To begin with, you do not have control over the situation. You are pushed into a crisis that you may or may not be prepared to manage. Your stress level increases significantly with the lack of control. Depending on a variety of factors, there may or may not be other good jobs immediately available. Your search for a position is marred by feelings of insecurity, low self-esteem, and anger, which firings always produce. Finally, your negotiation position is seriously eroded when you need a job. Financial realities, family pressures, and your own feelings can push you to settle for something that might not be in your long-term best interest.

If you do not manage the crisis carefully, being forced into a transition against your will can be a devastating experience. The principles and techniques for handling these situations are somewhat different from those involving changes that you initiate, and they will be discussed in more detail later.

Life Crises/Life Changes

A second form of involuntary transition occurs when you face a crisis or normal, but none the less difficult, change in your life. Psychologists have learned a lot about crises and their management. They are skilled at doing research and at helping both individuals and organizations surmount the difficulties that automatically arise in these situations; however, they are not always prepared to manage catastrophic changes in their own lives.

Crises come in many forms. Serious, life-threatening illnesses frequently cause you to rethink career aspirations and jobs. Sometimes, financial reversals and family problems arise suddenly to upset what had been a stable situation. The career plans and personal needs of a spouse can force you into a job change. Finally, problems on the job or with the organization in which you work can precipitate a crisis.

Life changes can present more subtle but equally difficult situations. Divorcing a spouse often leads to an examination of life style and goals. Changing jobs and locations can provide you with a new start. And the birth of a child will always force changes into your life. Sometimes, you may choose to stay home or to cut back at work so that you can spend more time with your child. At other times, changing jobs to work for a more supportive employer may be necessary. As you age, you will reassess your career periodically. At times, you may decide that it is time for a change even though no one is pushing you to move. Similar situations often arise at different points in your life cycle. What you want to do professionally at the age of 50 will probably be very different from what you want to do at 30, independent of the age dimension. Hollander, Blass, and I have described such situations in previous chapters.

Managing these crises and changes can be quite demanding. Although the emotional challenges are not usually as difficult as when you are fired, the physical and professional problems can be just as difficult. You must be prepared for crises in your life. This may seem to be a paradox; however, I believe that you can develop skills and abilities that will help you through any threatening, catastrophic change. Anticipating the need for such skills and realizing that life is ultimately unpredictable prepares you for difficult times, even if you cannot foresee the exact nature of the challenges.

Problems of Fit

As I described in chapters 2 and 3, we are all constantly working to adapt to the niches we create for ourselves in life. When the transformation process works well, you develop a very nice fit between your professional position and your own knowledge, skills, abilities, and needs. For a wide variety of reasons, the process can go wrong. When this occurs, you usually end up feeling like you did during your adolescence when your shoes and clothes always seemed too small or too big. Nothing fits. Somehow, you do not mesh well with the situation, the job, the colleagues, the boss, and the geographic location. A substantial number of job transitions are initiated because of poor matches. Most people who are fired are also victims of problems of fit.

Although the idea of building a successful niche in your professional career seems like an abstraction, we have discussed many of the characteristics that bring it to life. When there is a good match between what a job demands and what you can provide, you fit. When you like your colleagues and get along with your boss, you fit. When you enjoy where you live and the opportunities the location provides, you fit. When there is a sense of emotional fulfillment from your work, you fit. When any one or several of these features is missing, problems with fit arise. When they do, you may start to consider changing jobs.

Usually, problems of fit are not as apparent as during a crisis. Slowly but surely, you realize that something is wrong. The conclusions you reach are different than those when you recognize burnout or rust out, although burnout and rust out can be the result of a poor fit that has been sustained too long. When you aren't working well in a particular niche, there will be constant emotional pressure and a vague sense that the job is not going well. There may be concrete signs such as poor job performance, increased tension or poor relations with colleagues, or feedback from your boss that your performance is not meeting standards. One of the most difficult situations arises when you recognize that your own personal or professional ethics are being violated in or by an organization. When you start sensing that a position is not working out, pay attention to what is happening. A change in jobs may be necessary sooner rather than later.

Better Opportunities

The ideal way to change jobs is to leave one position for a better one. At times, your work may be recognized sufficiently so that you become the target of recruiting activity by a potential employer. This is the most flattering situation for professionals. Even if you do not accept a position that is offered to you, knowing that others are interested enough and think well enough of you to extend themselves is an enormous morale booster.

Most often, when you change jobs, you believe that you are going into a better situation. This is especially true when the niche that you are leaving leads to a burnout, rust-out, or kicked-out transition. The danger in accepting jobs under such difficult circumstances is that any job may look good if the position you currently have is very bad. Nevertheless, it's true that at times, any change is better than maintaining the status quo.

In her chapter, Dory Hollander described an effective methodology for systematically seeking better opportunities. She called it riding the upward curve to capstone. We do not need to reiterate her presentation here. However, it is crucial for you to understand that you can consistently and deliberately move to improve your career by changing jobs. Dory has demonstrated a solid conceptual and operational approach to the problem. The rest of this chapter will focus on some of the more important mechanics of the process.

Exercise 7.1 Analyze Your Niche

1. Take a sheet of paper and divide it into three columns. Head the first column "work characteristics." Head the second column "degree of satisfaction." Head the third column "need for change."
2. In the first column, make a list of the major duties and responsibilities that you have in your current position. Keep adding to the list until it is reasonably comprehensive (you might look at Hollander's chapter for some ideas to get started). Make sure you include the major work relationships you maintain in and out of your organization. Also include other characteristics of your work, including salary, benefits, support services, office conditions and location, commuting time and route, and so forth.
3. In the second column, rate each of the characteristics on a scale of 1 to 7. Scores of 1 should be given to characteristics that you absolutely hate, and scores of 7 should be given to those that you truly love. After you have rated each of the duties, total your score. Multiply the number of duties on your list by 7. The discrepancy between the two numbers can be interpreted as an index of your job satisfaction.
4. In the third column, rate each of the same characteristics on another scale of 1 to 7. Scores of 7 should be given to characteristics that must be changed immediately or you will do something drastic. Give scores of 1 to characteristics that you would hate to see removed. Again, total your score. The higher your score, the more you need to think about changing jobs.
5. These two scores should be considered together. You may find that your level of satisfaction is not very high, but that your need to change is also not very high. Keep the Doom Loop in mind. You might like to go back and review each of the quadrants to see if your scores tell you anything about where you are. High satisfaction will be associated with liking what you are doing. High need for change may spell boredom, burnout, or possible kicked-out situations.

Managing Change

Now that we have reviewed some of the major reasons for career transitions, we can spend a little time talking about the process of change and what it typically does to people. The discussion will focus on both planned and unplanned change. I will spend more time on unplanned change because of the potential for devastation if it is not handled properly.

Planned Change

In chapter 3, I provided a succinct overview of the nature of planning and its cyclic structure. You might like to go back and review the flowchart from that chapter before reading the rest of this section. In addition, the major exercise I provided concentrated on performing a WOTS UP analysis. These are two major tools for understanding, undertaking, and managing planned change.

In your career, there are going to be times when you recognize the need for change. As we saw in the first section of this chapter, these situations can vary widely. It could be that you want to move on to a more lucrative and challenging position. It could be that you are tired of what you are doing and simply want a change of any kind. It could also be the recognition that change in your organization is imminent and may have negative consequences for you. These situations and many others may push you into a cycle of planned change.

The flowchart in chapter 3 described this process well. For the most part, there are four major interacting components to the process. First, you must gather pertinent information. The importance of Mintzberg's (1973) informational roles is crucial here. If your information network is poor, you will not receive advance warning of impending changes that might affect you adversely. Similarly, if you are poorly connected outside of the organization, you will have a more difficult time moving if a transition is necessary.

Once you have the necessary information, you need to analyze it as is done in a WOTS UP exercise. This puts you in a better position to consider your options. Patience and creativity are called for when considering job changes. Remember, you may live with the choice you make for a substantial period of time. When you have the luxury of not being pressured to make an immediate decision, it is far easier to dream about alternatives.

The third major component of planned change involves making the decision. After the options are drawn up, you have the task of weighing the pros and cons of each. Keep in mind Hollander's notions about capstone and skill clusters. What knowledge, skills, and abilities do you need from your next position to move you forward to your capstone? What have you learned about your own needs, interaction style, and personal values that will help you avoid pitfalls in your next job? What is the next logical step that will give you both flexibility and bargaining strength in the future?

I have often found it useful to make a list of pros and cons concerning any position I take. I rank each of the items on a scale of 1 to 5. For pros, a 5 means that this feature is very attractive or excellent, and a 1 means that you don't like it very much, but it is still a plus.

A con is rated a 5 if it is a real stinker and you might not take the job because of it, and a 1 is given to items that may be annoying, but not fatal. I then sum up my ratings and get an overall idea about how I stack up the various features of the position (or positions). I am frequently surprised by how useful this exercise is. I have usually decided against taking positions where the pros did not substantially outweigh the cons. The ratings give the decision-making process visual substance. This can be very important because of the subtle influence that your emotions can have on the way you make decisions. Eventually, you must choose and trust the results of your planning.

Finally, you must evaluate the decision you made. You will begin doing this almost immediately upon entering a new position. How does your boss treat you? Do you like your colleagues? Are the tasks and activities meaningful and challenging? Do the physical surroundings and attributes of the geographic location meet your needs? Are you really making enough money? The list goes on and on.

It is important to keep the pros and cons exercise for future reference. You can go back to your original ratings and check them against the reality of your perceptions through time. I believe it is important to assess your job status at least once a year.

Managing Emotions and Mechanics

Your emotional responses to planned changes may vary widely. If you are being recruited by someone, you may feel surprised, pleased, and self-confident. If you are burning out in your job and recognize the importance of moving on, you may feel lethargic, depressed, and emotionally distant from work and people. It may take you a while to work up some enthusiasm for change. If you have come to the realization that your job may soon be in jeopardy, you may become quite anxious and angry. This array of feelings is quite natural even if they are difficult to manage.

Although space limitations prohibit me from exploring these emotional responses in great detail, there are several major strategies you can use to help manage them.

First, remember that you are a feeling creature. Your emotions can be your friends if you allow yourself to get to know them well. It is not a great idea to do this for the first time in the middle of a crisis. The power of our emotions can be overwhelming even in good times. Take some time now to get to know your emotional self. Try to identify the physical sensations that you associate with various emotional states, such as joy, surprise, curiosity, anger, anxiety, embarrassment, and sadness. Also, try to understand the internal and external events that lead you to experience these feelings. If you can do this, you will be building a road map of emotions that you can use in any situation. Remember, it is harder to find something without a map.

Second, once you have your map, experiment with it. Try to stretch your understanding and coping ability. If your boss is making you angry, ask yourself why this happens. See if you can identify other feeling states preceding your anger. How do you typically handle your anger? Do you suppress it? Do you complain about the boss to your colleagues or spouse? Do you confront the situation assertively and try to negotiate a better understanding or deal for yourself? Do this for your other major emotional states as well. If your responses to your emotions are stereotyped and rigid, begin to experiment with people in situations in which you feel safe.

Third, try to learn to balance your emotional responses. Your feelings are conditioned by your socialization, relationships, expectations, sex role, and biological makeup. Nevertheless, emotions are malleable. You can learn to find all of your feelings in almost any situation. Simply ask yourself the following questions: Where is my anger level? Do I feel any joy? Am I interested in what is happening? Do I seem embarrassed? Going through a checklist of emotional responses will let you know where you are and, simultaneously, lead you to seek other emotional states that may help safeguard you from the worst of the negative emotional reactions.

Fourth, if all else fails or if you are truly interested, you might like to seek a formal growth experience such as psychotherapy with a well-trained professional. Most metropolitan areas and quite a few rural areas have well-trained people available to help you. Overcoming the stereotypes involved in seeking assistance may be your biggest hurdle. However, anything that you can do to increase your emotional knowledge and ability to handle these powerful tools will eventually pay off when you enter into a change process.

The strategies for managing emotions will vary depending on the situation in which you find yourself. If you are being recruited, you may need to be on guard against overconfidence or pride. Carefully weighing the pros and the cons of the offer is an absolute necessity. If you are experiencing burnout, you may need to mobilize yourself to deal with your depression and sense of depersonalization before you can really begin to search for a job. If you believe you will lose your job soon, you will be very anxious. The irritation, humiliation, and anger that accompany such a situation can lead you to leap before you look carefully at a job. You may need to slow yourself down emotionally to handle a job search under these circumstances.

We will look at the mechanics of the job-search process later. They will be approximately the same regardless of what type of change you are making.

Crises

Figure 7.1 identifies the six stages of a crisis along with the typical events, activities, emotional responses, and phases that accompany them. This figure represents an amalgam of the work of Turner (1976) and Frederick (1980).

It is very easy to apply this framework to job-related crises that arise in psychological careers. This is especially true for burnout, rust-out, or kicked-out scenarios. We will use the kicked-out situation as a means to understand how a crisis can affect you.

In any job, there are a variety of situations that can lead to a particularly dangerous crisis for a person. For practicing psychologists, one of these situations could be an individual or organizational client that threatens your career through legal action. In academia, the situation might involve the failure to get the grants necessary for substantial financial support of your research. Psychologists in management positions frequently encounter problems when political or financial support is withdrawn from their organizations. Most frequently, there is no initial hint that there will be a problem. You proceed with your normal precautionary behavior and expectations of the job. Emotionally, you tend to deny that anything major could go wrong. Anxieties related to worst-case scenarios are repressed or only thought of in the context of "what could happen." Such thoughts are easily dismissed.

In the second phase, a series of events occurs that is at odds with your usual

1. NORMAL STARTING POINT

Events/Activities
- Your normal beliefs/expectations of the work world and its hazards
- Your normal precautionary behavior

Emotional Responses/Phases
- Repression, denial, projection, normal coping

2. INCUBATION

Events/Activities
- A series of events at odds with beliefs/expectations/precautions

Emotional Responses/Phases
- Repression, denial, projection, normal coping

3. PRECIPITATING EVENT

Events/Activities
- Something terrible happens

Emotional Responses/Phases
- Shock, psychic numbing leading to increasing anxiety, anger, anguish, and decreasing self-esteem, the stress response

4. ONSET

Events/Activities
- Effects of event and nature of crisis become known

Emotional Responses/Phases
- Coping: Heroic, honeymoon, disillusionment

5. INITIAL ADJUSTMENT

Events/Activities
- Preliminary post-crisis events: Assess damage, begin salvage

Emotional Responses/Phases
- Coping: Heroic, honeymoon, disillusionment

6. FULL ADJUSTMENT

Events/Activities
- Damage cleared, precautionary behavior assessed and changed

Emotional Responses/Phases
- Reorganization; increased self-esteem, decreased anxiety, anger, anguish; respite/rebound

Figure 7.1. Stages of a Crisis.

expectations of the job. In kicked-out situations, these events most often involve reversals of predicted performance or unexpected interpersonal problems with your boss. You may say or do something to make him or her angry, receive feedback that your performance is not up to standards, or notice that the funding that the organization expected to receive is not forthcoming. Often, the experience is not initially noted as something of import. You deny its significance, repress the potential consequences, and try to continue living as though everything is normal.

In the third phase, something terrible usually happens. You have an all-out fight with your boss, your grant does not receive a high-enough score to merit funding, or the budget of your organization is slashed terribly. Your response to the event is shock, "How could such a thing happen?" A sensation of numbness creeps into everything you do. Your emotions can whip you with anger, terrible anxiety, sadness, or a real sense of failure and embarrassment. You become immobilized.

This event is usually followed by the true onset of the crisis. As time passes, you become aware of the full extent of the problems and their consequences. In the kicked-out scenario, you may actually be informed that you are fired, or you can readily see the eventual likelihood of such an action. You immediately mobilize biologically, psychologically, and socially. In the next section of this chaper, I will describe the actual steps of mobilization used to find another job. For now, let us assume that you review your financial situation, contact friends to inquire about job possibilities, check the help-wanted ads, and prepare to search in earnest.

Your coping at this point may approach heroic proportions. You have plenty of energy and enthusiasm. You are optimistic. You follow the advice of friends and colleagues. You try to remain positive. You tend to concentrate on what you can do and not to think about the worst possible case. You have entered into the fifth stage.

Now you are accurately assessing the damage and trying to develop an action plan that will get you out of the crisis. Your emphasis is still on the positive yet, depending on how long this stage lasts, you can become quite tired. As you review what occurred, you may experience periods of extreme embarrassment and shame, especially if you must tell someone you know that you have lost your job. Anger over what did happen, anxiety about what might happen, and sadness about the losses you have experienced can be constant companions, making constructive action difficult. The longer this phase continues, the more likely it becomes that you will be confronted by serious emotional consequences. At its worst, you can become severely disillusioned and give up hope. Keep the coping strategies described earlier in mind if you find yourself in such a situation.

Eventually, you make proper connections, find a job and begin to move forward again. As Georgine Pion describes in her chapter, the unemployment rate in psychology remains quite low. It is extremely likely that you will find something to your liking. At that point, you will truly begin to recover from the crisis. You must engage in all of the constructive activities necessary to succeed at the new job. This absorbs time and energy. Your anxiety level decreases markedly as you make the transition. The process of behavioral transformation moves you to build a new structure in your job and the relationships attached to it. Your self-esteem rises. You can now tell others about your new challenge. Your anger at your old boss or oganization decreases as your attachment to your new job increases. A few successes have a wonderful cleansing effect on sadness and feelings of loss. You rediscover your sense of joy and curiosity as you settle into the new position.

Under the best of circumstances, you take the opportunity to sit down and analyze the early warning signals that preceded the crisis. You learn from that experience. You are better able to anticipate what might happen. You begin to take new precautions in your job based on the crisis. The next time, you might not be so surprised, shocked, and unprepared for a budget crunch, lost grant, or angry boss.

Managing a Job Search

Conducting a job search can be one of the most difficult, challenging, and, simultaneously, rewarding experiences of your professional career. The odds are that you will have several jobs during your lifetime. Although there are a number of decent, popular books available describing the mechanics of finding a job (Kennedy & Laramore, 1988; Bolles, 1988), I want to review the basics of the process with you. Familiarizing yourself with the necessary ingredients of a good search will help to demystify the process in advance of when you may need to use the information. You may also find that knowing about how to find a job may help you to do some things now that will make conducting a search easier if you find yourself in a crisis.

Phase 1—Knowing Yourself

Even in the middle of a major crisis, such as being fired from your job, you must begin the process of finding a new job by first finding yourself. In the emotional turmoil of a financial and professional disaster, this can be a very tall order under the best of circumstances. However, it is the single most important step that you can take in finding a new position.

If you complete Exercise 7.1 and go through the capstone exercises in Hollander's chapter, you will be off to an excellent start at getting to know yourself as a professional psychologist. You will understand your strengths and weaknesses, your likes and dislikes about your present position (or the one you have just left), and you will have some idea of what will make an excellent next job. This information provides the foundation on which you will build your search campaign. Without this information, you may charge into battle without any idea of what you are trying to accomplish, what your resources are, or how to engage your potential employers. Ideally, you now have a set of materials that provides the following:

1. *Self-definition*—who you are as a person; the nature of your strengths and weaknesses; what motivates you; how you can best present yourself to a potential employer.
2. *List of accomplishments*—the things that you have done and feel most proud of; what you did to make these accomplishments happen; what obstacles you overcame; what you have achieved.
3. *Knowledge, interests, and abilities*—what you know and can teach others; what excites you and motivates you to do things; what you do well (capacities, skills, talents).
4. *Desired working environment*—the degree of structure and support you need; the physical surroundings you wish to work in; the people you want to be around; the type of organizational climate you prefer; the types of

relationships you want; how you prefer assignments to be given; the motivational systems that work best for you.

It is equally important to understand yourself emotionally as you plan your strategy. The earlier sections of this chapter will help you to assess your feeling states and level of emotional comfort. Knowing who you are as a person and how you are likely to react emotionally to different situations gives you a big advantage in conducting a search. Let's assume then that you now have a pretty good idea about who you are as a person and what you have done and want to do as a professional.

Phase 2—Defining Your Objectives

In the crassest sense, you are going to sell yourself to potential employers just as any business attempts to sell its products. If you have done the work in phase 1, you have already started to define yourself as a product. This may sound a bit impersonal, but finding and getting a good job is bound to make you feel better about yourself.

As Hollander pointed out, at each stage in your career, you are trying to determine the correct position to take. Even if you are basically a beachcomber and are comfortable moving from job to job without an overall plan or capstone in mind, it pays to think carefully about what you want in a position.

You need to decide on the *stated objective* for the present stage in your career. This will cover the nature of the job that you are seeking without giving it a specific title. The objective becomes the central theme and guides the construction of your résumé. Some examples of objectives for various subareas of psychology are as follows:

Clinical or counseling.

1. To be responsible for a diverse outpatient caseload in a major health or human service organization, providing cognitive therapy to individuals, systems-oriented therapy to families, and supporting the development of colleagues through in-service education.
2. To manage the service and financial operations of a mental health agency in a major metropolitan area by creating innovative applications of computer software and hardware, building evaluation systems, and working with community leaders to define the best directions for the organization.
3. To establish an independent therapeutic and consultation practice specializing in services to chemically dependent families, education programs for schools and churches, and consultation to local businesses.

Industrial/organizational.

1. To contribute to the growth of a major international manufacturing corporation through the application of organizational and personnel development strategies and techniques.
2. To lead the human resource functions of a major corporation by helping to

solve the people problems of the organization, creating excellent performance-appraisal systems, and identifying strategies to find the best people for the jobs in the company.
3. To provide consultation, management training, and organizational development services to Fortune 1000 companies through the auspices of a well-known training and development firm.

School.

1. To play a principal role in the development and provision of school psychological services, such as consultation, evaluation, and psychotherapy in a large, urban school district.
2. To manage a broad array of consultation, evaluation, and therapeutic services in a rural school system.
3. To lead the educational programs of a progressive school district by working creatively with elected officials, creating innovative funding sources, and building a dynamic educational team.

Academic.

1. To be responsible for expanding a cohesive research program, training future leaders in neuroscience, and assisting in the development of a dynamic department of psychology.
2. To lead a large and diverse department of psychology to a new level of academic and professional excellence through grantspersonship, fund raising, and the identification and nurturance of the talents of individual members of the organization.
3. To develop an innovative, challenging, and dynamic research program in the area of the social perception of behavior, using the latest methods of research design, multivariate and path analysis, and building a team of dedicated faculty members and students.

Notice how these objectives are, simultaneously, general statements of positions desired and specific calls to action. Your own career objective must have some fire in it. It should communicate to a potential employer both what you want to do and your implicit attitude about how you will perform the job. Use action words such as *lead*, *create*, *manage*, *train*, *take responsibility*, *have authority*, and *establish* to convey a sense of direction and excitement. The technique may seem trite and manipulative, but it works. It will show your future boss that you have carefully considered what you want to accomplish.

Exercise 7.2 Define Your Immediate Career Objective

Take a few minutes to review the materials that you have generated. Sort through the lists of strengths, weaknesses, pros, and cons of your last job (or jobs). If it seems useful, create another list of potential jobs that you might like to do. Now, let's try to write several career-objective statements. Make sure that each of your draft statements attends to the following:

1. Find and use a term that defines a general career area. Some examples are research, teaching, clinical services, consultation, leadership, management, test development, and so forth.
2. Identify and list three major strengths that support your ability to perform the tasks of the potential job.
3. Indicate what you can do for your potential employer. Some examples include creating a research program, delivering high-quality services, and building a dynamic department of psychology.

Once you have written a statement that looks and feels right, you are ready to move on to the next phase of your search.

Phase 3—Building Your Résumé

There are many different types of résumés. Elliot Blass gave you some good pointers about how to create one for use in academic settings. Keep in mind that the expectations for a résumé may vary depending on the position you are seeking. Remember that the résumé is one of your major tools for conducting a successful search. It is an advocacy document supporting your claim to a particular position. A good résumé allows you to do the following:

1. Organize your objectives and the documentation supporting them.
2. Provide a guide for interviewers who may be uncomfortable with the process of reviewing your accomplishments and potential contributions.
3. Leave a piece of yourself behind or send it on for others to consider.
4. Remind a potential employer why you created such a wonderful impression.

For general business and most nonacademic settings, the format described below has proven to be very useful. Keep in mind that the information is organized to help you make your arguments look rock solid. The information should be action-oriented, which should help the reader to see you as someone who has significant accomplishments to your credit.

Format.

Heading: Provide your name, address, and home and office telephone numbers in an easy-to-read layout.

Objective: Make Exercise 7.2 work for you here. State your career objective in a clear, concise tone. Imagine that you are reading through a pile of résumés looking for someone to fill a position. What statements will make your résumé stand out from a pile of 40 or 50 others?

Qualifications: Next, state why you can achieve your stated objective. Identify the core of the knowledge, skills, abilities, and experiences available to you and a potential employer. Some examples might include the following:

1. Ten years of consulting and training experience with Fortune 1000 firms using a wide variety of organizational development and educational technologies.
2. Three years of clinical experience in an outpatient setting with individuals, couples, families, and groups from a variety of socioeconomic backgrounds.

Achievements: Now, list a series of specific achievements in the positions you have held that support your objective. These should be tied to the strengths you outlined. If you can provide statistical information that shows the magnitude of your contributions, do so. Use action verbs. State the results of your efforts in a framework that people can understand. Some examples include the following:

1. Carried a caseload of 50 patients with a wide range of diagnoses, averaging 30 hours of treatment per week.
2. Managed the outpatient services of an urban, community mental health center with a full-time staff of 15 clinicians, an annual budget in excess of $500,000, and an average caseload of 700 patients.
3. Taught courses in social psychology, personality psychology, statistics, multivariate design, small-group behavior, social perception, and advanced research techniques.
4. Led the design team to create a new testing and evaluation procedure for clerical staff at a major regional bank resulting in a 30 percent decline in staff turnover and a 25 percent increase in productivity.

Employment: Identify the major positions you have occupied. Do not list anything that would not be supportive to you. Omitting something that might be detrimental is wise in most situations. If it was a job you held for some time, you might need to think carefully about how you would handle a great gap in time on the document. Give the years that you were in each job—1983–1987. You do not have to account for every moment. Any gaps might lead a potential employer to start asking hard questions before you are even asked in for an interview. If it seems wise or appropriate, you can include a brief summary of the major duties you had in each position.

Education: Start with the highest degree obtained. List the area of major, the name of the school, and the date. You can give any other training or educational experience if it supports your stated objective.

Other relevant information: Select other experiences and qualifications that will support your application. Some potential sections include (a) licenses held, (b) special certifications, (c) offices held in professional societies or relevant organizations, (d) honorary societies, (e) appointments to national or state commissions, (f) membership in the National Academy of Sciences or other prestigious organizations, and (g) consultantships.

Bibliography: If you have published any journal articles, chapters, or books, you might provide a list organized in the manner suggested by Elliot Blass in chapter 5 of this book. For nonacademic positions, a bibliography is not usually necessary. However, keep in mind that one of the informal means that psychologists use to measure their value is the written contributions made to the literature. Knowing who will interview you will help to determine if this section is necessary.

I should make one final point. Of course, if you have not written anything, do not feel pressured to provide a list. Artificially padding your résumé can only lead to trouble. Leaving off something detrimental to you has far less negative implications than deliberately stating that you have done something you haven't.

Phase 4—Finding a Job

Congratulations, you have done your homework. Now, you can find a job. I am positive that many people have found great positions without going through the steps outlined so far. Yet, I am equally convinced that proceeding in a systematic fashion will make it easier to move closer to your dream job than an unorganized effort will. The fourth phase of a job search consists of most of the activities usually associated with finding a position.

There are two broad methods for conducting a search, direct and indirect. *Direct methods* include answering advertisements, contacting personnel departments, and filling out applications by using an employment agency or by trying to identify managers who may have a position available. *Indirect methods* capitalize on the networks of people you have created throughout your life. You try to increase the number of individuals who know that you are looking for a job and who might be in a position to create a job or to influence someone who has a position to offer.

As mentioned in chapter 5, many positions in psychology are advertised in *The APA Monitor*, *The Chronicle of Higher Education*, local newspapers, the state associations newsletters. Answering advertisements is a traditional way of getting a job. It is appropriate to answer an ad if there is a good fit between the stated requirements of the position and your qualifications, you have a highly desired set of skills and experiences, or you have time left over from your indirect methods. In answering an ad, remember that there are frequently a great many other candidates seeking the same job. You must meet the minimum qualifications in order to be considered. If you don't, you can save the postage in most cases. Keep the following things in mind as you apply.

1. Take a few days to send in your letter. It may have a better chance of ending up on top of the pile.
2. Send a letter, not your résumé (unless they ask for it). State your qualifications for the job and how you can help them.
3. Don't send your salary history. Outline your experience and say that you will call for an appointment.
4. If you don't hear anything, write a follow-up letter in a week or so. Be tactful. Let them know you are still interested.
5. If possible, identify the administrator responsible for the hiring decision. Write him or her a letter as well.

If you use an employment agency, remember that there are three basic methods of operation. Retainer companies are paid by an enterprise to find someone to fill a particular position. They are usually the only organization permitted to fill the job. Contingency companies get a percentage of the salary from the employer if their candidate is hired. Other companies will take a percentage of your salary for 6 months or a year as the fee for assisting you. Try to interview the agency before you send them anything besides a letter of inquiry. You may well be able to determine if this is an organization with which you want to work.

At times, you may know that someone has a job available. It is appropriate to directly approach the administrator who has the position. Send a letter of introduction organized specifically for the position and the person. If you know someone who can arrange an introduction, take advantage of the opportunity, call the person, and request help. Again, emphasize the potential fit between your abilities, achievements, skills, and the job requirements. In your letter or call, ask for an appointment to discuss the position. Don't try to talk money or discuss any of the details. Remember, you are trying to get in the door and create a competitive advantage for your candidacy.

In using indirect methods, you will be applying much of the knowledge covered in the earlier chapters of this book. You can constantly create networks of people you know regardless of the position that you hold. It is this network that you will use indirectly in finding a job.

You must put aside most of the emotional objections you have about calling people you know and telling them you are looking for a job. The anxiety, embarrassment, and potential hostility you might experience must be mobilized on behalf of your major objective. You are trying to find a good job. Most of the people you know will be glad to help you if asked. They can get you through the front door in many situations and make sure that your application or letter sits on top of the dozens of others in the pile.

With indirect methods, your initial step begins by making a list of people. First, there are the managers who have the available jobs. Second, there are people who know managers who might have these jobs. Finally, there are individuals who are in a position to identify potential companies or individuals by virtue of special information that they have obtained through social, professional, or other types of connections. You undoubtedly know some of these people. You can count on many of them to help you. You are depending on their networks to lead you to your dream job.

Exercise 7.3 Identifying Organizations and People

To begin an indirect approach to a job search, you must start by developing a road map or implementation plan. There are two essential ingredients to this part of your plan—a list of organizations that you might be interested in working for and a list of people you know who might be able to help you.

1. Start by making a list of organizations that interest you. Draw three col-

umns on a sheet of paper. In the first, place the name of the organization. In the second, put the organization's address and telephone number. In the third, identify the principal reason for your interest. There are a wide variety of sources for this information. Any reference librarian can help you find the published information on various organizations.

2. Now, take out several other sheets of paper. Draw four columns and head them as follows: person, rationale, how known, and title. Start with friends and relatives. Extend your list with colleagues—past and present, employers, and other professionals you know in various industries, such as law, medicine, accounting, consulting, insurance, banking, and so forth. Add members of professional associations, people you know from community affiliations, and any other individuals who might take an interest in you. Round out your list with contacts in the management of the organizations in which you are interested. Aim for 50 to 100 names. When you have finished, you have identified the people that will lead you to your next job.

The second step consists of making approaches via the mail and telephone. In most instances, you will first send a letter. It should be short, no more than one page, three or four paragraphs, pleasant in tone, and easy to read. It should lay out exactly what you want the reader to know, conserve the person's time and energy, show you in the best light possible, and open the door to a personalized follow-up.

The letter should start with a statement to seize the attention of the reader. Mention a mutual acquaintance, interest, how you know him or her, or a specific achievement in which he or she might be interested.

Next, shift the focus to yourself. Why are you making contact? For example, "I am planning to move from my present position at Southern University and would be interested in your ideas about other organizations and universities with research strengths in the following areas."

The third part of the letter should build the reader's curiosity about you. Mention two or three key accomplishments.

The fourth part should define the reader's role. Remember, you are not necessarily seeking a job from this person. You are seeking their advice about your plans. You expect them to use their knowledge to help you refine your approach to finding a job. If the person knows of a job, fine. However, you are not specifically asking for that. You want them to become involved with your efforts.

Finally, be sure that the person will remember the letter. Say you will call on a specific date to find a mutually convenient time to meet. Try to control your anxiety and sense of shyness. Most people you know or can make connections with will sincerely try to help you.

Step three consists of meetings and interviews. Congratulations, you now have your foot in the door. This person may not have a specific job for you; however, he or she will have information that you can use. This information could include other potential people to contact, organizations that might be recruiting, conditions in particular job markets, or problems with the type of job you are seeking. You are trying to get assistance in any form offered.

When you call to set up a meeting, refer to your letter. Suggest a brief period of time to further discuss the issues you outlined. People you know will gladly give you 30 or 60 minutes even from the most busy schedules. Others will usually help out of personal interest. Who knows, he or she may need to contact you sometime in the future.

Plan what you want to do during the meeting. In general, this will consist of letting the person know more about you, what you are capable of, what you are interested in, what you have been doing, and what you want from him or her. In some instances, you will only want responses to your ideas and plans. In other instances, you will be seeking potential contacts with others who may be able to help. In still other instances, you may be looking for information about an industry or a type of job you are considering. Do not be disappointed if you are not offered a job on the spot. This sometimes happens, but it is very rare. Your main goal is to get people to help you. Eventually, this will lead you to a job.

Remember, do not be late for the meeting. Take a little time to check out the surroundings. If you know you will be late, call in advance. If you are unreasonably late, try to reschedule the meeting.

Try to be friendly with the secretary. Often, they will have significant influence in the organization. Dress well and conservatively. Your career is on the line. This individual can both help and hurt you. You do not want to make an enemy. Don't smoke. It may offend someone or, even worse, violate a company or institutional policy with which you are unfamiliar.

Start the interview with a little conversation about the weather, your experience finding the office, observations about the company or organization, the building, or anything to break the initial tension and present yourself in a positive light. When it seems natural, explain the purpose of the meeting (e.g., I am planning to make a career transition and I am interested in your ideas and reactions to what I am considering). Take the person into your confidence. Even if it is someone you know, unless you have seen him or her very recently, you will need to paint a coherent picture of yourself if the person is to help you.

When making the request for assistance, leave the person room to say no gracefully—even your friends may not want to help. If you pressure someone, you may defeat your purpose. Assistance can come in the most unlikely ways. Your job is to stay open to the possibilities. At a minimum, ask the person to refer you to other people he or she knows who might be able to help you with your search. Clarify the information given. If names are offered, make sure you get the right spelling and an address and telephone number if available. Exchange business cards if you have one. Whatever happens, stick to the time schedule. If you have 30 minutes, watch the time carefully. Manage the appointment so that you accomplish your goals. Thank the person for the time he or she has given to you. It is, after all, a gift to you.

Step four consists of following up on the meeting. Send a short thank you note. If the person has helped you in a specific way, such as referring you to another person, identifying an organization that is looking for someone, or providing a particularly useful piece of information or criticism, mention it specifically. If appropriate or necessary, clarify or reinforce something from the meeting. Use the note to strengthen the impression you created during the meeting.

Let's assume that your indirect approach has led you to an organization with a job that might interest you. The fifth step consists of the job interview. This first meeting will usually be the initial part of the process of being offered a job. If you pass through the initial screening of résumés and contacts, you will be put on a short list of candidates and offered an interview. This is your major opportunity to impress a potential employer. If you are successful, it will lead to a follow-up discussion either in person or on the telephone and, eventually, to a set of negotiations about the position. You are managing a process. You are also forming what may be one of the most important relationships of your life.

Review your plan before the meeting. Keep your goals and career objectives in mind. Be sure you understand how you will present your strengths and achievements. Let the other person start the interview. Stay cool. Even if this is a job that you want, there will be others for you if the process does not go as planned. Emphasize your interest in the job, not your need for it. Be optimistic and positive.

Try to listen carefully for information about the organization that will let you make a case for how your strengths and achievements will help it. You will only be hired if you can help the organization. Don't talk about your personal problems. Don't reveal confidences about your past employer. Even if you greatly dislike your past employer and institution, remember that organizations value loyalty. You will demonstrate tact, maturity, and trustworthiness when you show an understanding of your ex boss and the factors that caused you to leave. Above all else, try to retain your personal authenticity. Being yourself is the best credential you have.

Figure 7.2 presents a list of typical questions asked during job interviews. Take a look at them. Spend some time thinking about how you might answer each question in a general way. Draft some initial answers. Once you know more about the company or position for which you have applied, rethink your answers to emphasize how you might fit comfortably into the niche they have created in the organization. You are trying to interest the interviewer in your ability to contribute to the organization. He or she will be watching every move you make, so preparation can help you handle the pressure.

A job interview should be a two-way street. The person conducting the interview will probably give you an opportunity to ask your own questions. This is another chance for him or her to evaluate your performance. It will give the interviewer a good idea about the types of concerns you have. It is an opportunity for you to shine. You want to appear savvy, smart, and experienced. Figure 7.3 provides a preliminary list of issues and potential questions. You might even take a list with you to the interview. If you do, be careful about how you present it. It is usually acceptable to take a few notes in a neat-looking portfolio. You can attach your list inside so that the interviewer will not see it. Try not to be obvious about looking up and down from your notebook after each answer. You may want to add to the list some technical questions applicable to your specialization.

You may not have time to ask all of the questions you have in the initial interview. Be selective and thoughtful when deciding what to explore. Also, be cautious when you respond to the answers. There may be information that you do not like. An overt demonstration of discontent or dissatisfaction may move you out

1. What are you looking for in a job?
2. Why did you or do you want to leave your present job?
3. What interests you about our organization or the job?
4. How did you obtain your last position?
5. What are your short- and long-term professional plans?
6. Design the best possible job for yourself.
7. What are your major strengths and weaknesses?
8. What do you like to do when you are not working?
9. What did or do your parents do professionally?
10. What do you hate to do at work?
11. How do you handle time pressure, deadlines, conflicting demands?
12. What kind of job are you looking for?
13. What is your approach to management (for administrative positions)?
14. How do you typically handle interpersonal or organizational conflict? Can you set limits, say no?
15. What types of clients have you served?
16. What is your therapeutic orientation?
17. Give us some examples of the work that you have done clinically, in consultation, administratively, in teaching, in research.
18. Do you have any health problems that could interfere with the job?
19. What salary are you interested in?
20. Can you give us some references?
21. If you got the job, what do you envision for the next year? Three years? Ten years?
22. How do you feel about working with minority groups?
23. How would you evaluate yourself as a psychologist?
24. What was your impression of your last organization? Your boss?
25. Why haven't you found a job yet?
26. Will you be after your boss' position?
27. Can you describe yourself? Your personality?
28. Have you ever submitted or gotten a research grant funded?
29. How would you deal with a suicidal client? Other difficult clinical situations?
30. When can you start?

Figure 7.2. Typical Interview Questions.

of direct consideration for the job. It is far easier to negotiate for change if you are being offered a position than if you are screened out because of a sour remark or a series of emotional responses that the interviewer can neither interpret nor tolerate.

Stay away from discussions of salary, benefits, and perks. The time to discuss these concerns is when you are being offered the job. Be as concise and thoughtful in your answers as possible. Don't ramble on endlessly, the interviewer might take it as a sign of disorganization, a poor ability to communicate, dissembling, or a lack of ability to perform under pressure. Even if the job seems unsuitable, be upbeat about the possibilities. Any job offer can be used as leverage and as a morale booster. Focus on your capacity to do the job once you have mastered the essentials. Finally, indicate your willingness to continue discussions about the position. You are interested, eager to get to know them, and have a great deal to offer them.

There will be clear indications if the interview is going well. If the person asks you to come in for another meeting with the boss, associates, or personnel staff,

1. What are the duties and responsibilities of this position?
2. With whom would I work most closely?
3. To whom would I report administratively?
4. Who would report to me?
5. What authority would I have in this position?
6. What are the strengths and weaknesses of the people who would report to me?
7. How does the budget process work in this organization?
8. What is the financial condition of the organization?
9. How would we know if I was succeeding or failing in the position?
10. How does the organization establish its goals?
11. How does the organization communicate?
12. Is there any growth potential in this position?
13. How would you describe the organizational culture here?
14. What are the objectives or mission of this organization?
15. What explicitly would I need to accomplish in the first 6 months? First year? Two years?
16. What does the chief executive of the organization like? Dislike? How does he or she operate? Management style? How long has he or she been in the position? How long will he or she stay in the position?
17. What are the major trouble areas that I would need to attend to?
18. What would be my case or client load?
19. How many billable hours will I need to generate per week or month?
20. Will I be expected to develop new business? Grants?
21. Will there be an employment contract? If yes, with what provisions? Is there a non-competition agreement?
22. What courses will I be required to teach? How many?
23. Will I have a budget to set up my laboratory?
24. To what office and or lab space will I be assigned?
25. What do you see as the future of this organization? This unit within the organization?
26. What characteristics are you looking for in a candidate?
27. Have I told you what you need to know to make a choice?
28. How seriously am I being considered?
29. What is the best way to follow up on this meeting?

Figure 7.3. Your Interview Questions.

this is a signal that you are making it onto a shorter list of most favored candidates. More subtle signs include the interview stretching beyond the time initially allotted for the meeting, more elaborate discussions of specific issues or problems facing the organization, and the interviewer going into more specific detail about you personally (e.g., when can you start, what are you looking for in a salary, what will it take to get you to accept this position). Never indicate that money or benefits are the primary consideration. This person is asking you to become a member of their family. The job and the relationships with colleagues will be uppermost in his or her mind.

If you have already left an organization, you will need an explicit explanation of why you left and why you have not found a job yet. Most people will be ready to accept a reasonable explanation. This is an era of mergers, acquisitions, downsizings, and of individuals staying in jobs on an average of 3 to 5 years. Over 1 million people have lost or left jobs in the last 4 years because of these trends. In a sense, you are expected to be in the job market. However, be careful and professional in crafting your explanation and make sure that your references are ready to back up your story. Even a company that has let you go will often cooperate in helping you find another job.

The sixth step consists of following up on the interview. Send a short letter of appreciation. Emphasize one or two important points and your enthusiasm for the position and organization. If another meeting has been offered, express your gratitude, and tell them you are looking forward to the interview. If a meeting has not been offered, suggest that you will be in touch shortly to follow up on the meeting. It is appropriate to call to find out how the recruitment process is going, but don't make a nuisance of yourself.

The seventh step consists of the final interview and position negotiations. Prepare for the next meeting as carefully as the first. Consult people you know who may have information about the organization, the individuals with whom you might be working, or the position. Review the information you obtained in the initial interview and create a list of additional questions. Be sure to include detailed inquiries about the nature of your responsibilities and authority. Identify your salary and benefit needs and any perks you may require. Many organizations have rigid salary and benefit structures. Your initial decision about salary level may lock you in for years to come, so be careful.

In a follow-up meeting, you may be interviewed by other individuals. All of the same rules for handling the process apply. This is also an opportunity for you to seek the opinions of others about the position and the organization. Pay attention if there are conflicting messages about duties, responsibilities, and authority. Listen closely for how they talk about each other and the organization. They will give you clues as to how they operate on a day-to-day basis. They are on their best behavior during an interview as well.

If everything goes well, you will be offered the job. Salary, benefits, perks, and logistics move to the center of the considerations. In the beginning, you can try to defer salary discussions by saying something like, "I would prefer to defer any discussions of financial considerations until we both have a better feel for the position and how I might fit into the organization." If they insist, ask about their salary ranges and how they administer salaries. If they force you to give a figure, tell them you prefer the high end of their range.

In the negotiations, you need to be firm, professional, and flexible. You are going to join their family, so it is important to start out on the right foot. How you conduct the final negotiations will give them very clear messages about how you operate. You must avoid any declaration of ambition beyond doing the specific job they are hiring you to do. Otherwise, they might feel or sense that you are merely trying to use them in a manipulative fashion.

Part of your firmness comes from a solid understanding of your needs. Elliott Blass described this very well in chapter 5 when he discussed the costs of setting up a lab. It does not pay to accept a position that will not work for you. You must have the tools and the social, financial, and administrative support to do the job well.

In all of your discussions, keep the concept of fairness squarely in front of you and them. The most important thing for you should be the definition of duties, responsibilities, and authority. Once you have settled the issue of what you will do and how you will do it, you can safely turn to compensation. You can usually get the person you are negotiating with to name a salary range. Do not leap in with a request for the highest figure. Take a few moments to mull over the amounts. Waiting may cause the other person to throw something else into the deal. Depending on how the position and salary structure has been presented, you may choose to settle on a figure then or to wait for a better offer. If the offer is fairly close to what you had in mind or is clearly the top offer they can make, further negotiations may not be appropriate.

If it seems like they might come up with something additional, review the job and its responsibilities, and suggest that the figures seem a little on the low side to you, but that you are willing to consider the offer. Tell them you would like a day or so to go over the details. It is appropriate to take your time and let them sweat a little. You may discover that they sweeten the deal when you call back. Do not wait too long to reply. You may well be in competition with others who would be happy to accept the offer.

Keep in mind that your negotiations should include benefits and perks. You must look at a total compensation package to judge its value accurately. Several extra weeks of vacation, paid medical benefits, a professional development fund, sufficient financing to start a lab, help in developing an initial list of clients, or other perks can make a job much more attractive than a few extra salary dollars. Do not be too tough in the negotiations. In emphasizing fairness, you want what will work well for both of you. If they resent how you handle the negotiations, you may destroy yourself before you ever show up for work.

Perks or other organizational benefits should be explored carefully. Depending on the job, you may be eligible for one or more of the following items: bonuses, moving expenses, sales commissions, company car, employment contract, minimum employment period, deferred compensation, extra insurances, clothing allowance, personal computers, computer time, personal secretaries, performance incentives, profit-sharing, stock options, assistance with child care, mortgage assistance, severance package, extra medical benefits, legal or investment services, professional development fund, funding for conferences, graduate assistants, and extra staff. Don't be afraid to ask. The list could go on. You must think about what you need to do your job well and ask the organization to provide these things for you. When the offer and the job seem right, accept it with grace and enthusiasm. Make sure they put the offer in writing, including the perks. You can avoid big misunderstandings if you have written documentation. Accept the offer in writing.

I'd like to add one final point on the negotiations. As I stated earlier, this has become an era of mergers, acquisitions, and downsizings. Make sure you ask if any such moves are anticipated. Try to clarify what will happen to you in the event of any such move. If you are accepting an executive position, this is crucial. You must understand how any transition will be handled. It is appropriate and acceptable to negotiate the terms of separation before you start to work. The agreement will bind and protect both parties. Compensation, out-placement services, period of notice, benefits coverage, letters of recommendation, etc. can and should be made part of your employment negotiations.

Settling In

In one sense, a major transition ends when you accept a new position. When you send the letter of acceptance, you close the previous chapter in your professional life and, simultaneously, open a new one. Although the worst part of the process may be over, you are starting an equally challenging step as you enter your new job.

We covered most of the issues and skills you will need in this phase in chapters 2 and 3. You are now managing a different process. Review and focus on the steps in behavioral transformation. In the beginning, your efforts will feel awkward. You may have a lot to learn about your new job, the people with whom you work, and the expectations you need to meet. Continued recognition of the key issues in careers, such as interdependence, power and dependency, relationships, ethical practice, planning, and solid decision making, can keep you out of most of the initial problems that develop in jobs.

Pay particular attention to the necessity of developing solid sources of information about what is happening within the organization. Remember, information brings the tremendous advantage of having time to respond to what is happening. This chapter should have made clear some of the difficulties of managing and living through crises. Avoid them if you can.

Information of this type can only come from good relationships with people who are informed and whom you trust. It will take time to develop such relationships. Put this at the top of your list of priorities. You will also need to pay close attention to your job performance. I take this for granted with most psychologists who are bright and well trained. It will rarely be job performance per se that gets a psychologist into trouble on the job. Most frequently, it will be a problem of fit, interpersonal relationships, politics, personal preferences, or burnout that leads to a job change in our field. Maintaining your own network of relationships can be the key to managing any transition in your career.

In a chapter of this size, it is impossible to cover every contingency you may encounter while conducting a job search and participating in position negotiations. Transitions are times of turmoil and excitement. Undoubtedly, you will face some of these situations in your own career. As you do, you may find some of the ideas in this chapter useful in successfully managing the transition.

References

Bolles, R. N. (1988). *The 1988 what color is your parachute?* Berkeley, CA: Ten Speed Press.

Carver, C. S., & Scheir, M. F. (1981). *Attention and self-regulation: A control theory approach to human behavior.* New York: Springer-Verlag.

Frederick, C. J. (1980). Effects of natural *vs* human induced violence upon victims. *Evaluation and Change: Special Issue*, 71–75.

Freudenberger, H. J., & Richelson, G. (1980). *Burnout: The high cost of high achievement.* Garden City, NJ: Doubleday.

Kennedy, J. L., & Laramore, D. (1988). *Joyce Lacy Kennedy's career book.* Lincolnwood, IL: Natural Textbook Company.

Maslach, C. (1982). *Burnout: The cost of caring.* Englewood Cliffs, NJ: Prentice-Hall.

Maslach, C. (1986). Stress, burnout, and alcoholism. In R. R. Kilburg, P. E. Nathan, & R. Thoreson, (Eds.), *Professionals in distress: Issues, syndromes, and solutions in psychology*. Washington, DC: American Psychological Association.

Mintzberg, H. (1973). *The nature of managerial work*. New York: Harper & Row.

Pines, A., & Aronson, E. (1988). *Career burnout: Causes and cures*. New York: The Free Press.

Turner, B. A. (1976). The organizational and interorganizational development of disasters. *Administrative Science Quarterly*, *21*, 378–397.

Part IV

Special Issues

8

Michael Owen Miller and Bruce D. Sales

The Importance of the Law in Psychological Careers

Malpractice, discriminatory personnel-selection procedures, licensing examinations, and cross-examination while testifying—these and other shibboleths are legal hobgoblins for the novice psychologist. It is no wonder that many psychologists, including some with impressive experience and sophistication, have elected to ignore the law that affects them and their practices. Their rationale is direct and unadorned: "I went to graduate school to study psychology. If I had wanted to be Perry Mason, I would have gone to law school."

Although the sentiment is understandable, it would be a grave error to adopt this attitude. Ethical, responsible, and successful practice requires that a psychologist (a) understand the basic legal tenets of relevance to psychology, (b) know how to find the law when unusual or new situations arise, and (c) have an advanced understanding of regulatory problems that are likely to arise in his or her career. This chapter addresses the first two objectives; discussion of the many specialized topics in law and psychology is not possible given space limitations.

The Need to Know the Law

The law directly and indirectly affects the professional and academic activities of every psychologist. Its impact has expanded with the growth in the influence and authority of psychology. For instance, licensing laws were among the first legal issues that confronted psychologists. As the number of practitioners increased, malpractice liability became a pervasive concern. This development was followed by antitrust concerns over the exclusionary practices of other professions—practices that placed unreasonable limits on the growth and scope of professional psychology. After initial victories (and some reversals) in the courts, psychologists became aware of the many benefits and responsibilities derived from the law. Today, the legal interests of professional psychologists include such diverse topics as hospital regulation of psychological practice, third-party reimbursement, professional incorporation, and privacy in the therapeutic relationship.

Nonclinical academicians have been less affected by the law, but have not escaped its purview. Academic researchers traditionally have been familiar with the ethical requirements mandating informed consent for human subjects (American

Psychological Association, 1981). They also must realize their need to be informed of the legal regulation of their experiments, as well. For example, state law may specify that particular information be provided to subjects during the informed consent process.

The need to know the law derives principally from three situations: direct control, indirect control or influence, and participation in the legal system. Although the first is the most important, the latter two will determine, many times, the effectiveness and satisfaction of one's career. At the least, knowledge of the law will usually help; total ignorance invites calamity.

Laws that directly affect psychologists usually concern prescriptive regulatory matters such as licensure. Although this topic may initially seem to concern only applied psychologists, it may also affect academics, whether they are acting in their roles as teachers, researchers, or consultants. For example, the designation by the legislature or state licensing board that a particular activity is primarily psychological in nature and limited to licensed psychologists would likely be interpreted to exclude all others from engaging in the activity, regardless of the qualifications of the psychologist or where the activity takes place. The only exception would be if there were exemptions from those regulations for some or all university psychologists. The moral of this lesson is that there is only one way to assure that one's activities are legal—that is, to learn about the laws that directly affect psychologists in your state or jurisdiction.

Psychologists may also find themselves indirectly affected when their clients become involved in legal entanglements that are related to the delivery of psychological services. For example, psychologists who provide services to persons at high risk of being in a lawsuit (e.g., psychologists doing marital counseling, neurological examinations for accident victims, and substance-abuse treatment) must educate not only themselves, but also their clients as to the possible uses of the psychological services and data by the legal system.

Finally, psychologists can be direct participants in the legal system as policy advisors to regulatory bodies, expert witnesses, trial consultants, or service providers. The purpose of this work is to apply their knowledge of human behavior in legal settings or to influence the policy process so that future laws more adequately represent the state of the art in psychological science and practice. Although pursuit of the first goal is purely dependent on a psychologist's interest in working within law-related settings—in some cases, to expand the scope of their practice, the latter, we believe, is an obligation that psychologists should share in improving laws that use or should use psychological information or that affect psychology and those who are in need of our services. In order to work in either capacity, psychologists must first understand the current status of the law. Although it takes considerable effort to become broadly educated in the law, it is reasonable to learn the law in a specific area, particularly when that law relates to an area in which the psychologist has scientific and professional expertise and experience.

Learning About the Law

Like scientific literature, the law is a multifaceted, ever-changing body of information. It is impossible to publish a general legal text that is not outdated as it rolls off the presses. In addition to the problems of outdatedness, psychologists and mental health attorneys face an additional hurdle: There are no compendiums that cover the variety of topics that are important to psychologists. Although there are an increasing number of very good general texts discussing mental health law, lack of specificity for a particular state or federal jurisdiction makes their usefulness limited in any given situation. For instance, one gains little guidance from a statement that in many states, a mental health professional has a duty to protect the intended victim when he or she predicts that a client will be violent toward that person, but not when the prediction is for violence randomly directed toward anyone. The statement begs the question: "What is the law in my state?" What the psychologist needs, therefore, is to understand the various sources of law governing his or her locale and how to find them.

There are eight primary sources of law: state and federal constitutional, statutory, regulatory, and case law. Constitutional law is rarely a direct concern, but because of its broad impact, the cases interpreting the Constitution must be consulted to determine its specific applicability. Statutory law is very important, because it generally governs professional licenses, protections for special groups, time limitations for lawsuits, and a myriad of major and minor provisions that affect psychologists and psychology. Regulatory law consists of administrative rules and regulations that provide the detail frequently absent from statutory law. It is promulgated by the government agencies responsible for enforcing particular sets of statutes. For instance, the Federal Trade Commission might issue regulations that directly affect a psychologist's use of advertisements; similarly, licensing boards generally issue regulations governing many aspects of a psychologist's practice. The final source of law, case law, is judge-made law that interprets all of the other types of law. Courts also have authority to make and modify what is known as the common law, a body of law separate from statutory or regulatory law that "derives its authority from usages and customs of immemorial antiquity, or from the judgments and decrees of the courts recognizing, affirming, and enforcing such usages and customs" (Black, 1979). *Tarasoff v. Regents of the University of California* (1976) is among the most well-known common law decisions affecting psychologists; it established the duty, referred to earlier, to protect an intended victim from the predicted violence of a client. *Tarasoff v. Regents of the University of California* is an example of a law emanating solely from the courts. In this case, it is the California Supreme Court, rather than a legislative or agency enactment.

The enactments of professional associations increasingly constitute an indirect source of law. Statutory or regulatory law may incorporate the ethical codes of a professional organization or the accreditation standards for a private group, such as the Joint Commission on Accreditation of Hospitals. Licensing boards routinely refer to practice guidelines, position statements, and codes of ethics of their profession. Similarly, trial and appellate courts will use those publications to adjudicate an individual case or to establish precedent. Because these sources of professional guidance are often referred to in the law, the psychologist who follows them closely will usually be in compliance with the law in those areas. Relatedly, major trends in the law often become subsequently incorporated into professional standards.

Finding the Law

As already mentioned, the absence of an encyclopedic compendium makes finding the law difficult, but not impossible. The reader should know, however, that the American Psychological Association is addressing this gap by publishing a series of books that comprehensively review and integrate all of the law that affects mental health professionals in each state, the District of Columbia, and the federal jurisdictions. The first two volumes of the Law & Mental Health Professionals series cover Arizona (Miller & Sales, 1986) and Texas (Shuman, 1989) law. New states will be added at the rate of two to three each year. If your jurisdiction does not have a published volume, more traditional and laborious methods will have to suffice for the present.

The library of any law school, a government library, or a county court library will generally have collections of primary legal materials. These collections of law can be found in the official reporters (i.e., books) for legislatures, government agencies, and the courts. There are usually private publishers that also compile this information and are equally accurate and much more timely. For instance, federal statutes have an official publication time of approximately 3 to 5 years in the official reporter, whereas the private reporters publish new laws in less than 2 months. It is particularly important to make up-to-date searches of these materials. We know of more than one instance where a statute or case caused someone great consternation, only to later discover that it had been repealed or overrruled.

We realize that in many situations where a psychologist needs legal information, it is not always realistic or practical to undertake primary research. It can be difficult, even for a lawyer, to know all the places to search. Fortunately, in many states, groups of psychologists have undertaken in-house publishing projects that narrow the search considerably. For instance, the state psychological association may publish or at least compile selected statutes and regulations that affect psychologists. These collections vary widely in the scope of coverage and accompanying commentary if any. Nonetheless, the collection will usually represent a core body of state law that the psychologist should have a general knowledge of. The state licensing board may also have a separately published collection of statutes and regulations that directly govern the practice of psychology in that state. Any psychologist whose psychological activities extend beyond teaching college or undergraduate students should have ready access to at least the material issued by the state board.

General discussions of legal issues that affect them will also help psychologists think about a particular situation by conceptualizing the issue, identifying major trends, and locating the most important cases or statutes. For example, Woody (1988) and Sales (1983) provided general materials that are relevant to the clinical practitioner. For the psychologist who will testify in court, whether by choice or subpoena, Blau's (1984) text on the psychologist as an expert witness is well worth reading, and Ziskin and Faust's (1988) classic diatribe will give a preview of the methods attorneys can be expected to use in cross-examining the psychologist.

Finally, a time-honored means of obtaining information can complement your own reading—ask or consult with someone about this. For a particular problem or situation, it is always advisable to consult with a knowledgeable colleague or attorney before, during, or after you undertake your legal research. But we are very reluctant to suggest that another person be used as the sole source of information. Colleagues are not always as well informed as they may appear to be. Additionally, there are relatively few lawyers who are well versed in the broad range of laws affecting psychologists; therefore, second-hand reporting of what an attorney may have told a psychologist must be regarded with caution.

Core Legal Materials

The competent, thoughtful psychologist may now feel that he or she is in a bind. On the one hand, it is obvious that a successful, satisfying career incorporates legal information, but the scope and sources of the information are so broad as to seem unwieldy. Proper classification resolves the dilemma.

A psychologist should have access to three kinds of legal information: information that is simple and immediately available in one's head, general and specific written materials in one's work setting, and a wide variety of primary legal information or the ready ability to consult with someone who has access to it. The first objective should have been met upon completion of graduate school. Classes on ethics and professional issues should have given the psychologist a working knowledge of the most important legal and ethical rules and guidelines in his or her specialization. If that is not true or one has concerns about the adequacy of his or her knowledge, completion of the second step will remedy any deficiencies.

Every psychologist should have an up-to-date set of core materials as well as specialized treatises that discuss legal and law-related issues in his or her field. The core should contain the "Ethical Principles of Psychologists" (American Psychological Association, 1981), the "General Guidelines for Providers of Psychological Services" (American Psychological Association, Board of Professional Affairs, Committee on Professional Standards, 1987), and the licensing law for the particular jurisdiction. Any psychologist who has a general knowledge of these rules and provisions will have fingertip access to the most important information. Although such reading is dry, it should be reviewed on a regular basis.

Within each specialization of psychology, there may be additional codes of ethics, specialty guidelines, and major discussions of legal and ethical topics. For example, clinical, counseling, industrial/organizational, and school psychologists must have, and be familiar with, the "Specialty Guidelines for the Delivery of Services" in their area (American Psychological Association, Committee on Professional Standards, 1981). Psychologists who are involved in creating, administering, or using psychological tests should have the *Standards for Educational and Psychological Testing* (1985). Social or experimental psychologists that testify as expert witnesses should be conversant with the unique problems of courtroom consultation and testimony, described in a recent issue of *Law and Human Behavior* (McCloskey, Egeth, & McKenny, 1986).

Psychologists wishing to participate directly in the legal system should have, in addition to the requisite skills and expertise, a specialized legal text in their area or, better yet, law–psychology texts relevant to their topics of practice. For instance, for a psychologist interested in forensic clinical practice related to criminal law, there are a number of law–psychology treatises that would be of help in ensuring expertise in providing services (e.g., Grisso, 1986, described various measures for assessing legal competencies; Melton, Petrila, Poythress, & Slobogin, 1987, provided a comprehensive discussion of psychological evaluations for the courts; and Monahan, 1981, described the research relating to prediction of violence). The psychologist must create a comprehensive bibliography of writings that is updated regularly to ensure currency and tailored to the type of issues being faced in his or her career.

Inevitably, of course, a situation will arise where it is necessary to seek legal assistance. For instance, before starting a new business, purchasing property, or becoming a party to a lawsuit, a psychologist must consider obtaining legal counsel. Whereas most people would not think of representing themselves in the courtroom, many professionals embark on business ventures without considering the legal ramifications of their type of business, relationships with colleagues and employees, or agreements with third parties. This decision is unfortunate. A skilled attorney attuned to the particular concerns of, and challenges and opportunities faced by, an academician or mental health professional can help him or her to maximize their effectiveness by reducing their likelihood of facing legal problems in the future.

Assuming that a psychologist takes a proactive, preventative approach, preliminary research with the materials we described earlier will make the "legal consumer" a more informed, efficient user of legal services. Although the attorney has a responsibility to translate the situation into a legal framework and a proposed solution, the psychologist's knowledge of legal issues will help the attorney to identify quickly the relevant issues. Additionally, if the attorney is inexperienced in the psychological issues that form at least part of the basis of your concern, it may be necessary to educate him or her in preliminary matters. The legal knowledge will provide the psychologist with a means to educate more effectively the attorney, as well as to test his or her knowledge and willingness to respond to input. Of course, there is a danger of second-guessing another professional, but it is more important to avoid the greater risk of being an uninformed client who blindly follows the attorney's advice.

Using Legal Information—Protecting Yourself From Liability

Knowledge of and adherence to your obligations as articulated in the law and professional standards is the best way to avoid illegal and negligent practice and liability. Indeed, following this simple admonition is critical because of the myriad parties who may sue psychologists: a governmental authority, the subject or recipient of psychological services, and third parties, such as insurance carriers and the potential victim of a client's violence. Because the duties and rights between psychologists and these other parties are defined almost exclusively by the law and professional standards, psychologists must be familiar with the regulations affecting their activities in order to avoid conflict with those authorities. Violation of a law or standard frequently carries with it the assumption that the person was acting in a negligent manner. This finding could result in civil liability, as well as in penalties or sanctions imposed by the government or by a professional association.

Once the psychologist understands these regulations, he or she will realize that the cornerstone of psychologists' relationships with others is that they ". . . respect the dignity and worth of the individual and strive for the preservation and protection of fundamental human rights" (American Psychological Association, 1981, p. 633). These goals are congruous with a psychologist's legal responsibilities. To meet them, there is a simple approach that, although not sufficient by itself, may be very helpful. The psychologist and the client or subject should each have a copy of a signed written document that describes the psychologist's relationship with the client or subject. This document should represent the product of the psychologist's review of the relevant professional guidelines and the law, agreements unique to the psychological activities in question, and any individual information that is relevant to the particular case.

Because it is impossible to create an all-purpose form, we can only indicate the areas that should be addressed. First, these forms should describe the psychological activity that will be engaged in. This section sets out the rights and responsibilities of the people involved and any attendant benefits or risks associated with the activity. It is usually helpful to include goals and time estimates, as well as any contingencies that may arise. Then, the responsibilities of the client or subject should be described. For instance, this section could describe when and how credit will be given for participation in an experiment or discuss fees, payment schedules, and collection procedures if any, for the delivery of psychological services. Finally, the document should explain how information obtained will be used. This section describes confidentiality, mutually agreeable releases of information, and unilateral releases of information required by law. Because a client's or subject's reluctance to sign the agreement will put the psychologist on notice that there is a problem, it should be addressed before anything else takes place. Obviously, if the client or subject refuses to sign the agreement, consent has not been given to proceed with the psychological service or activity.

This document, in and of itself, will not encompass all that the psychologist knows about the law and professional responsibilities, but its preparation and a willingness to explain and discuss it with the client or subject will bring to the fore most problems that are likely to be encountered. Additionally, it will force the psychologist to gather the materials that should be kept in the office and to consult others if there are issues that the materials do not address. As an important side benefit, many points will remain in memory, available for immediate access. In short, the psychologist will be better protected in a variety of ways, and the benefits will extend to those people with whom the psychologist interacts.

Conclusion

Psychologists need to know the law, not because it is the current paranoia, but to foster legitimate client and professional concerns, many of which were initially recognized by psychologists themselves. Although it is difficult to become widely educated on the variety of laws that affect psychologists and their clients, or even to conduct specific research with primary materials, it is possible to become generally educated on the majority of law-related topics that are most likely to cause psychologists problems. It is critical that all psychologists, especially those in the early stages of their careers, gather the most important, core materials so that they can be easily used. Finally, to make immediate use of the central legal information for a particular psychologist's career, that person should have a written document that describes the rights, responsibilities, and benefits for both the psychologist and his or her client or subject. Construction of this document will make concrete each of the points noted throughout this chapter.

References

American Psychological Association. (1981). Ethical principles of psychologists. *American Psychologist, 36*, 633–638.

American Psychological Association, Board of Professional Affairs, Committee on Professional Standards. (1987). General guidelines for providers of psychological services. *American Psychologist, 42*, 712–723.

American Psychological Association, Committee on Professional Standards. (1981). Specialty guidelines for the delivery of services. *American Psychologist, 36*, 639–681.

Black, H. C. (1979). *Black's law dictionary* (5th ed.). St. Paul, MN: West.

Blau, T. H. (1984). *The psychologist as expert witness.* NY: John Wiley & Sons.

Grisso, T. (1986). *Evaluating competencies: Forensic assessments and instruments.* NY: Plenum.

McCloskey, M., Egeth, H., & McKenny, J. (Eds.). (1986). The ethics of expert testimony [Special issue]. *Law and Human Behavior, 10*, 1–181.

Melton, G. B., Petrila, J., Poythress, N., & Slobogin, C. (1987). *Psychological evaluations for the courts: A handbook for mental health professionals and lawyers.* NY: Guilford.

Miller, M. O., & Sales, B. D. (1986). *Law and mental health professionals: Arizona.* Washington, DC: American Psychological Association.

Monahan, J. (1981). *Predicting violent behavior: An assessment of clinical techniques.* Beverly Hills, CA: Sage.

Sales, B. D. (Ed.). (1983). *The professional psychologist's handbook.* New York: Plenum.

Shuman, D. W. (1989). *Law and mental health professionals: Texas.* Washington, DC: American Psychological Association.

Standards for educational and psychological testing. (1985). Washington, DC: American Psychological Association.

Tarasoff v. Regents of the University of California, 131 Cal. Rptr., *14*, 551 p. 2d 334 (1976).

Woody, R. H. (1988). *Fifty ways to avoid malpractice.* Sarasota, FL: Professional Resource Exchange.

Ziskin, J., & Faust, D. (1988). *Coping with psychiatric and psychological testimony* (4th ed., Vols. 1–3). Venice, CA: Law and Psychology Press.

9

Richard R. Kilburg

Financial Performance and Professional Life

Of all the commonly known hallmarks of professional life, the keystone, in the perception of many people, involves the ability of professionals to assert their independence and competence in the financial sphere. This is not to say that the expression of one's talents and training or the contributions to clients and society via professional activities are not important. Rather, it acknowledges that one important measurement of how any person is doing is the amount of money he or she makes. The fundamental point to be made in the following discussion is that one major way of assessing and managing your professional performance involves handling your financial life. The purposes of this chapter then are to review the need for financial planning and budgetary skills for professionals, explore some of the major purposes and procedures of accounting, examine budgets in operation, and provide some information on methods to assess your professional performance from the financial perspective.

However, before beginning, it is important to note that I am not a financial professional (CPA, tax attorney, economist, etc.). Consequently, I have had to rely on other authorities in the preparation of the technical material offered in this chapter. Regardless of the novelty of some of the information presented, it is my belief that every professional must have some rudimentary knowledge and skill in the financial area in order to perform effectively.

As is the case with a great deal of the information in this volume, these financial skills are part of what makes for improved professional performance. Yet few if any education and training programs in psychology offer information regarding money to their graduates. Recognizing the deficit in my own professional training and the need to develop these skills to help manage my professional life led me to prepare the following basic materials.

Creating a Financial Road Map

Most psychologists are acutely aware of the status differentials in their subfields. Some measure these differentials via the type of reputation they have among colleagues. Others score themselves according to known criteria, such as size and diversity of caseload, number of publications, and frequency of grant awards. However, most of us also measure ourselves and our career progress via financial benchmarks.

These benchmarks may be direct, such as the level of your salary, fringe-benefit package, or bonus compared to your contemporaries, or indirect, such as the neighborhood you live in, the car you drive, or the type of vacations you take. All of these signs are external measures of the level of recognition a psychologist has achieved in his or her professional life. They certainly are not the only way of gauging performance, and I would argue strongly that they are not the most important. Yet they are a factor for nearly all of us.

The world of finance is a strange place for everyone except those few professionals who specialize in this type of work. To the rest of us, the jargon, the technicalities, and the fact that it is all tied up with the manipulation of money—even when it is our money—makes it a difficult world to understand and with which to be comfortable. As a result, almost every successful professional relies on experts in this financial world to help guide him or her. In fact, if you take nothing more away from this chapter than an understanding of the need at times for expert advice, I will have done a good job.

One of the important steps that you must take for yourself during your career involves formulating your financial plan. This process includes many of the steps outlined in chapter 3 in the section on the planning process. Spiro (1978) offered additional insight into the requirements for your financial plan. He emphasized that financial plans are developed "to assure that financial resources are available at the time desired" (p. 214). This involves an attempt to anticipate, to the best of your ability, the kind of resources you are likely to need at various stages in your life. Looking at this problem from the perspective of the cycle of behavioral transformation and the normal developmental tasks of adult life, you can anticipate that the need for money will increase at certain times and decrease at others. Your financial plan then includes goals, objectives, and specified activities designed to address your developmental needs.

It is comparatively easy to anticipate the following common events: marriage; the acquisition of a house, cars, and other assets; building a family, and meeting the needs of children for food, clothing, education, entertainment, and medical care; caring for one's parents as they age; meeting your own goals or desires for a particular lifestyle; and the occurrence of major crises, such as periods of economic hardship, health problems, and deaths in one's family. Finally, and perhaps most importantly, you must plan your own retirement. These events can be anticipated, and reasonable financial plans can be made to meet them. Let's address some of these events in Exercise 9.1.

Exercise 9.1 Analyze Your Financial Challenges

1. Take out a sheet of paper, and divide it into three columns. Give careful thought to your personal and professional goals in light of the work you have done in previous chapters. Include such issues as the place you want to live, the car you want to drive, whether or not you want to marry or

have children, where you want to retire, your age, your health, and the financial status of parents, etc. Take into account the need for financial support during times of emergency and during the normal occurrences of a human life. List these events in the first column.

2. Now, try to anticipate the year in which each of these events will occur given your current age and status. If you are just starting a career, your list may be longer than if you are in your 50s and have already reached many of your objectives. Write down the anticipated year opposite each of the events. Remember these are targets not prescriptions.
3. Finally, try to estimate the cost of each event. Use your best judgment knowing the current prices of housing, transportation, clothing, and education. Check the *Consumer Price Index* and other sources of information available in any library. Put the estimated price in the third column opposite the date for each event.
4. Take a look at the totals in the years of major expenditures. For example, your costs will be higher the year you decide to buy a house, purchase a car, or send a child to college. This will give you an idea of the type of income you will need at different stages of your life and the savings you will need to accumulate.

Determine your insurance needs, retirement plans, and the requirements for ready financial reserves; enter them into your calculations in Exercise 9.1. Two rules of thumb are that you should be insured at 3 to 5 times your annual gross income, and you should have sufficient funds to cover at least 6 months of normal expenditures in the face of major illness, job loss, or any other emergency.

Retirement planning is complicated by a number of factors. Two major issues are the age at which you plan to retire and the standard of living you want to maintain. Although these are somewhat difficult to determine because of shifting goals, responsibilities, and perspectives as we age, it is nonetheless crucial to attempt to do so because these decisions/goals then provide a guide for a realistic set of financial decisions and tasks throughout one's life.

The primary method for addressing financial goals, of course, involves making money. Having made an effort to determine your needs and goals for financial outlays, you must realistically assess your ability to earn money on an annual basis. This evaluation includes a determination of how you are likely to work, that is, as an independent practitioner or in an organization, and the salaries, fees, and other sources of revenue likely to be available to you. Your anticipated earnings can then be compared with the expenditures outlined earlier, and you will have a good, general picture about the financial component of your professional life.

The financial road map you began to create in Exercise 9.1 serves as a yardstick with which you can measure your progress over a lifetime. The accumulation of wealth through the effective management of salary and other income will enable you to meet your needs throughout your life cycle. Insurance is purchased to guarantee financial resources in case of emergencies or to meet long-term needs with limited monthly payments. A reasonable savings plan helps to meet retirement, crisis, education, child-care, and lifestyle-consumption needs.

One final factor that must be addressed involves the effect of inflation on accumulated wealth. Inflation decreases the value of accumulated savings over time. The past 2 decades have witnessed significant increases in the rate of inflation, and all financial sectors have been severely affected. There are ways of coping with inflation, because some investments tend to perform better during periods of inflation than others. This issue should be weighed carefully as you put your financial plan together.

As we have seen in previous chapters, power accrues to professionals through the acquisition and management of resources and through the identification and sophisticated handling of dependencies. A power–dependency analysis usually begins with an assessment of the resources at your command and moves from there to a determination of other factors. Let's examine the relative power positions of two psychologists in parallel positions at the same organization, but who have taken different approaches to financial planning.

Mary Hartman designed a careful financial plan, which she implemented over a number of years. She set annual targets for the development of resources, such as savings, insurance, and major capital outlays. Several years ago, she purchased a condominium, which she subsequently parlayed into a house. She takes the financial side of her life quite seriously, and her savings plan has led to the accumulation of approximately a year's worth of financial reserves. Mary has made the necessary life-style sacrifices to accomplish these goals by economizing on vacations, clothing, luxury items, and leisure activities.

When comparing her approach with that of her colleague, James Browning, who has a similar record and position with the university, one can readily grasp the difference in power and dependency. Jim has no financial plan. Although he has no major debts, because his salary is sufficient for his needs, he has not accumulated a stock of wealth. He relies on the university's disability insurance plan for emergency coverage, drives a marvelous sports car, and updates his wardrobe every season. He enjoys life to its fullest, taking major vacation trips annually and travelling whenever and wherever he has the opportunity. His attitude is that he is still very young and has many years in which to become serious about money. He participates in the university retirement plan at a minimal level, and any savings accumulated are spent in the pursuit of pleasure.

It is easy to see which of these psychologists is positioned to weather a forthcoming storm. In the face of not getting tenure, personal emergencies, and in terms of lifelong financial goals, Mary is in a better position. She also has more flexibility. If she confronts work situations that make her uncomfortable, she could survive a major period of unemployment and could also manage a job search without the support of her present position. She can afford to be somewhat more assertive on the job and less fearful of superiors' demands and collegial competition.

However, Jim is not in the position to do any of these things comfortably. Depending solely on his salary, with no accumulated assets, he lives from paycheck to paycheck. He has fun to be sure, but this lack of a financial strategy leads to high levels of tension and anxiety on the job. He feels much less freedom to say "no" to any demand and, consequently, works significantly longer hours to please everyone. With no resource base, he can ill afford a period of unemployment and is thus highly dependent on the university.

In terms of power and dependency, it is easy to see the contribution that a solid financial plan, implemented effectively, can have on your life. The next step in constructing a good plan consists of creating a balance sheet for yourself.

Exercise 9.2 Building a Balance Sheet

Construct a list of financial assets and liabilities.

Assets	Amount
a. Checking account	________
b. Savings account	________
c. Certificates of deposit	________
d. Stocks and bonds—no. of shares, cost, market value	________
e. Life insurance—premiums, death value, cash value	________
f. Real estate—description, location, cost, balance of mortgage, market value	________
g. Business interest—(corporation, partnership, etc.) percentage of ownership, cost, estimated value	________
h. Personal property—jewelry, boats, cars, collector's items, antiques, receivables, art	________
i. Trust funds, inheritances—actual or expected	________
j. Employee benefit plans—present value, yearly retirement receivable now, future benefits expected, death benefits	________
k. Car—market value	________
l. Insurance—cash value	________
m. Pension, retirement plan—amount vested	________
n. Other—stock options, deferred compensation	________
TOTAL	____________

Liabilities	Amount
a. Mortgages	________
b. Bank loans—cars, furniture, vacations	________
c. Life insurance loans	________
d. Installment debt	________
e. Bills other than installments	________
f. Other—including divorce agreements, others who are dependent on you, other debts owed	________
TOTAL	____________

NET WORTH as of ______________, 19 ___
(total of assets less liabilities) .... ____________

In Exercise 9.1, you began to build your financial plan by organizing what you believe will be your future financial needs. Exercise 9.2 provided a strong evaluation of where you are now with regard to the plan. Your net worth—the bottom line of your balance sheet—tells you how you are doing at the task of accumulating wealth to meet the objectives you have set for yourself.

If you are interested in charting your progress, simply do Exercise 9.2 on an annual basis and graph the results. The trend line should be consistently upward if your plan is working. You should be aware that assets, such as homes, jewelry, cars, and art, may be carried on both sides of the balance sheet. These items will contribute positively to the bottom line as they appreciate or increase in value. However, the payments for them reduce your net worth.

When combined, these two exercises tell you where you think you need to go financially and where you are now. In a sense, they orient you to the world of money. If the results of the two exercises make you think that you are not doing enough to plan for your financial security, don't panic. You can't do everything at once. Improving your position may take time, but you can definitely accomplish a great deal. The key is to take it one step at a time. The following sections of this chapter will give you some ideas about how you can move toward your goals and systematically and steadily improve your balance sheet.

Finally, it is extremely important that, as part of your financial plan, you establish a will in order to provide explicit instructions to your survivors for the distribution of your assets when you die. No one likes to think about this. However, if you do not make the decisions yourself, a court will decide for you. Competent legal assistance can be obtained readily and fairly inexpensively.

The next phase of managing the financial side of your career consists of establishing short- and long-range budgets, which are consistent with your financial goals. We shall examine the budgeting and accounting process in the following section.

Budgeting and Accounting Concepts

The information presented in this section and subsequent ones involves a distillation of a variety of concepts and techniques commonly known in the financial world. Because I am not a financial professional, I have gone to a number of sources to determine the kind of material that would be most helpful. I discovered that most of the texts provided similar treatment of these topics. As a result, I believe that what follows is a fairly standard description of some basic accounting and budgeting concepts. In order to provide some consistency and clarity, my discussion will follow closely the approaches described by Horngren (1978) and Spiro (1978).

Major Functions

Accounting systems provide quantitative information for a variety of purposes. The first major function of a system is to generate internal reports for planning and controlling the operations of the individual or the organization. The ready availability of critical information from budgeting and accounting sources can automatically direct your attention to trouble spots.

These reports provide fuel for the process of "management by exception" in which you direct your efforts at coping with the results and problems that were not in your plan, such as an unanticipated car-repair bill or a lack of cash because insurance checks have not arrived. This problem-finding and -solving approach to financial management complements the second major function of accounting systems—goal setting and strategic planning. We discussed this in the first section of this chapter.

The third major function of the accounting and budgeting system is to provide information for reporting to outside parties. The individual psychologist working in an organization or in solo practice has some, even if minimal, responsibilities to others. The main responsibility that the psychologist has is to report finances to state and federal tax authorities to whom everyone in the country must report.

Beyond these reports, psychologists in more complex organizations or who carry formal managerial responsibilities in an enterprise have a variety of external parties to whom they must report. Examples include boards of directors, funding sources, stockholders, and a number of government agencies in addition to the Internal Revenue Service. A good accounting system allows you to collect, categorize, and evaluate financial information to help you make decisions.

Budgeting and accounting systems play a central role in your capacity to develop and survive. In keeping with the major theme of this volume, you are the executive officer of your career. Paying careful attention to these financial functions provides you with the freedom and flexibility to pursue the goals that are central to your life.

The functions of management, budgeting, and accounting are interrelated. As we saw in chapter 3, the management process emphasizes planning, decision making, implementing, and evaluating results. These elements flow into each other in a natural and spontaneous fashion even though the chart in chapter 3 specifies that certain steps always precede others.

The components of an accounting system consist of budgets, records, a classification system, and reports on performance. The system begins with a budget, the formal specification of the financial plan of an organization or an individual. More information will be provided on budgeting later. Budgets lead to the planning and resource-allocation decisions central to the performance of your work. Resource allocation involves spending money. The expenditures produce source documents (bills, checks), which become records of the various financial actions you take. These source documents are classified in the process of bookkeeping, which consists of recording the transactions in general and subsidiary ledgers. Performance reports can be constructed on a regular or as-needed basis with the information you collect and organize in your ledgers.

These management and accounting processes operate simultaneously. You plan goals and activities and construct a budget for how much they will cost you. You implement the plan by spending money in the pursuit of the goals and through your various activities. You keep good records of what you spend, and then you construct reports that let you evaluate your goals and decisions.

What follows is a rudimentary presentation of some of the major features of the budgeting process. It is important that you understand that this information is a condensed synthesis of just a few of a wide range of budgeting and accounting concepts and conventions. These are provided in order to demonstrate the utility and importance of the budgeting and accounting processes to your professional performance. You must be familiar with these procedures if you are to survive. There is no substitute for competent financial judgment. It is part of the foundation of your professional performance.

Familiarity with these procedures can best be likened to a minimal competency in a foreign language. You must become budget and accounting literate. Similarly, you must also be aware of the limits of your literacy and arrange for competent financial experts to assist you in these functions. Providing for a financial advisor to help you with the planning, budgeting, and record keeping of your business is a key step in the assurance of your professional success.

It is necessary for most psychologists to obtain this assistance. Unfortunately, when we are just beginning our careers, we usually feel financially pinched and are unable to allocate the resources necessary for such services. This is when the rudimentary skills covered later will be most helpful. They also should enable established psychologists to interact more effectively with their accounting consultants.

Budgets. In their simplest form, budgets consist of two major lists. One list specifies all of the revenue you expect to receive from various sources. This constitutes the revenue or income statement. It can be very detailed, providing projections for each account managed by a professional, or quite simple, consisting of a summary across major categories of income. Revenues come from salaries, bonuses, stock options, interest or dividends on investments, rent on properties owned, profits on properties sold, and cash or accounts receivable for goods or services delivered (fees). In complex, entrepreneurial organizations, revenues can also be raised through the sale of stocks, bonds, or other forms of sold equity (shares or values in the company's activity). Your income budget lists each source of revenue and the amount of money expected to come from that source for the year.

You should immediately grasp the information, utility, and power that are derived from such a list. The income statement clearly depicts your major financial dependencies. It directs attention to your expected sources of survival for the following year. It provides a crude but effective road map of your financial objectives for the year. It literally shows us where we need to go in order to succeed in the financial sphere.

Similarly, the expense budget also begins with a list. However, instead of identifying where the revenue or money will come from, this budget depicts all of the major categories in which you expect to spend the money obtained from the sources of revenue. Expense budgets can be very simple for households or solo, professional practitioners. These budgets will consist of several dozen categories at most. For large businesses, these budgets sometimes contain several thousand categories spread across hundreds or even thousands of operating units that form the structure of the organization. The expense categories can be grouped together in any fashion, as in dealing with revenues. Expenses usually include salaries, fringe benefits (insurances, pensions, social security payments, etc.), mortgages or rents, utilities costs (heat, cooling, electricity), telephones, equipment, printing, consulting services, transportation (travel), professional development, computer or other purchased services, depreciation, etc. For both types of budgets, you need to summarize the major choices and decisions you make about where you hope to obtain money and where you expect to expend it.

Whereas budgets can be somewhat global or general in their categories, the accounting system usually has a separate listing for each specific item of revenue received and each specific expense disbursed. The accounting system listings are tabulated and summarized in various formats to provide reports on how well you are doing in light of what you budgeted. These reports form the foundation for many management decisions that you make in order to guide yourself or your organization toward the goals stated in the budgets.

Budgets can be short-term, listing the financial exchanges expected during a day, a week, a month, or a year. Most often, they reflect the decisions made for about a year of financial activity. Budgets also can and should reflect the long-term goals of the enterprise. Long-term budgets are usually statements of targets one hopes to reach over several years of financial activity. Long-term budgets usually contain fewer categories than short-term budgets, because they are broad statements of expected performance rather than detailed road maps that provide decision-making flexibility on a daily basis.

Let's examine an example of a budget of a psychologist in independent practice. Familiarity with the elements of the budgeting process in this type of setting can help to prepare you to manage more complex budgets in larger, organized settings.

As can be seen in Figure 9.1, our psychologist, Robin Williams, expects revenue from six major sources during 1990. Because he has been in professional practice for some time in a small city, he has developed consultation agreements with two local firms and one local business person who owns several enterprises. They pay him a fixed retainer for a set number of hours of work on an annual basis. Hours

Revenue

	Item	Amount
1.	Consulting Retainer L.W. Manufacturing	$ 30,000
2.	Consulting Retainer P.A. Retailers, Inc.	$ 25,000
3.	Consulting Retainer R.W. Jones	$ 5,000
4.	Other client fees (accounts receivable)	$120,000
5.	Interest	$ 6,000
6.	Rent	$ 14,000
	TOTAL	$200,000

Figure 9.1. Sample 1990 revenue budget for Robin Williams, PhD.

expended over the contracted number are billed at Robin's regular rate of $100/hour.

These retainers, amounting to $60,000/year, add great stability to Robin's practice, because they are billed in two installments at the beginning and middle part of the year and allow for effective cash flow and interest-rate management. Other fees account for the bulk of expected revenue. Robin bills by the clock, recording time in 15-minute segments and charging clients at the rate of $100/hour. This flat fee includes the services of a secretary, a part-time, paraprofessional assistant, and all overhead charges. Robin has cash-flow and billing-management approaches that allow the retention of an average bank balance of $60,000. This translates into an additional $6,000/year interest income via management of short-term investments. The final category of revenue consists of $14,000 in rent from the tenants in the office building that Robin owns. Thus, the total expected revenue for this psychological practice in 1990 is $200,000.

The expense budget (see Figure 9.2) comprises 14 separate categories. Each item has an amount budgeted for the year. The primary expenses are salaries, fringe benefits, and the mortgage on the building Robin owns. These three categories account for approximately 70% of his anticipated expenses. The other 11 categories are the relatively minor, but nonetheless important, areas of operating expenses. The number of categories is totally flexible in that any item can be added if a professional believes it will be useful to help track expenses. Adding categories usually occurs when particular items in "miscellaneous" or "other" accounts begin to accumulate significant amounts of expense and a psychologist or his or her accountant wishes to gain better information and, therefore, control these expenditures. A separate account is usually created that allows for monitoring all of the activity in that category. These budgets can obviously be as global or as detailed as you wish. In the end, the number and types of categories depend solely on you and your particular pattern of revenue and expenses.

These 14 categories can be separated into two different types of items, *fixed* expenses and *variable* expenses. Fixed expenses represent major areas in which the level of commitment is known and is relatively unchangeable. Items such as salaries, fringe benefits, mortgages, and insurances tend to be known in advance and require major allocations of funds. Another name for fixed expenses is the *uncontrollable* items in the budget. This title refers to the fact that once the commitments are made (a salary established, a lease signed, a fringe benefit agreed on), you agree to provide that amount for the period specified. The only control exerted is in the initial decision to expend funds in this area.

Variable expenses frequently are called *controllables*, because greater discretion can be exercised over these amounts. This control is obtained through a number of smaller decisions made more frequently. Expense discretion, therefore, is obtained each time a decision is made for these items. Substantial savings can be realized by saying no to expenditures or reducing the amounts to be spent in these categories. Finally, you can see in Figure 9.2 that $30,000 has been budgeted in the miscellaneous and depreciation categories together. This $30,000 represents 15% of the total budget. These categories also are controllable in major ways, adding greater flexibility to the budget-management process. It is generally a good idea to plan for considerable flexibility in certain categories to gain this control. A good rule of

Expenses		
	Item	**Amount**
1.	Salaries	$ 110,000
2.	Fringe benefits (insurance, pensions, social security,etc.)	16,500
3.	Mortgage	14,000
4.	Insurance (liability, mortgages, etc.)	5,000
5.	Utilities (heat, air conditioning, lights)	4,500
6.	Telephone	5,000
7.	Equipment total	
	a) New	1,500
	b) Leased	3,500
8.	Printing	2,000
9.	Postage	1,000
10.	Transportation	2,000
11.	Professional Development (books,workshops, etc.)	3,000
12.	Computer expenses	3,000
13.	Depreciation of building and equipment	15,000
14.	Supplies and Other (miscellaneous)	15,000
	TOTAL EXPENSES	$200,000

Figure 9.2. Sample 1990 expense budget for Robin Williams, PhD.

thumb is that budgets are managed on a 5% to 10% margin of error. Therefore, the amounts allocated in variable categories should allow for this margin so that control can be established quickly when needed.

In Exercise 9.3, you can practice budgeting skills with your household expenses and revenues. Try to create an average monthly budget based on your current living arrangements.

Exercise 9.3 Preparing a Monthly Budget

EXPENSES

Item	*Amount*	*Item*	*Amount*
1. Mortgage/Rent	______	17. Dental Care	______
2. Food	______	18. Education	______
3. Lunch	______	19. Credit Cards	______
4. Telephone	______	20. Other Bills	______
5. Heating Fuel	______	21. Maintenance	______
6. Gas/Water/Electric	______	22. Contributions	______
7. Property Tax	______	23. House Expenses	______
8. Insurance	______	24. Church	______
9. Auto Expenses	______	25. Memberships	______
10. Clothing	______	26. Vacations/Travel	______
11. Laundry	______	27. Savings Plan	______
12. Hair Care	______	28. Other	______
13. Liquor	______	29. Other	______
14. Entertainment	______	30. Other	______
15. Subscriptions	______	31. Miscellaneous	______
16. Health Care	______	TOTAL CASH OUT	________

INCOME

Item	*Amount*
1. Net Pay	______
2. Fees	______
3. Royalties	______
4. Dividends	______
5. Interest	______
6. Other Investments	______
7. Other Income	______
TOTAL CASH IN	______
DIFFERENCE (Cash in–Cash out)	______

Ledgers. After the budget is created, either the financial consultant or the professional must create a series of ledgers in which the expenditures in each of these expense accounts and the receipts (or cash received) in each revenue category are listed as they occur. The general convention is to keep an account ledger for each separate item in the revenue and expense budgets and a general ledger that tracks the amount of activity in each account on a monthly basis. These ledgers are usually summarized on a monthly and quarterly (every 3 months) basis. You will need to develop reports containing these summaries regularly. They form the foundation of your financial-management system.

If you follow Exercise 9.3 with this step, you will create a separate ledger and file for each of the 31 categories in your household-expense budget and each of the seven items in the revenue budget. All transactions for the month are recorded in a general ledger. The general ledger is organized with the 31 categories of expense or seven items of revenue arrayed along the top, each with its separate column. Each financial transaction from your checkbook is then listed below in the appropriate column. Figure 9.3 gives an abbreviated picture of a general ledger for your household-expense budget. Four categories of mortgage, food, auto, and clothing are identified. Expenditures for the month are placed in each column as they occur, and the method of payment, usually a check or receipt for cash or credit card, is identified in the row. The general ledger lets you track expenditures closely every month. There are now a number of inexpensive software programs available for home or office computers that can automate these financial chores for you.

Knowing the location and size of financial transactions enables you to make the decisions necessary to keep your budget within its targeted boundaries. The absence of such reporting and budgeting tools puts you in the position of a ship captain, who has no stated port of call, no compass to steer by, and a broken rudder. Such situations clearly can and frequently do lead to disaster.

In order to better understand the ledger systems and certain other concepts I will discuss, I will need to present some additional material on accounting conventions. These concepts are more or less standard in the field. Additional information can be obtained in almost any accounting textbook.

Some Accounting Methods

The field of accounting has evolved into a profession of singular importance to all areas of human endeavor. It is the job of an accountant to determine the financial status of individuals or organizations. To accomplish this task, accountants have evolved a body of knowledge and practice that includes generally accepted account-

		Categories			
	Item	**Mortgage**	**Food**	**Auto**	**Clothing**
1.	Check # 1	$1000.00			
2.	Check # 2		$100.00		
3.	Check # 3			$250.00	
4.	Check # 4				$75.00
	TOTALS	$1000.00	$100.00	$250.00	$75.00

Figure 9.3. An abbreviated general ledger, June 1990.

ing principles. There are two professional organizations, the Accounting Practice Board and the Financial Accounting Standards Board that help to establish these principles and resolve particular problems. Accountants working with and for professionals will follow these principles.

Two major documents form the foundation of an accounting system and help to transform the budget from a planning to an operating tool. The first document is called the *balance sheet.* Balance sheets are the statements of wealth possessed by an individual or organization at a particular point in time. The second document is called an *income statement.* Income statements present the flow of money through an individual or organization over a particular time period. Balance sheets are constructed at least on an annual basis, but usually on a monthly basis. Income statements are prepared monthly, quarterly, and annually.

In order to understand balance sheets and income statements and, therefore, the implementation of budgets, we must explore some additional accounting principles.

T Accounts. To create a balance sheet or income statement, indeed, to create any major financial document, an accountant begins with a list. We have seen this process in operation in the creation of budgets. Accounting conventions require these lists to be split into separate but equal columns. Thus, accounting documents are presented in the form of a *T*. On the left-hand side of the *T*, the accountant lists assets. On the right-hand side of the *T*, the accountant lists liabilities and ownership. There is no real explanation for this arrangement, accountants have simply all agreed to use this method to create their lists. In addition, by tradition, entries on the left-hand side of the *T* are termed *debits*, and entries on the right-hand side of the *T* are called *credits*. You must remember that assets are listed as debits on the left side and liabilities and ownership are listed as credits on the right. Figure 9.4 presents this arrangement of the classic *T* account format.

A major portion of the accounting process consists of creating accurate and useful *T* accounts that list assets and liabilities in a variety of ways at different points in time. Additions to the list of assets are made by debiting the asset or left side of the *T* account, that is, simply adding the proper amount of money to the correct category on the lists of assets. Similarly, additions to the lists of liabilities

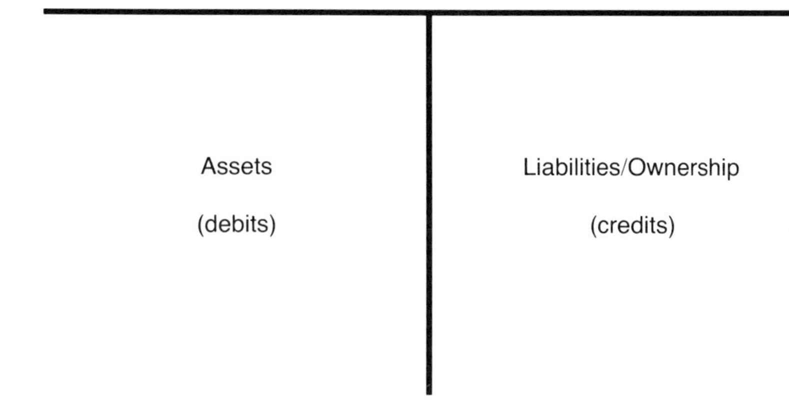

Figure 9.4. The T-account format.

and ownership are made by crediting the liability side or the right side of the proper *T* account. This is done by adding the new amount to the appropriate item on the lists of liabilities or ownership.

Most accountants will begin their work with a client by asking him or her to help create lists of assets and liabilities. As we saw in the first part of this chapter, assets consist of such items as cash on hand or in banks, accounts receivable, inventories, investments, land, buildings, equipment, and so forth. Liabilities and ownership involve such items as accounts or bills payable, mortgages, bonds outstanding, preferred stock, common stock, and retained income. Balance sheets are built from these lists of assets and liabilities.

A simple equation governs all transactions involving the balance sheet, *assets = liabilities + equity*. This is called the balance-sheet equation. The *T* account formation for the balance sheet is as follows:

Assets	Liabilities Equity (ownership)

Each asset, liability, and equity listed on the balance sheet will also have its own *T* account kept by the accountant. These accounts or specific ledgers back up the general ledger that, as stated earlier, records all of the financial transactions in an enterprise, usually on a monthly basis. Transactions are recorded in the specific ledgers as they occur. Additions and subtractions are made to the assets and liabilities columns for each transaction so that the balance-sheet equation is maintained in each account and, therefore, also maintained for the overall enterprise. We can see these principles in action in the following example.

Our psychologist, Robin Williams, and his accountant have created *T* accounts for each client in the practice. These appear as separate pages in the accounts receivable section of Robin's records. Several of these accounts are displayed here:

Client #1		Client #2		Client #3	
Date $1,000		Date $500		Date $1,500	

Accounts receivable appear as debits on the left side of the *T* accounts. These are monies owed to Robin by clients for services rendered. They are all grouped together or summarized in the accounts receivable *T* account or ledger as shown here.

Accounts Receivable	
Date $4,000	

This is done for record-keeping and reporting purposes. Balance sheets rarely show all of the back-up accounts kept by the enterprise, but usually provide summaries of major items that are integrated to give a broader and more useful picture of financial status. Accounts receivable is one of these categories.

The accounts receivable *T* account is usually balanced by a *T* account kept for cash. The cash account provides a record of all of the monies actually paid to the enterprise, in this case, the enterprise is Robin Williams, PhD. Suppose, for example, Robin kept $10,000 in cash on hand in an interest-earning checking account to pay bills and meet emergencies. And suppose in a given month, Robin received payments of $500, $200, and $300 by the three clients described earlier. Robin's cash *T* account would look as follows in recording these transactions.

Cash	
Date $10,000	
Date 500	
Date 200	
Date 300	

These amounts are debited in the cash account. In order to keep the balance-sheet equation, they must also be credited somewhere, usually, in each client's receivable account. This is illustrated here.

Client #1		Client #2		Client #3	
Date $1,000		Date $500		Date $1,500	
Date	500	Date	200	Date	300

Each of these transactions is dated for record-keeping purposes. The purpose of adding and subtracting the various debits and credits is to maintain the balance-sheet equation for the enterprise. This process describes what has become known as *double-entry bookkeeping*.

Transactions, as stated earlier, are dated and summarized at regular intervals in financial reports of various types. This description should begin to give you an idea of the power that budgeting and accounting systems give to an individual trying to manage an organization or business. The budgeting process and methods allow you to establish clear financial goals in any number of areas for income and expenditures. The accounting system keeps a running tally of financial transactions and, at any time, can provide a detailed evaluative report of the progress made toward those goals.

Balance sheets. As described earlier, the major progress reports used to measure the financial status or health of the organization are the balance sheet and income statement. A balance sheet usually is done on a monthly basis. It lists the status of current assets, which are accounts expected to turn into cash within 1 year, and fixed assets, which have longer life expectancies. Similarly, it lists the current liabilities, those needs for cash that should be provided in 1 year, and long-term liabilities, which are to be met over longer time periods. Current assets consist of such accounts as cash, inventories, and accounts receivable. Fixed assets are equipment and buildings. Current liabilities are accounts payable and mortgages. Long-term liabilities usually consist of equities commitments, such as stocks, bonds, and paid-in-cash surpluses.

For the sake of simplicity, this chapter will only cover a balance sheet with current liabilities and paid-in surpluses. Readers can refer to Spiro (1978), Horngren (1978), and other sources for more detailed treatments of equities and long-term liabilities. In my judgment, these issues are not central to this discussion, but the reader must be aware of the role that equities play in the finances of larger enterprises where they often provide major sources of capital upon which organizations operate.

The balance sheet in Figure 9.5 gives a statement of Dr. Williams's assets and liabilities heading into the 1991 calendar year. It is his monthly balance sheet.

This report reveals current assets of $82,000, including $60,000 in cash and short-term securities and $22,000 in accounts receivable or cash owed to Robin from various clients and tenants. Fixed assets include $25,000 in office equipment and his office building, valued at $300,000 (both are partially depreciated for tax purposes). As of December 31, 1990, Robin's total assets equal $407,000.

On the liability side, the balance sheet reveals $17,000 in accounts payable or bills owed by Robin and a mortgage on the building of $200,000 on which he pays monthly installments. Because Robin is practicing as a sole practitioner rather than in some form of partnership or corporation, he has no outstanding equities in the form of stocks. In the past, he decided to use $30,000 in profits generated by the business to invest in his enterprise in the form of his building, so he has a $30,000 paid-in surplus in the equity category. In other words, his practice owes him the $30,000 he loaned to it for the building. His balance sheet therefore shows $247,000 in total liabilities. Subtracting liabilities from assets reveals a balance of $160,000 as of December 31, 1990, the majority of which represents appreciation in the value of his building. As of this month's report, Robin's business looks pretty sound.

Balance sheets are also calculated on a quarterly and annual basis in order to give a picture of organizational performance that stretches over a longer period of

Cash & Short Term Securities	$ 60,000	Accounts Payable	$ 17,000
Accounts Receivable	22,000	Mortgage	200,000
Current Assets	$ 82,000	Current Liabilities	$217,000
Equipment	25,000		
Building	300,000	Paid in Surplus	30,000
Fixed Assets	$325,000	Equities	30,000
Total Assets	$407,000	Total Liabilities	$247,000

Figure 9.5. Sample balance sheet as of December 31, 1990, for Robin Williams, PhD.

time. Annual reports constructed in this fashion can be compared to give an idea of how the enterprise has done over a 3-year, 5-year, or even longer time period.

Income statements. The second major financial report, the income statement, presents a summary of the flow of money through an organization during a given time period. These reports are constructed at monthly, quarterly, and annual intervals and are used with the balance sheets for the same period to assess progress. The flow of money in a professional practice usually involves income from the sales of services, rents, and other revenues, and payments in the form of salaries, mortgage or interest notes, and bills paid. Again, the income statement starts with a list of these types of transactions. The records for this list are obtained from the general ledger that records all such transactions as they occur. In Figure 9.6, the list contains a summary of all recorded events for the period of November 30 through December 31, 1990, the same period used for the balance sheet in Figure 9.5.

As seen in Figure 9.6, Robin's business earned $11,700 during the last month of fiscal year 1990. His primary source of revenue came from fees of $10,000. Rents from building tenants and interest from his short-term deposits accounted for $1,700, bringing his total revenue for the period to $11,700. His expenses included $10,600 in salaries and fringe benefits, including his monthly draw, $1,500 in mortgage payments, $1,700 in depreciation, and $2,100 in accounts payable that represent his office bills for the month. Thus, expenses totaled $15,800. Subtracting expenses from revenue gives a figure of minus $4,100, represented here by parenthesis around the number, a net loss for the month. Each of these categories is, of course, backed up by entries in the appropriate *T* accounts and ledgers.

As we described earlier, Robin's practice has three big clients who take up substantial amounts of his time. In those months in which he receives no retainer or fees from these clients, his income statement shows a net loss. This is to his advantage, despite its impact in some months, because he is able to raise his annual revenue through the management of short-term investments that yield substantial amounts of interest each year. Thus, a monthly balance sheet or income statement can be somewhat deceiving, because the financial status of the business can be severely distorted in short time periods.

This illustrates the need for quarterly and annual statements, which give a generally better picture of business health. Annual statements can be accumulated and compared over time to give an idea of how the enterprise is doing over longer periods of time when compared to forecasts or plans.

These reports are part of the financial management system you must have in order to assess your fiscal progress in your chosen niche. Without such a system, it is impossible to determine whether your goals are being met or even if the basic needs of survival are being addressed over time. These tools permit you to identify major sources of financial dependency in the environment and to formulate activity plans to manage these dependencies so that they do not become overwhelming or sources of pain or failure. The annual budget, balance sheet, and income statement are three of the four principal, reporting components of the financial management system.

Monthly financial reports. The final component of an accounting system is a monthly financial report that presents a listing of the budget categories, the amounts

Revenue

	Item	**Amount**
1.	Retainer L.W. Manufacturing	0
2.	Retainer P.A. Retailers	0
3.	Retainer R.W. Jones	0
4.	Other fees	10,000
5.	Interest	500
6.	Rent	1,200
	TOTALS	11,700

Expenses

	Item	**Amount**
1.	Salaries	9,200
2.	Fringe Benefits	1,400
3.	Mortgage	1,500
4.	Insurance	500
5.	Utilities	700
6.	Telephone	300
7.	Equipment	0
8.	Printing	200
9.	Postage	0
10.	Transportation	200
11.	Professional Development	0
12.	Computer Expenses	0
13.	Depreciation	1,700
14.	Other	100
	TOTALS	**15,800**

Income for December 1990 = revenue – expenses.

$11,700
–15,800

($ 4,100)

Figure 9.6. Sample income statement covering November 30–December 31, 1990, for Robin Williams, PhD.

planned to be spent in each of them, the amounts spent in each category for the report period, and, usually, monthly and year-to-date totals in each category. Some financial reports also present the percentage of variation in each account for the time period. Figure 9.7 presents such a financial report for Robin's practice.

As you can see, this report is a powerful tool for fiscal management purposes. Arrayed before Robin is a summary of his financial and program plans and the results of his financial and program decisions for the month and for the year. The report tells him where his money came from and where it went to. It also gives him an assessment of how accurate his planning process was and how successful his management decisions were in variances between the budgeted and year-to-date amounts. These variances are expressed as the percentages, plus or minus, by which the amount collected or spent in a budget account deviated from the plan. The variance column thus gives a reading on the specific areas of program and budget and an overall reading on the general status of the practice. Let us review Figure 9.7 in more detail in order to get a better idea of the usefulness of this type of report.

The revenue and expense report contains an itemization of the amounts summarized in the balance sheet and income statements reviewed earlier. On the revenue side, we see zero income from his retainers and a total of $11,700 for the month from other fees, interest, and rent. Actually, this is a simple repetition of the income statement provided earlier in Figure 9.6. Budgeted amounts are depicted to provide a baseline for analysis and problem identification. The year-to-date column arrays the total sum accumulated in each category for the year as of that report period. In this case, Robin's fiscal year coincides with the calendar year, so the year-to-date column actually presents a preliminary summary of financial activity for all of 1990. We clearly see that income in all categories is pretty much on target with the amounts originally forecast in the budget column. The only deviation from predictions comes in the other-fees category, which reveals that Robin has earned $10,000 more in other fees than he anticipated a year earlier.

The variance column reports these results in a different form, stating that for five out of six categories, there was 0% deviation between the amount budgeted and the year-to-date sums, thus demonstrating the accuracy of Robin's budgeting process. The sixth category, other fees, reports a positive variation or increase of 8.3% over the amount budgeted. This has a direct positive effect on the total revenue for the year, increasing it by 5%. Thus, the revenue report shows that, although Robin may have had a poor revenue month in December, his overall revenue budget was right on target. In addition, it tells him that his business, other than for his three major clients, was better than he expected. An analysis of his *T* accounts will give him a more detailed look at where his revenue came from and perhaps some idea of how to maintain these new clients or sources of income.

On the expense side of the report, a more detailed, yet generally similar, picture emerges. Total expenses for the month were $15,800, representing 7.9% of the $200,000 budgeted for the year. This is approximately 1/12 of the total budget and, therefore, is probably a fairly average month. Utilities were high, reflecting increased fuel bills for a winter month. All other categories appear to be in reasonable shape for this period. Again, the budget column presents the expense baselines or targets for the year. Year-to-date figures offer a nice portrait of how his expense budget held up for the year.

Revenue

	Item	Amount	Budget	Year-to-Date	Variance
1.	Retainer L.W. Manufacturing	0	30,000	30,000	0%
2.	Retainer P.A. Retailers	0	25,000	25,000	0%
3.	Retainer R.W. Jones	0	5,000	5,000	0%
4.	Other fees	10,000	120,000	130,000	+ 8.3%
5.	Interest	500	6,000	6,000	0%
6.	Rent	1,200	14,000	14,000	0%
	TOTALS	11,700	200,000	210,000	+ 5%

Expenses

	Item	Amount	Budget	Year-to-Date	Variance
1.	Salaries	9,200	110,000	110,000	0%
2.	Fringe Benefits	1,400	16,500	16,500	0%
3.	Mortgage	1,500	14,000	14,000	0%
4.	Insurance	500	5,000	6,000	+ 20%
5.	Utilities	700	4,500	5,000	+ 11%
6.	Telephone	300	5,000	4,500	– 10%
7.	Equipment	0	5,000	4,200	– 16%
8.	Printing	200	2,000	4,000	+ 200%
9.	Postage	0	1,000	700	– 30%
10.	Transportation	200	2,000	2,400	+ 20%
11.	Professional Development	0	3,000	2,400	– 20%
12.	Computer Expenses	0	3,000	1,500	– 50%
13.	Depreciation	1,700	15,000	15,000	0%
14.	Other	100	15,000	12,000	– 20%
	TOTALS	**15,800**	**200,000**	**199,200**	**– 0.4%**

Figure 9.7. Revenue and expense report covering November 30–December 31, 1990, for Robin Williams, PhD.

Here, we see a more detailed and better illustration of the power of this financial report and of the importance of variance analysis. Immediately, we are drawn to the pattern of plus and minus percentages reflected in the variance column. Salaries, fringe benefits, mortgages, and depreciation categories were all on target and represent fixed costs that are very predictable. All of the other categories vary from the budgeted amounts, some as much as 200%. These are controllable accounts and give a summary of what happened in the business on a daily basis.

Obviously, Robin had an unexpected rise in insurance payments (+20%) and utility bills (+11%). He was able to cut back expenses in his telephone (−10%), equipment (−16%), and computer (−50%) budgets more than expected. His printing bills were much higher than expected (+200%), probably reflecting increased copying and training work. Postage was under budget (−30%), while transportation was over budget (+20%). Professional development (−17%) and the other miscellaneous category (−20%) were all under budget, thus balancing the increases. The total result of his expenses for the year, $800 under his budget (−.04%), reflects astute planning and good judgment.

Note that in the categories that Robin had significant control—telephone, equipment, postage, professional development, computer expenses, and other—he exercised great restraint, which allowed him to meet his budget targets. The overall results for the year show an excess of $10,800 in revenue over expenses, a good year for our psychologist.

This report gives Robin an important way to manage his business on a monthly and annual basis. It facilitates financial and program decisions by providing a clear idea of the impact these decisions have on the financial status of the business. Without such information, it would clearly be harder for Robin to adapt to changing environmental conditions and, hence, to survive. It also gives him a good tool for analyzing and managing his major dependencies, thus increasing the power he asserts over his own destiny.

Beyond these functions, the revenue and expense report enables Robin to plan more wisely for the next fiscal year and to adjust his professional goals. The increases in certain expense categories must be carefully scrutinized to determine if they represent permanent changes that must be accommodated by increases in the budget or whether they were idiosyncratic or one-time occurrences that can be ignored in budget planning. The same goes for the increases in other fee revenue. If the income was obtained from new clients who are now likely to produce more business, budgets can be increased. If the revenue represent a one-time bonanza, say from the fees generated by a lengthy and unexpected consultation, appropriate adjustments can also be made.

The important point here is that Robin has the data he needs to make these decisions. Without such information, any evaluation of his performance is likely to be less accurate and objective. Thus, one role that financial planning and assessment plays is in helping to provide a more empirically based appraisal of how well the professional is adapting to his or her niche. In a certain sense, the information can be used to make probability statements about survival in the niche. Without successful financial performance, survival is not possible. To be sure, there are many other attributes of successful adaption; however, all other means of assessing the adaption process are not as empirical and as easy to obtain. Although professionals must obviously have a command of the financial-planning and analysis tools, they cannot afford to ignore other types of information regarding their performance.

Audits. The final piece of the financial puzzle involves an annual audit performed by an independent and certified accountant. For corporations, partnerships, and other large enterprises, the annual audit is frequently required by law or by the by-laws or articles of incorporation for the organization. For solo practitioners, it may not be a requirement, but it is still a good idea. The auditing process consists of a complete financial assessment of the status of the business. It checks the sums in all the T accounts and ledgers. It cross-checks the paperwork documenting each financial transaction, such as the checks written, invoices received, bills sent out, etc. The audit makes sure that categories, such as depreciation and equities, are properly labeled and appear on the balance sheet in the appropriate area. It also checks to see if such activities are conducted within the bounds of local, state, and federal laws regulating financial transactions. One must not underestimate the importance or difficulty of complying with these legal requirements, because they change all the time in response to new case law, regulatory rulings, and statutory modifications.

The end result of the audit is a formal, written summary of the accounts of the business in the form of a balance sheet and income statement for the year. This represents the judgment of an independent professional about how well a business or professional performed financially for the year. It is a financial report card and the equivalent of a thorough physical examination. It will not give you all of the information you need to manage yourself, but you cannot perform well without the data it does provide. In addition, the audit analyzes financial procedures and makes recommendations for changes. It highlights areas of strength and weakness and is very important in planning for the future.

If you are working for a salary in an organization, these methods and principles remain useful to you. You should still have access to competent financial advice. You still need lists of your assets and liabilities. And you must carry on your private financial life in a responsible and thoughtful fashion. This requires the use of budgets, accurate record keeping, and, hopefully, the production of useful periodic reports. At a minimum, on an annual basis, you are required to pay your taxes. This necessitates a review of income and expenses and can be turned into a broader and more useful process with the expenditure of a little more time and effort and the use of some of the principles and techniques illustrated in this chapter.

Concrete Steps for Professionals

In this chapter, I have attempted to present the basic foundations of financial management and planning. I believe that the ability of all professionals to actualize themselves and survive is highly dependent on effective financial performance. The information in this chapter is not complex by design, because relatively simple financial systems are very powerful tools in the hands of a professional who has a clear idea of how to use them. Financial information and skills always increase the power of those who have them. In closing this chapter, I would like to leave you with a simplified checklist of steps you can take to develop and use a financial plan.

First, as I have stated before, obtain competent, professional, financial assistance. Even though many planning and accounting tasks can be done by anyone with a pencil and some rudimentary knowledge, skilled consultation is always useful, because the rules in the financial world change periodically, and it is important to have an objective view of one's performance. Experts, such as certified public accountants and tax attorneys, help to assure that you are meeting your financial obligations, while simultaneously facilitating the accumulation of wealth. The information and services provided help to assure that competent decisions are made and that financial plans stay on track. You may wish to contact your state psychological association, the state bar association, or the state association of certified public accountants to find people who will work with you.

Second, create lists of all of your assets and liabilities. This will serve as a baseline balance sheet against which future performance can be measured. It also gives you some idea of the financial goals you may wish to pursue.

Third, think about and then write down a list of your financial goals. This list could include a statement of salary or income needs and desires, a listing of expenditures desires or plans, a statement of pension, insurance and emergency-cash plans, and other needs or desires, such as health maintenance and education.

Fourth, provide yourself with a statement of the specific activities and methods you will use in pursuit of these goals. Statements such as purchase annuity plan, arrange $ worth of life insurance, and save $ per month in the following ways will give you a set of behavioral steps to take in pursuit of your goals. Such a list will eliminate much of the fog and anxiety surrounding procedures in the financial area.

Fifth, list your sources of anticipated income and expenses for the year, and create your budget. This is how you make your goals and activity plans tangible for a given time period.

Sixth, create your record-keeping system. Everyone has a way of keeping records even if it involves throwing everything in one drawer until tax time. Remember, your records tell you what decisions you have made and how they affect your performance.

Finally, do periodic reports of your performance. At least once a year, you should drag out your records and summarize where you are. You should always compare this statement of performance with the goals that you have established. In this way, you can assess progress over time and make corrections if problems have arisen.

Following these seven steps, most of which appear in the exercises of this chapter, will not guarantee you financial success. As you have seen, financial success is dependent on a larger array of variables. However, financial systems are a necessary part of every professional's life. I hope this chapter has given you some understanding and appreciation of the major characteristics of these systems and how you can put them to work.

References

Horngren, C. T. (1978). *Introduction to management accounting* (4th ed.). Englewood Cliffs, NJ: Prentice-Hall.

Spiro, H. T. (1978). *Financial planning for the independent professional.* New York: Wiley-Interscience.

10

Georgine M. Pion

Psychologists Wanted: Employment Trends Over the Past Decade

In the early 1970s, career opportunities in psychology were relatively clear. The large majority (58%) of doctoral psychologists were faculty in college and university psychology departments, with another 25% working in hospitals, clinics, schools, and human service agencies. Only small minorities were employed in other non-academic sectors (8%) or as independent practitioners (7%).

Since that time, however, the employment options for psychologists have changed dramatically. The academic marketplace began to contract as higher education was confronted by a shortage of resources, an expanding middle-aged and tenured faculty, and shrinking enrollments. In contrast, opportunities in the mental health sector began to flourish in response to increasing demands for psychological services, a shift from institutional settings as the primary locus of care to community-based services, and the passage of laws and regulations favorable to psychologists involved in delivering services. For example, the eligibility of psychologists to receive payment from third-party insurers suddenly made independent practice a more viable career option.

At the same time, other nonacademic sectors began to place a higher premium on the skills associated with advanced psychological training. Corporations, contract research firms, and nonprofit organizations needed individuals with expertise in personnel testing, program evaluation, and organizational development. Moreover, psychologists themselves continued to carve out new roles and functions that had never been envisioned by their faculty mentors—in consulting firms catering to the needs of the legal profession, in museums, in architectural design firms, and in congressional staff offices.

Such changes in the employability of psychologists were stimulated by more macrolevel shifts in society, and demographic, economic, and sociopolitical trends will continue to influence where psychologists will be working. In order to identify future employment scenarios and how psychologists can best exploit emerging career opportunities, it is useful to examine trends in society and in the employment of psychologists over the past decade.

Major Societal Shifts and Their Implications for Psychologists

American society is a product of two major transformations: (a) a shift away from an economy heavily dependent on agriculture or manufacturing to one driven by the delivery of services, particularly such human services as education, health care, and government; and (b) a growing reliance on the application of specialized scientific and technical knowledge in all arenas (Pion & Lipsey, 1984). These two trends have had a profound impact on all major disciplines, and psychology is no exception. In fact, psychology has stood much to gain from these trends, given that it has both strong professional and scientific underpinnings.

The increasing emphasis on services is evidenced by several developments. For example, the growing share of the U.S. labor force that is devoted to service-related activities has grown from 55% in 1960 to 68% in 1985. The fastest growing occupations have been those in the professional and technical areas; this group has more than doubled in size, rising from 7.5 million in 1960 to 17.3 million in 1986 (Silvestri & Lukasiewicz, 1987). Much of this growth occurred in the human services occupations.

Concurrent with this trend toward a services-based economy has been an increasing commitment to generating and applying scientific knowledge by all major sectors. This is reflected, for example, in the changing use of scientists. Whereas colleges and universities employed 42% of all scientists in 1968 (Pion & Lipsey, 1984), this percentage had declined to 29% by 1986, and industry had emerged as the largest employer (48%) of scientific personnel (National Science Board, 1987). Further, investment in the production and application of scientific knowledge by all sponsors has continued to grow, rising from $62 billion in 1970 to $102 billion in 1986 (constant 1982 dollars; National Science Board, 1987).

Such trends have presented considerable opportunities to psychologists. For example, the shift toward an economy based on human services had several implications. During the past 20 years, a multitude of programs have been launched to resolve major problems plaguing society (e.g., drug abuse, alcoholism, family violence, and AIDS), many of which focused on changing maladaptive or harmful human behaviors. Thus, psychologists trained in the practice specialties were needed to assess and treat clients, as well as to provide consultation and preventive services. Another area where psychologists could make significant contributions involved developing and testing better theories on which to base these interventions. Similarly, there was a growing recognition that effective services delivery also required program planning, services coordination, program monitoring, and outcome assessment. This led to opportunities for psychologists skilled in program development, administration, and evaluation.

The view that scientific knowledge was indeed a national resource that could improve decision making, along with the development and implementation of policy, further accentuated opportunities for psychologists. In addition to the need for basic and applied research on human behavior, individuals skilled in policy analysis and knowledge dissemination were in demand by a variety of nonacademic employers. Given psychology's contributions in such areas as survey design, measurement, organizational functioning, and social experimentation, the discipline should have been among the first of the social sciences to profit from these developments.

Psychology's Response

Given these major societal shifts, we might expect changes in the field of psychology over the past decade—in the way psychologists are trained, in the fields of study they pursue, and in the activities in which they are involved. Let's see what happened.

Size and Strength of the Psychological Work Force

Since the early 1970s, psychologists have become an increasingly visible component of the professional and scientific work force.[1] In 1973, the number of employed PhD psychologists totaled about 24,000, but by 1987, this figure had more than doubled to over 56,000.

During the past decade, the demand for doctoral psychologists appears to have kept pace with this expanding population. Since 1977, the employment of psychologists increased more rapidly than did the employment of all other doctoral scientists (5.3% vs. 3.9% per year). Compared with other scientific and engineering fields, unemployment rates during the last decade for psychologists have remained remarkably low—about 1% for all doctoral psychologists and 2% for new doctorate recipients (Pion, Bramblett, & Wicherski, 1987; Stapp, Tucker, & VandenBos, 1985).

There has also been a growing trend toward part-time employment. In 1977, 87% of all doctoral psychologists were employed full-time, and 6% were working part-time. Only 10 years later, these percentages had shifted to 83% and 11%, respectively. Although increasing part-time employment can signal a tightening marketplace, this does not seem to be the case for psychology. New doctorate recipients, the group perhaps most sensitive to fluctuations in demand, have not experienced increasing part-time employment; the percentage who were employed part-time (9–10%) has remained relatively stable since 1975 (e.g., Stapp, Fulcher, & Wicherski, 1984). The majority of psychologists working part-time do so by choice rather than because they are unable to find a full-time position (Stapp & Fulcher, 1983). For these individuals, part-time employment appears to offer a more flexible work schedule for personal or other interests.

Other indicators point to the strength of the marketplace for psychologists. For example, individuals want to work in jobs that are related to and commensurate with their training. In 1986, an overwhelming majority of doctoral psychologists (94%) were indeed working in psychology—the highest percentage of any scientific field (National Science Foundation, 1988). In addition, large majorities of 1977–1986 doctorate recipients with full-time positions have continued to report that their job was in their field (97%), that they were not underemployed (74%), and that their current position was their first choice (74%).

Assessments of employment prospects made by new doctorate recipients have also steadily improved over the past 10 years. The percentage rating the job market as "bleak" or "poor" declined from 31% of 1977 doctorates to 10% of 1986 recipients, whereas the percentage judging it as "good" or "excellent" climbed from 32% to 57%, respectively. Overall, psychologists have been functioning as psychologists in jobs that use the considerable number of years (the median is now 7 years) required to earn the degree.

---

[1] This chapter will restrict its attention to doctoral psychologists, given the predominant doctoral orientation of most career roles in psychology and the relative lack of data on other degree holders. Furthermore, the majority of the analyses focus on PhD recipients, given the relative recency of the PsyD degree and the limited amount of information on PsyDs.

Changes in Subfields

Another major transformation in the discipline has concerned the fields chosen by psychologists. Table 10.1 illustrates the increasing concentration of psychologists in the practice-oriented specialties. Since 1977, the number of doctoral-level psychologists in clinical, counseling, and school psychology has more than doubled, rising at an annual rate of almost 7% overall. In fact, nearly 70% of the growth in the number of employed doctoral psychologists can be attributed to the increasing number working in these specialties. The rates at which new doctorates are being produced in each of these three fields have also been much higher than that for psychology as a whole.

The shift toward the professional side of the discipline is even more pronounced than the figures in Table 10.1 suggest. In response to the expanding service-based economy, the number of doctoral programs in clinical, counseling, and school psychology increased from about 250 in 1975 to almost 350 in 1989.

Perhaps the most noticeable aspect of this growth has been the proliferation of professional schools of psychology. These free-standing and university-affiliated schools, most of which were established in the 1970s, sought to prepare students solely for practitioner careers—a departure from the traditional scientist-practitioner programs that aspired to produce individuals who would be actively involved in both research and practice.

During the past decade, doctoral production by these programs has accelerated. In 1979, 62 PsyDs and 189 PhDs in clinical psychology graduated from these programs—about 25% of all doctorates awarded in this specialty (Howard et al., 1986). By 1987, these numbers had increased to 311 PsyDs and 266 PhDs, representing 39% of all clinical psychology doctorate recipients. Thus, not only has psychology produced more doctorates in the direct-service-provider specialties, but an increasing proportion of these are being trained as practitioners rather than as researchers or teachers.

Among those fields that do not involve a strong services-delivery component, however, the picture is quite different. Although Table 10.1 shows that the total population of doctoral psychologists in these areas did increase, the annual rate of growth was much slower (about 4%). Moreover, trends differed for individual specialties within this group.

In fields with a long history of academic and research employment, the total numbers of new doctorates have actually declined, primarily due to a tapering off in doctoral production. For example, the pool of new PhD graduates in social and personality psychologists has shrunk since 1977 by an average of 12 individuals per year. An even sharper decline is true for new PhDs in experimental, comparative, and physiological psychology.

In contrast, those fields characterized by both research and applied orientations have not witnessed as much (if any) erosion. Industrial/organizational psychology—a field long known for its research on "real world" problems—has inched upward in terms of individuals working in these specialties. Developmental psychology, which has recently incorporated a distinct applied component, has experienced an average annual growth rate of about 5%. It is interesting to note that growth in these fields cannot be primarily attributed to surges in doctoral production. Rather,

Table 10-1. Major Fields of New Psychology Doctorate Recipients and All Doctoral Psychologists: 1977–1987

	1977		1979		1981		1983		1985		1987		Average Change per Year	
	N	%	N	%	N	%	N	%	N	%	N	%	N	%
All psychologists[a]														
Clinical	13,378	39.8	17,389	45.9	19,369	45.2	21,461	46.0	25,260	48.4	28,147	49.9	+1,477	+7.8
Counseling	2,712	8.1	1,949	5.1	2,079	4.9	2,300	4.9	2,842	5.4	2,735	4.9	+2	+0.5
School	1,084	3.2	1,293	3.4	1,542	3.6	1,965	4.2	2,006	3.8	2,001	3.5	+92	+6.5
Developmental	1,728	5.1	1,957	5.2	2,256	5.3	2,175	4.7	2,570	4.9	2,903	5.1	+118	+5.4
Educational	1,622	4.8	1,201	3.2	1,462	3.4	1,074	2.3	1,453	2.8	1,438	2.6	−18	−0.3
Social and personality	2,450	7.3	2,384	6.3	2,565	6.0	2,501	5.4	2,834	5.4	3,066	5.4	+62	+2.3
Industrial/organizational	1,974	5.9	1,805	4.8	2,235	5.2	2,650	5.7	2,709	5.2	2,714	4.8	+74	+3.4
Experimental, comparative, and physiological	4,598	13.7	5,144	13.6	5,787	13.5	5,051	10.8	4,839	9.3	4,959	8.8	+36	+0.9
All other	4,106	12.2	4,726	12.5	5,534	12.9	7,468	16.0	7,669	14.7	8,415	14.9	+431	+5.3
Total	33,652		37,848		42,829		46,645		52,182		56,378		+2,273	+5.3
New psychology doctorates[b]														
Clinical	981	32.3	1,117	35.4	1,377	39.3	1,409	38.8	1,375	40.2	1,484	41.5	+50	+4.4
Counseling	269	8.9	315	10.0	351	10.0	434	11.9	432	12.6	485	13.6	+22	+6.5
School	148	4.9	139	4.4	159	4.5	243	6.7	223	6.5	243	6.8	+10	+6.5
Developmental	203	6.7	221	7.0	201	5.7	219	6.0	176	5.1	200	5.6	0	0.0
Educational	136	4.5	163	5.2	180	5.1	154	4.2	127	3.7	89	2.5	−5	−1.4
Social and personality	265	8.7	258	8.2	229	6.5	223	6.1	188	5.5	157	4.4	−11	−4.8
Industrial/organizational	81	2.7	87	2.8	87	2.5	90	2.5	102	3.0	105	2.9	+2	+3.8
Experimental, comparative, and physiological	491	16.1	416	13.2	396	11.3	314	8.6	255	7.5	224	6.3	−27	−7.4
All other	460	15.2	437	13.9	522	14.9	546	15.0	544	15.9	592	16.5	+13	+2.7
Total	3,034		3,153		3,502		3,632		3,422		3,579		+55	+1.8

Note. Source of data for new doctorates: National Research Council (1988, 1989) and data from *Graduate Study in Psychology and Associated Fields*, respective years. Source of data for all doctorates: National Science Foundation, Division of Science Resources Studies (unpublished analyses).

[a] Major fields for all doctoral psychologists refer to the field of employment rather than the field of the doctoral degree. Data pertains only to individuals with the PhD.

[b] Included are both PhD and PsyD recipients. For School Psychology, PhDs who reported their degree field as School Psychology, whether they used the codes listed under the major fields of Psychology or Education, were included. It should be noted that these totals are undercounts, given that data were not available for a small number of doctoral programs.

it appears that psychologists in other specialties (e.g., social psychology) have switched into them, possibly because of new research interests or the perception of more promising career opportunities.

Apart from the practice specialties, the other major area of growth has been the category of "other subfields." Here, the increase is primarily fueled by the emergence of several new areas of specialization in psychology. Some of these areas (e.g., clinical neuropsychology and rehabilitation psychology) again reflect the increasing participation of psychologists in providing direct services to meet the needs of special patient populations. However, others represent either new research specialties, many of which are interdisciplinary (e.g., psychology and law and cognitive science), or traditional subfields that have adopted new orientations more geared toward "giving psychology away."

Changes in Where Psychologists Work

Another significant shift over the past decade has been in terms of where psychologists work. As Table 10.2 shows, the primary change has been the continued erosion in academic employment—a trend that began in the early 1970s. In 1973, almost 60% of all psychologists were working in academic settings. Four years later, this percentage had declined to 51%, and by 1987, it had dropped even further to 41%.

However, it is important to note that this was only a relative reduction. Although a decreasing proportion of psychologists were working in colleges and universities, the actual number increased at an average rate of about 3% per year. It is only with regard to new doctorates that the number hired into academic positions has steadily declined—from an estimated 1,013 in 1977 to 769 in 1986.

While the academic marketplace was tightening for new graduates, employment in nonacademic settings was on the rise. Looking at all doctoral psychologists, the majority of growth between 1977 and 1987 has been in the number of psychologists who were self-employed. This group has burgeoned, almost quadrupling in number and replacing hospitals and clinics as the second largest employer of psychologists. In 1987, one out of every four doctoral psychologists was self-employed.

The exact meaning of these shifts is difficult to interpret, given that employment opportunities available to individuals in the health-service-provider specialties differ from those existing in other subfields. Thus, it is useful to look at employment trends separately for (a) psychologists with doctorates in the practice specialties, and (b) those with doctorates in the nonpractice areas of psychology (e.g., cognitive, developmental, educational, experimental, industrial/organizational, and social).

The Health Service-Provider Specialties

As shown in Table 10.3, the bulk of the increase in employed doctoral psychologists has been in the health service-provider fields, with this group expanding at a rate of nearly 7% per year. The largest increase in both absolute numbers and percentages has been in the number of psychologists who are self-employed. In fact, this group has almost quadrupled in size since 1977, and self-employment is now the

Table 10-2. Type of Employment Sector of Doctoral Psychologists: 1977–1987

	1977		1979		1981		1983		1985		1987		Average Change per Year	
Employment Setting	N	%	N	%	N	%	N	%	N	%	N	%	N	%
Academic settings	17,247	51.3	18,255	48.2	20,021	46.7	20,328	43.6	22,624	43.4	23,122	41.0	+588	+3.0
Hospitals/clinics	5,386	16.0	5,881	15.5	6,183	14.4	6,042	13.0	6,379	12.2	7,155	12.7	+177	+2.9
Nonprofit organizations	1,272	3.8	1,725	4.6	1,679	3.9	1,773	3.8	2,084	4.0	2,501	4.4	+123	+7.2
Self-employed	3,637	10.8	5,151	13.6	7,091	16.6	9,455	20.3	12,009	23.0	14,272	25.3	+1,064	+14.7
Business and industry	1,891	5.6	1,926	5.1	3,031	7.1	3,565	7.6	3,521	6.7	3,109	5.5	+122	+5.6
Government	2,556	7.6	2,760	7.3	2,926	6.8	3,339	7.2	2,965	5.7	3,585	6.4	+103	+3.6
Other	1,663	4.9	2,150	5.7	1,898	4.4	2,143	4.6	2,600	5.0	2,634	4.7	+97	+4.9
Total	33,652		37,848		42,829		46,645		52,182		56,378		+2,274	+5.3

Source of data: National Science Foundation, Division of Science Resources Studies (unpublished analyses).

Note. Included in this table are individuals who have earned a PhD and who indicate that their current major field is psychology. Percentages may not total to 100.0% due to rounding.

Table 10-3. Type of Employment Sector of Doctoral Psychologists by Major Field Grouping: 1977–1987

	1977		1979		1981		1983		1985		1987		Average Change per Year	
Employment Setting	N	%	N	%	N	%	N	%	N	%	N	%	N	%
Health service provider fields														
Academic settings	5,658	32.9	5,983	29.0	6,353	27.6	6,752	26.2	7,942	26.4	8,293	25.2	+264	+3.9
Hospitals/clinics	4,939	28.8	5,421	26.3	5,636	24.5	5,422	21.1	5,814	19.3	6,546	19.9	+161	+2.9
Nonprofit organizations	649	3.8	1,066	5.2	1,021	4.4	1,187	4.6	1,201	4.0	1,441	4.4	+79	+8.8
Self-employed	3,157	18.4	4,745	23.0	6,135	26.7	7,961	30.9	10,350	34.4	12,336	37.5	+918	+14.7
Business and industry	438	2.6	439	2.1	856	3.7	988	3.9	1,105	3.7	522	1.6	+8	+4.4
Government	1,167	6.8	1,453	7.0	1,539	6.7	1,828	7.1	1,703	5.7	1,736	5.3	+57	+4.2
Other/not specified	1,166	6.8	1,524	7.4	1,450	6.3	1,588	6.2	1,993	6.6	2,009	6.1	+84	+5.8
Total	17,174		20,631		22,990		25,726		30,108		32,883		+1,571	+6.7
Other fields														
Academic settings	11,589	70.3	12,272	71.3	13,668	68.9	13,576	64.9	14,682	66.5	14,829	63.1	+324	+2.5
Hospitals/clinics	447	2.7	460	2.7	547	2.8	620	3.0	565	2.6	609	2.6	+16	+3.2
Nonprofit organizations	623	3.8	659	3.8	658	3.3	586	2.8	883	4.0	1,060	4.5	+44	+5.9
Self-employed	480	2.9	406	2.4	956	4.8	1,494	7.1	1,659	7.5	1,936	8.2	+146	+16.9
Business and industry	1,453	8.8	1,487	8.6	2,175	11.0	2,577	12.3	2,416	10.9	2,587	11.0	+113	+6.3
Government	1,389	8.4	1,307	7.6	1,387	7.0	1,511	7.2	1,262	5.7	1,849	7.9	+46	+3.4
Other/not specified	497	3.0	626	3.6	448	2.3	555	2.7	607	2.7	625	2.7	+13	+2.8
Total	16,478		17,217		19,839		20,919		22,074		23,495		+702	+3.6

Source of data: National Science Foundation, Division of Science Resources Studies (unpublished analyses).

Note. Included in this table are individuals who have earned a PhD and who report that their current major field is psychology. Percentages may not total to 100.0% due to rounding.

single largest employment setting of provider psychologists. For the most part, these individuals are in private and group psychological practices.

Although the numbers of psychologists in all other employment sectors have also increased, the large migration of individuals into independent practice has caused the actual proportions, for the most part, to decline. Clearly, the demands of a service-based economy where health care is a major priority, coupled with the recognition of psychologists as independent providers and the lower salaries paid by the public sector, have all been at least partly responsible for these changes.

For new provider doctorates, the trends are similar (see Table 10.4). Between 1977 and 1986, the total number of full-time employed individuals in these fields increased by an average of 72 each year. This increase consisted almost entirely of expanded employment in human service settings (hospitals, clinics, independent practices, and schools). It appears that new graduates in these specialties are preparing themselves for careers as full-time practitioners, spending their first year accumulating supervised postdoctoral hours so as to be eligible to take the licensing exam.

Psychologists with training in many of the new practice-oriented specialties (e.g., clinical neuropsychology, rehabilitation psychology, and sports psychology) are also finding jobs in settings that previously had not made great use of psychologists. As Figure 10.1 shows, new doctorates are now working in head-injury programs operated by medical schools, as staff members in oncology units in children's hospitals, and in medical practices specializing in neurology. Those interested in academic careers not only are limited to positions in psychology departments, but are also being sought after by schools of social work and family practice departments in medical schools.

The Nonpractice Areas

Employment of doctoral psychologists in other major subfields (e.g., developmental, experimental, and social psychology) has continued to grow, albeit at a much slower rate than that of their practitioner counterparts. For these psychologists, although academic settings have remained the largest employer, this market's share has declined during the past decade. In 1977, 71% of all doctoral psychologists in the nonpractice specialties were in colleges and universities as compared to 63% in 1987.

Over half of the increase in the number of employed doctoral psychologists has consisted, however, of individuals moving into nonacademic settings. Employment by nonprofit organizations and businesses have all experienced average annual growth rates equal to or greater than that for all psychologists in these fields. Similar to the practice specialties, the major shift once again, however, has been toward self-employment. Although the survey data are not clear about what exactly these individuals are doing, it is likely that more and more psychologists are serving as consultants to organizations (e.g., statistical analysis, organizational development, and research methodology).

The picture for new doctorates in these fields, however, is distinctly different. The effects of a contracting academic marketplace can be seen most clearly by looking at new psychology doctorates as a whole (see Table 10.4). Since 1977, the

Table 10-4. Type of Employment Setting of New Doctorate Recipients in Psychology by Major Field Grouping: 1977–1986

	1977		1979		1981		1983		1986		Average Change per Year	
Employment Setting	N	%	N	%	N	%	N	%	N	%	N	%
Health service provider fields												
Academic settings	275	24.7	270	19.8	266	17.1	236	14.3	261	14.6	−2	−0.0
Schools and school systems	104	9.4	160	11.8	157	10.1	178	10.8	152	8.5	+5	+6.4
Organized human service settings	553	49.8	708	52.1	880	56.6	916	55.6	962	53.8	+45	+8.2
Independent practice	NA	NA	76	5.6	89	5.7	152	9.2	273	15.3	+28	+30.0
Business, government, and other settings	179	16.1	145	10.7	163	10.5	166	10.1	139	7.8	−4	−0.8
Total	1,111		1,339		1,555		1,648		1,787		+72	+5.7
Other fields												
Academic settings	738	61.2	630	55.1	643	52.9	524	48.6	508	47.7	−26	−3.6
Schools and school systems	65	5.4	61	5.3	77	6.3	83	7.7	52	4.9	−1	−2.2
Organized human service settings	106	8.8	133	11.6	168	13.8	143	13.3	143	13.4	+4	+5.7
Independent practice	NA	NA	11	1.0	5	0.4	29	2.7	29	2.7	+2	+63.2
Business, government, and other settings	297	24.6	309	27.0	323	26.6	299	27.7	333	31.3	+4	+1.5
Total	1,206		1,144		1,216		1,078		1,065		−17	−1.2

Source of data: American Psychological Association, 1977–1986 Doctorate Employment Surveys.

Note. Included are individuals who received a PhD or PsyD in psychology in a respective year. Percentages of those respondents who indicated full-time employment and type of work setting were applied against estimates of the total number of new doctorate recipients to produce the *n*s reported in this table.

Health service provider doctorates:

- Trained in clinical psychology, John currently is director of a program for adolescents with head injuries. He works with a team of physicians, speech therapists, social workers, and other health care professionals. His job is multifaceted, involving psychotherapy, neuropsychological testing, assessments of patients' rehabilitation needs, and research.
- Susan, a clinical psychologist, works at a children's hospital in the area of pediatric behavioral medicine. Both a clinician and a researcher, her work centers around how to best prepare these young patients and their families for major surgery and treatment.
- A PhD in counseling psychology, Matthew's chief responsibility is to provide services in a psychiatry inpatient program serving the elderly.
- Brian, a clinical psychologist, specializes in sports psychology and directs a sports psychology program for athletes wishing to compete in the Olympics.
- A community psychologist, Jane is a faculty member in a graduate school of social work.
- With his own office-based practice, Dave uses his training as a clinical psychologist by consulting with the state attorney's office in providing expert witness testimony and training police how to manage stress in their jobs.
- Sam is a clinical neuropsychologist in a large group neurology practice of physicians.

Doctorates in other specialties

- An educational psychologist by training, Terre is a full-time technical consultant for a company that develops software for computer-based education.
- After receiving his PhD in physiological psychology, Don now works in a government research laboratory. The research team of which he is a member includes other staff who are clinical optometrists, vision specialists, psychologists, and engineers.
- A psychopharmacologist, Jim is a full-time researcher and in charge of clinical investigations for a medical device firm.
- After receiving her PhD in developmental psychology, Marlene now works in a program evaluation and planning office for a major private school system.
- A social psychologist, Karen is on the faculty of a marketing department in a business school of a university.
- A cognitive psychologist by training, Mary is employed by the automotive industry, applying her training in perception and physics.
- Frank is a social psychologist, working for a health maintenance organization, doing patient attitude studies, organizational analysis, and marketing research.

Figure 10.1. Examples of innovative and nontraditional jobs of 1986 doctorate recipients.

number of individuals locating full-time academic jobs has dropped by 28 positions each year. Although not shown in Table 10.4, this reduction has resulted primarily from shrinking opportunities in psychology and education departments, which are the traditional academic employers of psychologists, rather than from other academic units. In fact, the number of individuals hired by medical schools has actually risen since 1981.

In conjunction with the declining number of doctorates produced in the non-practice subfields (an average annual reduction of 29 individuals), there have been 26 fewer doctorates going into academic settings. It appears that these fields may have simply reacted to what was perceived as a shrinking academic marketplace in psychology departments. Although there were ample opportunities for individuals with appropriate training (as exemplified by the shifts in the entire doctoral population), relatively little appears to have been done by many training programs in exploiting the opportunities available in other employment sectors.

Some training programs have, however, been active in terms of capitalizing on the growing opportunities for research, policy analysis, and other applications of psychology. As Pion and Lipsey (1984) documented, a growing proportion of doctoral programs have begun to train students for nontraditional applied or alternate careers. Although still a minority (16% in 1983), there is clearly a demand for individuals from these programs.

Figure 10.1 presents examples of job positions and activities reported as innovative by new doctorate recipients who responded to recent APA employment surveys. As can be seen, psychologists in such fields as social, physiological, and cognitive psychology are working in innovative and nontraditional roles. They are in computer technology firms, in the automotive industry, in health care organizations, in business schools, and in criminology departments. Clearly, the opportunities have existed for those individuals with the appropriate configuration of skills and the willingness to take advantage of them.

Changes in What Psychologists Do

One consequence of the macrolevel societal trends previously described should have involved the nature of psychologists' roles and responsibilities. For example, the increasing demands for service delivery, along with the need for effective management of these services, should have allowed individuals in the practice specialties to become involved not only in services delivery, but also in program development, administration, and research. The emphasis by all employment sectors on the production and application of scientific and technical knowledge should have resulted in psychologists in almost any specialty becoming increasingly active in research and other applied psychology efforts.

Figure 10.2 compares the percentages of all doctoral psychologists in 1977 and 1987 who reported that their primary work activity was either research, management–administration, teaching, professional services, or other activities. What is most clear is the substantial growth in the number and percentage of psychologists

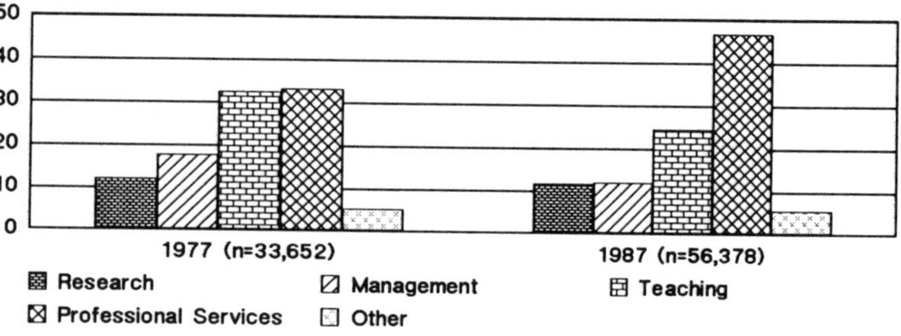

Figure 10.2. Distribution of doctoral psychologists' primary work activities, 1977 and 1987.

whose major function is to provide direct services. These figures are what we might expect in a field where an increasing concentration of psychologists are in the practice specialties. However, there appeared to be little shift in terms of individuals assuming managerial responsibilities, conducting research, or becoming more involved in consulting activities. Perhaps this lack of change is to be expected given the large increases in independent practice, a setting where the median number of hours spent in direct service is the highest reported (Stapp et al., 1985).

However, it may be the case that a focus on primary work activity only masks any real changes in responsibilities. Psychologists typically are involved in multiple activities. Information depicting involvement in all types of efforts is available from APA surveys of new doctorate recipients. Looking at the functions of new entrants into the labor force, in fact, may be quite instructive, given that the positions assumed by these individuals may be more indicative of new skills demanded by employers.

Table 10.5 shows the percentages and estimated numbers of 1981 and 1986 doctorate recipients reporting any amount of time in research, direct services, other types of applied psychology (e.g., personnel selection), educational activities, administration, or other efforts. As can be seen, individual psychologists are involved in many capacities. Almost 2/3 of those individuals receiving their doctorate in 1986 were involved in human services, 1/2 were spending at least some time in teaching and other educational activities, and 1/2 had some administrative responsibilities. Approximately 46% were conducting research, and 17% were engaged in personnel assessment, systems design, organizational consultation, or similar types of activities.

There were, of course, fairly predictable differences across the various subfields. Overwhelming majorities (at least 80%) of clinical, counseling, and school psychologists were involved in human services, whereas research was the most typical activity for developmental, experimental, comparative, physiological, personality, and social psychologists. Industrial/organizational psychologists were most likely to be involved in applied psychology activities, and these individuals also had the most varied responsibilities, with at least 60% reporting that their jobs involved research, applied psychology, and administration.

Looking at the actual numbers involved in various efforts, it is clear that psychology's participation in various functions has changed somewhat since the early 1980s. Not surprisingly, given the major growth in doctoral production in the practice specialties, the number of new doctorate recipients involved in direct-services delivery has grown. There has also been an increase in the number reporting involvement in other types of activities; although it is difficult to interpret this change, it may signal such new functions as computer software development, consultation, and program evaluation.

In contrast, the number involved in teaching and research has declined. This is partly due to the decline in academic positions previously discussed. However, it also may reflect changes in job responsibilities (e.g., clinical and counseling psychologists may have work schedules that heavily focus on direct services) or a waning in the interests of new doctorate recipients in being actively involved in research activities.

Table 10-5. Involvement in Various Work Activities by New Doctorate Recipients With Full-time Positions by Major Field: 1981 and 1986

	Research		Human Services		Other Applied Psychology		Educational Activities		Management or Admin-istration		Other Activities		N	N
Employment setting	1981	1986	1981	1986	1981	1986	1981	1986	1981	1986	1981	1986	1981	1986
Percent indicating involvement														
Clinical	48.2	33.9	92.4	87.9	16.6	12.9	63.9	49.8	59.5	49.8	22.8	24.5	1,103	1,179
Counseling	46.8	27.3	84.0	84.1	19.2	13.6	60.9	56.8	61.5	55.1	26.9	27.8	299	400
School	38.9	31.5	90.3	83.3	13.9	17.6	51.4	38.0	43.1	42.6	15.3	35.2	131	189
Experimental, comparative, and physiological	84.0	70.6	13.0	14.7	20.0	13.2	48.0	52.9	35.0	48.5	27.0	29.4	217	140
Developmental	70.6	81.9	45.1	26.4	10.8	12.5	65.7	65.3	40.2	52.8	27.5	26.4	142	137
Educational	70.3	47.9	43.2	54.9	17.6	15.5	66.2	59.2	48.6	62.0	24.3	28.2	151	97
Industrial–organizational	75.0	66.7	7.5	7.6	65.0	60.6	55.0	39.4	57.5	63.6	35.0	25.8	84	99
Social–personality	81.0	82.9	20.7	11.0	17.2	17.1	66.4	46.3	45.7	48.8	33.6	35.4	155	133
Other	77.3	71.8	31.1	34.4	24.2	19.0	52.3	42.9	53.0	50.9	31.8	33.7	423	460
All fields	59.8	45.8	63.7	65.1	18.1	16.5	60.7	50.1	52.9	50.8	25.9	27.8	2,705	2,834
Estimated numbers involved														
Clinical	532	400	1,019	1,036	183	152	705	587	656	587	251	289	1,103	1,179
Counseling	140	109	251	336	57	54	182	227	184	220	80	111	299	400
School	51	41	118	109	18	23	67	50	56	56	20	46	131	189
Experimental, comparative, and physiological	182	99	65	21	43	18	104	74	76	68	59	41	217	140
Developmental	100	112	64	36	15	17	93	89	57	72	39	36	142	137
Educational	106	46	65	53	27	15	100	57	73	60	37	27	151	97
Industrial–organizational	63	66	6	8	55	60	46	39	48	63	29	26	84	99
Social–personality	126	110	32	15	27	23	103	62	71	65	52	47	155	133
Other	327	330	132	158	102	87	221	197	224	234	135	155	423	460
All fields	1,618	1,298	1,723	1,845	490	468	1,642	1,420	1,431	1,440	701	788	2,705	2,834

Source of data: American Psychological Association, 1977–1986 Doctorate Employment Surveys.

Note. Included are individuals who received a PhD or PsyD in psychology in a respective year. Percentages of those respondents who indicated full-time employment and involvement in activities were applied against estimates of the total number of new doctorate recipients to produce the *n*s reported in this table.

What Does the Future Look Like?

Making predictions about future employment opportunities for psychologists, as well as for any other occupational group, is akin to gazing at crystal balls and reading Tarot cards. Many of the demographic, economic, and sociopolitical factors that influence the marketplace (e.g., inflation and political philosophies) are difficult to predict over the long term. However, certain trends in society and psychology have already begun to surface and help to identify some issues to consider in speculating about what opportunities and challenges psychologists may have over the next decade or so.

At present, all standard indicators point to the continued growth of the services component of the economy over the next 10 to 20 years (Johnston, 1987). Within this sector, one of the fastest growing areas will be professional services, and the number of professional workers is expected to increase more rapidly than total employment between now and the beginning of the twenty-first century (Kutscher, 1987). In conjunction with an economy increasingly focused on services is the continued growth of sophisticated technologies (e.g., computers, superconductivity, and biotechnologies).

As a result of these trends, employment in many occupations is expected to rise sharply, particularly those in engineering, computer specialties, and health care. Growth in computer and research services delivered by business and industry is also anticipated to be stronger than average, and this should increase demand for scientific personnel, including social scientists in independent research laboratories and management-consulting firms. Along with these changes, demographic changes are expected that will affect the academic marketplace.

The Future of Psychology in the Health Care Arena

Although the market for health care professionals is expected to remain strong for the remainder of this century, it is quite likely that factors different from those experienced in the 1970s will govern the operation of this marketplace. The major shift will be toward increasing competition; in fact, this trend has already surfaced and will have major implications on how psychologists will participate in the health care delivery system.

Increased competition has been prompted by the escalating costs of health care and has spurred vigorous attempts at cost-containment—efforts aimed at shifting the locus of control over costs from providers to the insurers and the actual consumers. As cogently identified by Kiesler and Morton (1988), the result has been a restructuring of the health care industry around the corporativism of health care (e.g., managed care settings and large, private hospital conglomerates) and the emergence of health care structures that provide a range of services (e.g., the merger between a hospital corporation and an insurance company).

It is quite likely that these developments in the health care field will also spread to the mental health service delivery sector. Mental health care costs have also been increasing, and mental illness is now the third most expensive category of illnesses (Mechanic, 1987). Thus, it is only a matter of time until more stringent cost-containment strategies will be implemented. The most likely scenario is that these measures will result in decreasing provider autonomy (in terms of setting fees), in greater emphasis on demonstrating successful treatment outcomes, and in the locus of care shifting to community settings, primarily, managed-care settings (Kiesler & Morton, 1988).

Given these developments, it is doubtful that the rapid expansion in independent practice that has occurred over the past decade can continue at its present pace. Although many students currently enrolled in direct-service-provider doctoral programs envision careers of independent practice oriented to psychotherapy (Fitzgerald & Osipow, 1988), it is likely that the majority will be working in HMOs, employee assistance programs, nursing homes, and alcohol and drug abuse rehabilitation programs. Successful work and career advancement in these settings will require an understanding of how the health care system operates, the ability to work as part of a team with several health and mental health care professionals, and a knowledge of treatment-outcome assessment. It will also require prior experience with special patient populations (e.g., the aged, the seriously mentally ill, and drug abusers) and interventions (e.g., cognitive assessment and neuropsychological assessment). Much of this specialized knowledge will need to occur at the postdoctoral level through working in organized settings. The recent trend toward movement into independent practice immediately upon receipt of the degree may become less and less an adaptive career choice.

Changes in the Academic Marketplace

Recently, there has been much talk about projected faculty shortages. However, it remains unclear when these shortages will occur. Currently, 20% of psychology faculty are 55 years or older. What this means in terms of the number of new faculty positions and when they will become available, however, depends on many factors.

First, it depends on trends in student enrollments, the composition of these enrollments, and other demographic trends. Second, it also depends on the number of people with PhDs who will be produced and who are interested in academic positions. Third, it is contingent on whether current retirement behavior on the part of faculty continues (the median age of retiring faculty is now 67 years), particularly when the mandatory retirement age is abolished in 1993. In addition, growth in the academic marketplace also depends on institutional practices—that is, replacing a retiring, full-time faculty with another full-time, tenured or tenure-track faculty member rather than several persons who can teach one or two courses on a part-time basis.

Available information to date provides some insight into these factors. Current demographic trends suggest that college enrollments will continue to decline through 1996, but then will increase through the first decade of the twenty-first century (U.S. Congress, Office of Technology Assessment, 1985). The composition of the undergraduate population, however, will change; the proportion of minorities will increase, and enrollment increases will be concentrated in specific geographic regions (e.g., the Northwest and Southwest).

Projections as to increases in psychology graduate enrollments and thus the number of doctorates produced also indicate little growth over the next decade. In fact, the number of psychology baccalaureates (the primary source of psychology doctorates) has declined rapidly over the past decade, dropping from 50,000 in 1976 to 41,000 in 1986. At present, unless students' career plans change, there is no indication that this situation will change over the next decade. Thus, the previous decline in the number of doctorates in the nonpractice fields may continue throughout the next decade.

Looking at factors related to when existing faculty may retire and how they might be replaced, information to date does not suggest any radical changes in the age of retirement. However, willingness to retire also depends on inflation, and if inflation begins a steep climb, retirement rates may slow down. Little change is also expected in how institutions replace retiring faculty; currently, only a handful of universities have implemented any policies that would radically change the faculty hiring or tenure policies (Pion, Kohout, & Wicherski, 1989).

Thus, if current trends continue, somewhere between 4,000 and 5,000 faculty positions will become available in psychology departments. It is expected that the peak of openings will not occur until after the year 2000.

Given the data on declining number of PhDs in the research specialties, there is concern over whether there will be a sufficient number of qualified individuals to fill these openings. Furthermore, the undergraduate psychology majors in colleges and universities today will be the pool from which future faculty members will come. We already know that the size of this pool is dwindling, and other factors suggest that these individuals will not choose to pursue a doctorate in psychology. For example, support for graduate training in the social and behavioral sciences has declined over the years, and as a result, the time required to earn the doctorate has increased. Also, the increasing specialization of research, coupled with advancements in highly sophisticated instrumentation and the advantages of additional time to develop a research program and a network of colleagues, may make additional postdoctoral training a necessity in order to obtain an academic position and successfully receive tenure, particularly in such hot research areas as cognitive sciences and neuroscience. In fact, 30% of the new full-time faculty hired by graduate psychology departments in 1988 to 1989 came from postdoctoral appointments (Pion et al., 1989).

Apart from concerns over future faculty shortages, psychology needs to be concerned with its ability to maintain a strong research presence and advance its knowledge base. As previously reported, the number of doctorates in many of our major research specialties is declining, and fewer and fewer new doctorate recipients are becoming involved in research. In addition, the results of a recent study by Uebersax and Ferguson (1989) indicated that the number of young investigators applying for research grants is declining. This is particularly disturbing inasmuch as research supported by these institutes addresses many of the urgently pressing problems of today and forms the basis for advances in the practice of psychology.

The next 2 decades appear very promising for psychology in terms of employment opportunities as practitioners, faculty, researchers, consultants, and so forth. Whether psychology will be able to exploit these opportunities, however, is dependent on each and every one of us working actively to ensure its success—by exciting students about the benefits of a research career, by ensuring that psychologists are actively involved in meeting the needs of populations who currently remain underserved, by working toward psychologists' full participation as direct mental health professionals in the newly emerging health care settings, and so forth.

References

Fitzgerald, L., & Osipow, S. (1988). We have seen the future, but is it us? The vocational aspirations of graduate students in counseling psychology. *Professional Psychology: Research and Practice, 19*, 575–583.

Howard, A., Pion, G. M., Gottfredson, G. D., Flattau, P. E., Oskamp, S., Pfafflin, S. M., Bray, D. W., & Burstein, A. G. (1986). The changing face of American psychology: A report from the Committee on Employment and Human Resources. *American Psychologist, 41*, 1311–1327.

Johnston, W. B. (1987). *Workforce 2000: Work and workers for the twenty-first century*. Indianapolis, IN: Hudson Institute.

Kiesler, C. A., & Morton, T. L. (1988). Psychology and public policy in the "health care revolution." *American Psychologist, 43*, 993–1003.

Kutscher, R. E. (1987). Overview and implications of the projections to 2000. *Monthly Labor Review, 110*, 3–9.

Mechanic, D. (1987). Correcting misconception in mental health policy: Strategies for improved care of the seriously mentally ill. *The Milbank Quarterly, 65*, 203–210.

National Science Board. (1987). *Science & engineering indicators—1987* (NSB 87-1). Washington, DC: U.S. Government Printing Office.

National Science Foundation. (1979). *Characteristics of doctoral scientists and engineers in the United States: 1977. Detailed statistical tables* (NSF 79–306). Washington, DC: U.S. Government Printing Office.

National Science Foundation. (1988). *Characteristics of doctoral scientists and engineers in the United States: 1987. Detailed statistical tables* (NSF 88–331). Washington, DC: U.S. Government Printing Office.

National Science Foundation. (1988). *Profiles psychology: Human resources and funding.* (NSF 88-325). Washington, DC: U.S. Government Printing Office.

Pion, G., Bramblett, J. P., & Wicherski, M. (1987). *Preliminary report: 1985 Doctorate Employment Survey.*

Pion, G., Kohout, J., & Wicherski, M. (1989). *Characteristics of graduate departments of psychology: 1987–88.* Washington, DC: American Psychological Association.

Pion, G. M., & Lipsey, M. W. (1984). Psychology and society: The challenge of change. *American Psychologist, 39*, 739–754.

Silvestri, G. T., & Lukasiewicz, J. M. (1987). A look at occupational employment trends to the year 2000. *Monthly Labor Review, 110*, 46–63.

Stapp, J., & Fulcher, R. (1983). The employment of APA members: 1982. *American Psychologist, 38*, 1298–1320.

Stapp, J., Fulcher, R., & Wicherski, M. (1984). The employment of 1981 and 1982 doctorate recipients in psychology. *American Psychologist, 39*, 1408–1423.

Stapp, J., Tucker, A. M., & VandenBos, G. R. (1985). Census of psychological personnel: 1983. *American Psychologist, 40*, 1317–1351.

Uebersax, J., & Ferguson, L. (1989). *ADAMHA and NIH research grants to psychologists.* (N-3031-APA). Santa Monica, CA: The RAND Corporation.

U.S. Congress, Office of Technology Assessment. (1985). *Demographic trends and the scientific and engineering work force—A technical memorandum.* (Report No. OTA-TM-SET-35). Washington, DC: U.S. Government Printing Office.

Index